THEM WAS THE DAYS

THEM WAS THE DAYS

An American Saga of the '70's

MARTHA FERGUSON McKEOWN

University of Nebraska Press, Lincoln

1961

Orginally published by The Macmillan Company.
MANUFACTURED IN THE UNITED STATES OF AMERICA

First Bison Book printing September, 1961
Most recent printing shown by first digit below:
6   7   8   9   10

DEDICATED TO

THE MEMORY OF MY BLIND GRANDMOTHER

MARTHA LUPHER HAWTHORNE

WHO TAUGHT ME TO SEE

A NOTE TO TEACHERS OF SOCIAL STUDIES

The westward movement in American history and the main lines of development in American life in the latter part of the nineteenth century have been explored and interpreted in any number of profound scholarly works. There is as well an abundance of first-rate textbooks and standard sources available to the teacher and student in subject-matter fields dealing with the American West. But what does seem to be hard to locate—at least, if I may judge from my friends and acquaintances among teachers of history and other social studies—are supplementary readings of a kind which will grip and engross the mind of adolescent youth: specifically, authentic personal accounts which have sufficient vitality, narrative interest, and detail so that the scene becomes real, the events exciting, and the young reader is led to a sense of identity with the men, women, and children who migrated westward to claim more than half the land of our nation.

THEM WAS THE DAYS is just such an account. In its pages Martha Ferguson McKeown has re-created the experiences of a homesteading family, the Hawthornes, and more particularly, of her uncle, Mont Hawthorne, from whose point of view the story is told. Mont was born in 1865 on an old land-grant claim in Pennsylvania. When he was five the family moved to Virginia, but the new West, not the Old Dominion, was the land of opportunity, and in 1873 the family moved on again to Nebraska where they settled on a homestead near present-day Loup City. For the next eight years, in Mont's own words, "I done my learning on the plains."

The first lesson the family had to learn was simply how to survive. The struggle of the pioneers to adjust to a new and harsh environment. their problems in adapting eastern woodland farming techniques to a region where timber and water were in short supply, the blizzards, droughts, and visitations of grasshoppers they were called on to endure, all are familiar aspects of an oft-told tale, but as they are narrated here they have the freshness and force of a story told for the first time. In part, this is due to the engaging personality of young Mont. Observant and perceptive, with a boy's curiosity and relish for adventure, he early acquires the paradoxical outlook of the pioneer: to be eternally optimistic and always prepared for the worst. In great part, too, the narrative owes its impact to the author's success in capturing the flavor and cadence of Mont's speech—the homely but precise and telling imagery, the humor (conscious and unconscious) , and the unsparing directness that goes straight to the heart of things.

There was, of course, more to life on the homestead than the never-ending battle to wrest a living from the soil—the gruelling round of breaking and planting, harvesting crops, and preserving food against the Nebraska winter. The great tide of western emigration eddied around the Hawthorne claim; and the "long drive" of Texas herds northward to Union Pacific shipping points brought a new breed of man to the Nebraska frontier. Despite the isolation of the life, there were encounters with the military, with traders, land-speculators, and rustlers, and—in times of drought—a steady trickle of dispirited settlers heading back east the way they came. The mid-years of the '70's saw the Battles of the Rosebud and the Little Big Horn; and for months on end the family lived in fear of raids and reprisals from the hostiles. After Crook's campaign and the opening of the Black Hills there was the heady, unsettling excitement of the gold rush.

In contrast to the overt drama of such events, the process of transforming the wild country into the abiding place of an organized society went forward in unspectacular fashion; yet with the establishment of mail routes and school districts and the location of the county seat—steps characteristically accompanied by a good deal of local politicking as well as many a tart comment about the state and national governments—young Mont was witnessing, and living in, the central drama of the period of settlement.

Although still a boy in years, Mont was doing a man's job long before he left the homestead in 1881. For him, as for many pioneers, the land beyond exerted a powerful pull. After working with a railroad grading crew in Colorado and in the mines at Carbon, Wyoming, in 1883 he headed west on an emigrant train bound for San Francisco and, ultimately, the Hood River Valley of Oregon. It was on his farm there, many years later, that he told the story of his adventures to the niece who has so brilliantly re-created it in the pages that follow.

Teachers who are interested in supplementing course work with a truthful, accurate, and immensely readable account of what it was like to be living in a crucial decade of our history can do no better than to call this book to their students' attention. Mont was right, no doubt about it; there was plenty of learning to be done on the plains in the '70's, and what he learned has been distilled by the author into the essence of the pioneer experience.

Royce H. Knapp

Professor of Secondary Education,
University of Nebraska

This is the story of Mont Hawthorne's boyhood. It is recreated from family memory records, authenticated and supplemented by my own research that has taken me from coast to coast.

My Uncle Mont was born on an old land-grant claim in Pennsylvania in 1865. The family moved to Virginia when he was five years old; they lived there for three years before moving on again to Nebraska. Uncle Mont says, "I done my learning on the plains."

By the time he was twelve years old he was doing a man's work and was treated as one by the miners he met during the gold rush into the Black Hills of Dakota. Then he joined the trail blazers into the Far West. He worked with the railroad builders in Colorado; he spent two years in the mines at Carbon, Wyoming, before going to San Francisco in 1883.

From there his Trail Led North. He became a part of a sweeping tide of men who put a bend in the trail as they moved along a rocky, wind-swept coast to spread out into the Pacific Northwest and into the Far North.

Uncle Mont, now eighty-four years old, lives on a farm next to ours, in the Hood River Valley in Oregon. When I started writing *The Trail Led North,* he said: "Now, remember, I ain't no storybook hero, I'm just an old-timer who remembers good."

But to me, our family adventurer, Mont Hawthorne, is a hero. He's one of many heroes Arch and I have learned to know among the old-timers out here in the West, or up in Alaska, or along the Yukon River in Canadian Territory. This is their history, written in their language, based on life's experiences of one of them.

Thoreau said: "I should not talk so much about myself if there were anybody else whom I knew as well." And so, my Uncle Mont becomes a symbol. He is one of the nameless thousands who helped settle America for us.   *M. F. M.*

CONTENTS

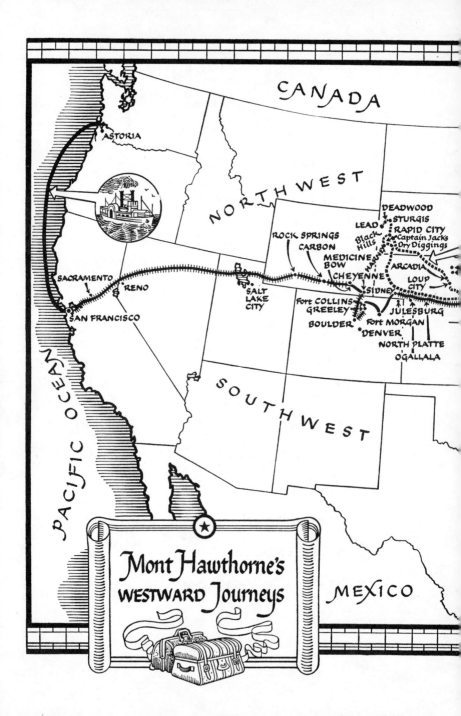

CANADA

NORTHWEST

ASTORIA

ROCK SPRINGS
CARBON

DEADWOOD
STURGIS
LEAD
RAPID CITY
Black
Hills
Captain Jacks
Dry Diggings

MEDICINE
BOW
CHEYENNE
ARCADIA
LOUP
CITY

SACRAMENTO
RENO
SALT
LAKE
CITY
SIDNEY

SAN FRANCISCO
Fort COLLINS
GREELEY
BOULDER
Fort MORGAN
DENVER
JULESBURG

NORTH PLATTE
O'GALLALA

SOUTHWEST

PACIFIC OCEAN

Mont Hawthorne's
WESTWARD Journeys

MEXICO

CANADA

ERIE
CORRY
WATER
FORD
PITTSBURGH

Fort HARTSUFF
ORD
OMAHA

WASHINGTON
FARMVILLE
AQUIA
CREEK

LINCOLN

GRAND
ISLAND

RICHMOND
KEYSVILLE
MEHERRIN

CONFEDERACY

ATLANTIC OCEAN

N
NW NE
W E
SW SE
S

ONE

MOVING SOUTH

One of the best fights I ever seen in my whole life happened way
back in 1870. I ain't ever forgot it, and I ain't likely to; but I better
tell you how we happened to get mixed up in it to begin with. You
see, we was moving at the time. Father had sold our farm up near
Edinboro Lake in northwestern Pennsylvania because everybody,
including the dogs, was shaking so bad with the fever ague that he
figgered he'd better get us out of there quick. Besides, Father wasn't
no man to stay put anyhow, and that time he had a good reason to
move. They'd dammed up the lake for water power, so the water
run out in the marsh land and the mosquitoes moved right in and
took over.

Mama had the ague the worst. Why the doctor told Father she
wouldn't last out the year if he didn't get her out of there fast to
a warmer climate. So, he went scouting around and he met a real-
estate fellow. Next thing we knowed he come back home to move
us. We packed some of our stuff, sold most of it, throwed away the
rest, and got ready to head south to live on a plantation that Father
had bought sight unseen.

Father didn't get much out of our farm. We had good dairy and
grazing land, too. A couple of years later, after we was gone, trading
picked up and boats from all over the world come into Lake Erie.
Our kin folks who'd stayed behind done real well. But we wasn't
there.

Of course, Mama had been wishing for good weather for our
moving. She didn't get it. Spring come late in 1870. There was still

a lot of snow on the ground when Father's brother, Charley, come to take us and our stuff to Waterford in a bobsled that was drawed with horses. Mama took all kinds of pains wrapping up her Singer sewing machine and it come through the moving just fine. Some of the other stuff didn't do so good.

About six hundred folks lived in Waterford. They made shoes, and firkins, and tubs. Mama said when she used to live with her folks they had a man come and make their shoes up, right on their farm from leather they had tanned theirselves. But after her and Father got married they just sold their hides to the tannery and then bought shoes from the fellows who was making them right there in Waterford, where we went to take the train to Corry where we was to transfer to the main line. It was in Corry I seen the fight I was telling you about.

We got to Corry in the late afternoon. The train taking us south wasn't due until one a.m. Mama was too sick to walk around and she wouldn't let me go out alone, so I didn't have nothing to do but set right there and wait. The depot was made double, with two waiting rooms; one side was for the married men and their families, the other side was for the single men. The ticket agent was caged off separate in between. A lot of men was traveling through Corry alone, because a bunch of new oil wells was being opened up a piece above there.

You could see Father was sort of itching to take off with them fellows, too, but Mama didn't see nothing to get excited about. She said her folks had knowed all about oil. They used to put an old wool blanket on top of the water in their spring. The oil would stick to it, then they'd wring it out into a pan, and pour it into a bottle, and keep it handy to rub on the children when they had the croup.

So many strange men was in town that the railroad kept a woman on duty in the family side of the depot day times. When a man come in there alone, she'd say, "Is your wife with you?"; or she'd point to the "No Smoking" sign on the wall, and she'd say, "The smoking room is next door." A lot of rough-looking fellows was coming and going, but everything went along fine as long as she was there. Come dark, she went home.

Most everyone else had cleared out of there on a train taking them up north, so we had the waiting room to ourselves. There was

Mama, who was terrible sick, and there was Father, who was getting sort of frazzled and short with us. Then there was my half-sister, Julia; and my sister, Sadie; and Aaron Crouch, a neighbor boy that my folks had took to raise; and then there was me. Everyone of us children was restless. Mama tried putting us to sleep on benches, but she didn't have no luck at it. The girls would whisper and giggle, and I'd set up and look around.

I was wishing something would happen so I wouldn't have to lay there on that hard, old bench, when who should walk in but a big stranger, smoking one of them bad-smelling, real-long, five-cent seegars. Now Mama was dead set agin smoking anyhow, but after she had the fever ague, it appeared like the least little whiff of tobacco smoke set her off into one of them ague fits. It was so cold outside, the windows had been nailed shut. It was tighter than a drum in there, and that seegar stunk something awful. Mama's teeth begun to chatter. I could see her knuckles turning real white as she set trying to hold her hands still in her lap. She says to my Father, "Sam, do I have to put up with that smell in here?"

She looked right straight at the big stranger, standing there leaning agin the wall beside the "No Smoking" sign. I could tell that she aimed for him to hear her and take the hint, but he never so much as batted an eye. I noticed Father sizing up the stranger, too, and I could see he didn't like his looks. Then when he looked at Mama, he didn't like the way she was looking, neither. So he got up, and he walked over to the stranger and he says, real polite: "Maybe you can't read. That's a 'No Smoking' sign on the wall beside you. My wife is sick. Please put your seegar out."

Well, that stranger's face got so red it run clean down on his neck. He blowed hisself up just like an old bull frog. Then he took a terrible big puff on his seegar and he blowed a whole mouth full of smoke right into Father's face, and he says: "No, I ain't putting my seegar out. But I'll be glad to put you out!"

Now Father had promised Uncle Charley that he wouldn't get into no more fights. Besides he didn't exactly hanker to take on that big stranger and mess up his homespun suit, so he sort of stepped back to talk things over with Mama. But Mama wasn't in no talking mood. All she says was, "What's the matter, Sam, are you afraid of him?"

Then she leaned back, real weak and sick-like, and closed her eyes. That left everything right up to Father.

So, he walked back to the stranger, and he says, "Either you, or your seegar, or both of you, are going out of here right now!"

That stranger was one of them lightning strikers. Quicker than a flash he swung on Father and got him right in the face. It throwed Father back across one of them benches, and his nose started bleeding all over his beard.

But Father got up again fast. He took a big swing; it was a regular hay-maker and would of knocked that stranger flat, but blamed if he didn't step back so that Father missed. Now Father was a powerful man and a good fighter when it come to slugging it out with a man who would come straight in with his two fists. The only reason he'd promised Uncle Charley not to fight no more was because he had pretty near killed one of the neighbors during a little argument over some cattle getting into the wrong field. But this stranger handled his feet more like a boxer; when he come in, he'd come in fast. Then when Father would get set and ready for him, he'd be gone. Blamed if he didn't draw blood four times before Father had a chance to lay a hand on him.

Then the stranger brung his knee up fast. But Father dodged back out of the way. By that time Father seen he'd tackled a mean one; so he got all set. The next time the stranger come in, Father let him have it right in the belly. He throwed his whole weight behind it, and sunk his fist into that fellow's middle clean up to the wrist. It was a corker and lifted him plumb off his feet and throwed him back onto the red-hot stove that stood in the corner. While the stranger was yelling and trying to get hisself off the stove before he fried, Father jumped in and grabbed him by his long hair and drug him right down onto the floor. Father always figgered getting ahold of that fellow's hair was what saved the day for him, because, after he once took hold, he never let go. He held him down on the floor and he started right to work kicking his face in with the toe of his boot. Father didn't dare take no chances; he knowed he had a tough one to handle. Them days, no one never heard of rules in fighting. You just licked the other fellow any way you could.

When Father was finishing the job, the door flew open and in come three policemen swinging their clubs. They grabbed Father and drug him out of the corner. Then they gathered the stranger up off the floor. He started spitting out some teeth so they seen he wasn't in no condition to talk. They asked Father what was wrong and he started to tell them that his wife didn't like tobacco smoke. Blamed if they didn't arrest Father, too. By that time another deputy had come in, and two of them had the stranger by the arms leading him off to jail. The other two had grabbed Father; they was taking him right along to jail, just like it was his fault.

Mama and the girls and me clumb down off the benches where we'd been keeping out of the way while we was watching the fight. We was all yelling and telling them policemen that they couldn't arrest Father but they wouldn't listen to us. Finally, after he could see that everything was safe outside, the ticket-taker come out of his coop and started talking. He told the policemen he'd seen the whole thing happen and that this fellow was in where he hadn't no business to be and they should of been on hand to put him out theirselves. He sounded like they ought to be thankful to Father for doing their work. He said if they didn't let Father go, he'd report them for failing to police the depot.

Just then the train come in, so they turned Father loose, and we gathered up our stuff and clumb on board. Father was cut up considerable, but Mama got out her kit and went right to work doctoring him just as soon as we got on the train. He always said it come in real handy, him marrying a woman who was a nurse.

Mama said with as much bad luck as he had, she figgered it was a good thing she could save on doctor bills, too. It did seem like all the luck he ever had was bad. Of course, he never stayed no place long enough to cash in on the hard work he done. Just like with that fellow he licked there in the depot at Corry. After we got down South Uncle Charley sent us a paper from back in Pennsylvania, and there was a story about how the police at Corry had captured "a dangerous criminal in the depot" and how he was a bank robber and all sorts of things, and how they'd risked their lives and then got a big reward. And Father wasn't even mentioned when he was the one that licked that fellow single-handed. Why, when Father got done with that bank robber, all them police had to do was sweep him up off the floor and carry him off to jail.

But I was telling you about Mama being a nurse. You see, she got a lot of experience nursing when she was just a girl. Her folks had eleven children of their own, then they adopted one more to make an even dozen. Because Mama was one of the oldest, she had a chance to learn to be real handy with sick folks right there in her own home. Her folks lived on a Revolutionary land-grant claim out from Franklin, Pennsylvania. Her father seen that land when he fought with Perry's fleet, and he figgered that country in around Sugar Creek had springs and good soil and just about all a man could ask for. The Lupher School there is named for her father because he give the land where it was built. Kinfolks of ours still live on the place.

When Mama was growing up, she got to be what you'd call a practical nurse because the doctor used to stop by and take her along when he needed her to help out at the neighbors; he said she had a feel for the sick. Then when soldiers was dying uncared for, and they didn't have nothing much to do with, and was short-handed during the Civil War, she helped nurse in the hospitals. She figgered it was her duty. One of her brothers was killed in the battle of Bull Run; another one chewed his fingers to the bone before he starved to death in Libby Prison. Father's brother, John, was an awful fine fellow, Mama always said, but he died in the Civil War, too.

Her and Father had lived neighbors to each other all their lives, but they didn't do their first courting with each other. It was after his first wife died, that she married him and started right in taking care of his little girl, Julia. Not long after that a neighbor boy, Aaron Crouch, come in one day with everything he owned tied up in a little bundle, and he says, "I come to live with you." He didn't have no real home; there wasn't nothing else to do but move over and make room for him, too. So by the time she got around to having Sadie, Mama already had two children in her family. But she never thought nothing of setting extra places at her table or of doing things for anybody that needed her. Mama was always one of them women who was taking care of folks, especially sick ones.

Aaron was an awful fine boy, and more than paid his way. Children did, them days. We paired off good, too. Just like after we got on the train that night at Corry—Father and Mother could set together; Julia was older and she could look after Sadie; and Aaron was ten years older than me, so I could lean up agin him and get some sleep. Blamed if I know whether they had sleepers on that train. We set up. Folks, them days, didn't waste their money.

From Corry to Washington, D.C., we was on the main line of the Pennsylvania Railroad. Our car was lit by coal-gas lamps. There was a good stove in each end of the car, bolted fast to the floor. Father looked close at the fire doors, and they was good ones with heavy gratings. Everything was fixed up fancy and kept clean, too. Setting up all night on a train ain't so hard on well folks, but with Mama and Father both sick, we was real glad to get off in the morning.

We had a full day's lay-over in Washington. Soon as we got to the depot we separated, and Father and Aaron and me got back first. While we was setting there on a bench waiting for the women to get theirselves tidy, a great big tall man in a high hat went right by us a-twilling a gold-headed cane. Golly I'd like to know for sure if he was the President. I always figgered he must of been 'cause he handled that cane like he'd been practicing for a long time.

Washington was chuck full of buildings. We walked and we walked and we walked, just gandering around to see all we could. Every once in awhile we'd stop on a street corner to get a drink. Why, they had regular pumps and wells. Mostly they was used enough so you didn't have to do no priming, you just drank out of a dipper hanging along side like you would at any well.

After awhile, Mama said her feet couldn't take it no more. So we went into a place where we could get some victuals. Father bought a copy of *The Evening Star* for two cents. He started right in to read to us about what was going on in Congress, and how there was a new party, the Liberal Republicans, going to make things so hot for President Grant that he'd never get hisself elected again. But all the time he was reading, Mama and the girls kept shoving over agin him reading over his shoulder about Mrs. Blaine's reception and who was there and what they wore. Father got real cross with them because he said the Fifteenth Amendment was up and that would decide who could vote, Negroes as well as whites. Them days the papers had more news, they never had no pictures, you just read the ads like you was reading a book. Most ads was about the price of gold, or cotton, or provisions, or patent medicines. They wasn't cluttered up with pictures of women getting married, or just setting around, or of their dresses, or shoes, or hats.

Usually Mama was a real sensible woman, but when Father took time out to eat she got hold of the paper herself. And when she read about the Whitehurst Gallery where they give back half of what they took in at each performance in prizes, and where you could see the "Panorama of the Moving of the Capitol and the Illuminated War Views, and the Pictures of the Statuary," she was dead set on going. Julia and Sadie backed her right up in it, too, but Father said, "No!"

He was a man who could put his foot down hard; I always figgered that that time maybe he was right. Anyhow he headed us straight back to the depot, and he left us setting there while he hired a dray. Then we helped load our stuff. Some of it was real heavy, Mama had her flat irons and a bunch of things along that weighed considerable. We drove clean across town, and unloaded our goods right at the boat, then Father found a place for us to lodge for the night in close to the landing, and him and Aaron took the team back to the fellow they had hired it from.

Early the next morning we had our breakfast and went down to the Potomac River where we was to take the boat to Aquia Creek, where we had to change to the railroad that was to take us to Richmond. That boat wasn't a bit like the little ones I'd seen up on the lakes in Pennsylvania. Why it had a regular house built on top and was big enough to haul a whole village full of folks and their stuff, too. When we was pulling out from the shore, Father had me stand by the railing so I could get a good look at the buildings in Washington. But I was putting in my time looking at the cannon lined up along both sides of the river bank. After the Civil War was over the Northern troops moved all them cannon up there close to the Capitol to be handy in case they ever needed them again.

That trip down the Potomac didn't last near long enough to suit me. All along the way we seen forts that had been built to protect Washington. A man on the boat said that during the war cannons was hid among the trees on most of the points along the river. The steamer made one real long stop at Alexandria, Virginia, seven mile below Washington, where we unloaded some iron parts for a steam brewery.

A big crowd of folks, both black and white, was down watching the boat come in. A bunch of little pickaninnies was there trying to earn a few pennies from the folks around by doing different stunts. A crowd of them was acting like a regular band, one pounded on an old kettle, another had a piece of an old saw. But the one I remember best was a little fellow about my size. He'd turn summersets backwards, and he'd walk on his hands, and do all sorts of things like that. Then he'd run along the edge of the dock and hold out his cap for pennies to the folks lined up watching them from the deck of our steamer. There was only about three foot of space between, and we was glad to have a show while we was waiting for the freight to get unloaded. The crowd wasn't putting out many pennies, and the boys kept trying harder and harder. The little fellow turning the back flip-flops had been doing three of them regular in a row. But that wasn't enough to suit a big, old, beer-bloat of a fellow standing up on deck close to us. He had enough pennies in his hand to make a jingle, and he kept calling to that little boy everytime he'd finish all them summersets and be so winded all he could do was to roll his eyes, and he'd say: "Make it four for my money."

That had been going on for a long time and you could see the little boy was so beat he couldn't hardly keep on turning over no more, but that big fellow kept egging him on and promising him them pennies. Just then the whistle blowed, and that little Negro boy made one last try. He turned over three times again, and we was all watching him make the fourth turn, when we seen he'd miscalculated and wasn't going to have no place to land. I'll never forget how his face looked, and the whites of his eyes stood out, as he turned over that last time and come down in between our boat and the dock, and then made a big splash as he went under.

Some sailors throwed a rope but he never showed again. I've always hoped he got ahold of one of them pilings underneath and hung on until someone got him out of there. But folks figgered he must of come up in under our boat. Because when we throwed off the line and swung out in midstream some men in a little boat was going around in under the dock hunting for him, and we never seen them haul him aboard. Us children felt pretty bad about that little boy, but we never could figger out why that big fellow, after holding onto them pennies all that time, just stood there looking down into the water, and then opened his hand and let that money drop into the Potomac River.

It wasn't long after that when a man on the boat told us that the big old house on the hill above us was Mount Vernon where George Washington used to live. We didn't get to stop there, but because this man I was telling you about would talk to us we knowed what we was seeing. Julia and Sadie got to feeling real proud about moving South to live in a plantation house because of them big houses we could see up on high ground and back in the trees while we was going down stream.

Father was generally a pretty good one to start up a conversation with strangers, but them Southerners on that boat sure froze up on him. Why he started to talk to a man and his wife standing next to us by saying real pleasant: "We're the Hawthornes from up in Pennsylvania and we're moving to Virginia on account of my wife's health."

This man said real quick, "It's not the best climate for folks who come from the North."

Then him and his wife got up and moved clean over on the other side of the boat. That was the first time I learned how the Southerners felt about carpet-baggers. It wasn't long though before we could pick them grafters out ourselves. Why them fellows went swarming down there after the Civil War was over, just carrying what they could in a carpet bag, and acting like they owned the place. They'd moved South under the Acts of Reconstruction that give the Negroes the vote—before they even had it up North—and during the time that the army was running the country and the Southerners who took part in the Civil War couldn't vote, they got theirselves and a bunch of Negroes elected to offices and just picked the country clean as a bone. It wasn't no wonder them people on the boat figgered we wasn't to be trusted.

The boat we was on from Washington, D.C., to Virginia was run by the Washington and New York Fast Lines. It connected with the Accommodation Train at Aquia Creek. We got off the boat and onto the train at four p.m. It was all steamed up and ready to pull out. It had an engine that burned four-foot cordwood sawed in two in the middle so it would be short enough to fit in the firebox. We set in a car that had sort of slat seats that pitched back some, then there was a freight car on in back of us. It didn't go so very fast, but it was considerable better than walking.

Mama had a hamper of provisions for our supper. We rode all night and got to Richmond about nine o'clock the next morning. That give Father plenty of time to look around and bargain for a place for us to stay. He got a boarding house to give us a real good rate because there was six of us and we agreed to stay for a full week. He said we'd better lay over there and give him a chance to figger things out and get our supplies together before we moved to our plantation at Meherrin Depot, just sixty-nine miles southwest of there. Besides Mama was so sick she needed to have a few days rest to sort of get herself pulled together again. Most of the time on the boat she'd been terrible quiet, just setting there with her shawl pulled up around her, trying to keep out of the wind. I always figgered moving away from her home and her folks was harder on Mama than it was on the rest of us.

In Richmond the peach trees was all in bloom, while up in Pennsylvania we'd left Uncle Charley waving at us through a snow storm. I kept hoping Mama would stop shaking with the ague, but she stayed in bed the first few days we was there. Father said for Aaron and me not to bother her, but just to walk around town and look at things; only to be sure and keep out of mischief and not get in older folks way.

Aaron and me figgered we had a lot to see in Richmond. The trouble was Julia and Sadie tagged after us all the first afternoon. They kept poking along, dragging their feet, looking in the windows, and turning around to stare at folks. When we passed the Magic Soda Fountain with fruit syrups, Sadie begun to beg and cry. She didn't understand how dear things was. By the time we got to C. Zimmers Confectionery she'd wore Aaron down. He had a little money he'd earned off of Uncle Charley and so he took us right inside. It was an ice-cream saloon with tables for ladies. We set on that side of the partition and we et our ice cream real slow so's to make it last.

Our feet was terrible tired. We'd been used to going barefoot summers up in Pennsylvania, and we'd always done all of our walking on dirt roads. But them brick streets and cobblestones wore us into blisters in no time. Father had told us about Richmond being a big city with about 50,000 folks living there. Only half of them was white though, and part of them sort of lived to theirselves in the big houses. Up where we come from the men worked in the fields all day, but in Richmond we seen folks everywhere. There was street auctions, and a big political meeting in front of the Capitol, and gangs of men sort of bunched together talking or just standing looking into windows.

Sadie and Julia wasn't missing no windows neither. They liked the ones that had muslin and calico, and mourning goods for sale, but Aaron and me liked the drug store best where they had rows of bottles with folks names on them and little rocks inside. The sign said

CURED OF GRAVEL.
FLUID EXTRACT OF BUCHER,
MANUFACTURED IN NEW YORK.
STONES PASSED AND TO BE SEEN.

Aaron spelled it all out for us. Them days folks didn't have operations. They just took patent medicines.

Then we come to a great big sign on a tree. It said

$200.00

TWO HUNDRED DOLLARS REWARD
FOR INFORMATION ABOUT THE MAN
WHO SHOT RICHARD KENNEDY.

When Julia read that one out loud, her and Sadie wanted to go home. Aaron and me walked them back to the boarding house. We figgered on getting rid of them, but by that time it was almost dark, so Father made us stay in, eat our supper, and go to bed.

After we'd blowed our candle out, Aaron and me layed there a long time talking about how we'd find the man who killed Richard Kennedy and how we'd buy things with our two hundred dollars reward. Come morning we got dressed, et breakfast, and snuck off early to run down the clues.

We hadn't no more than got started when some men on horseback come riding by as abreast as they could make it. Aaron pulled me

off to one side out of the way. You could see from their faces they was
terrible excited. We followed along after them, heading the way
everybody else was. Pretty soon I begun to think everyone in Richmond was out after that reward, too.

Next thing we knowed the crowds got thicker. Men was running
back and forth and yelling at each other. Aaron and me wanted
to see what was going on so we started running and yelling too,
then some other fellows come out of a side street, and there we
was right in the thick of it, and plenty scared.

Then somebody started shooting close by and a Negro fell dead!

Aaron and me run back across the street, and hid between the
front steps of two brick houses that had fancy iron railings, and
we stayed there a long time and watched until the soldiers come
and cleared the street and took over and told us to go home. I didn't
know until a long time afterward that what we seen didn't have
nothing to do with Richard Kennedy getting murdered. We never
did hear nothing more about him.

No, sir, what Aaron and me seen, right there in Richmond, on
March 16, 1870, was the beginning of the Radical Rebellion. You
see, after the Civil War, Richmond was put under military rule and
them carpet-baggers moved in from up North and run things their
own way until January, 1870, when Virginia was admitted back
into the Union and elections was to be held so that regular men
instead of the army would run the city again. The state had already
picked a new governor. March sixteenth was the day when George
Chahoon, the army mayor, was supposed to turn the government
over to H. K. Ellyson, who was the one the people had elected. But
he never done it. So they had two mayors and two city councils.

The army bunch held onto the books and the desks. The townsfolks turned out to put their friends into the offices. The Negroes
come along and got mixed up in it, too. John Henderson, the Negro
that the military man shot, wouldn't move on when he was told to.
I've heard he drawed a gun first on the soldier, but I never seen him.
When the soldiers come in from Camp Grant to take charge, the
Negroes begun throwing things at them. Then a policeman got
shot. Then another Negro got killed. Then the rioting went on for
a couple of days with our folks setting inside that boarding house
not knowing a soul in Richmond. Why, even the boarding-house

keeper didn't want to have nothing to do with us because she knowed we was Yankees.

Finally they got things under control outside, after they put a lot of folks in jail to cool off until they got around to holding a trial. By that time Mama was feeling better, so Father took her out and bought her a cook stove because she said she'd never be able to keep house without one. Why, her folks hadn't cooked in a fireplace since she was a little girl. Her folks didn't even believe in using a fireplace to heat a room—they was Pennsylvania Dutch and thrifty. They closed up all their fireplaces and put sheet metal in front, and set some of them Franklin stoves right out in the room so that heat could come out from them in all directions. She hadn't been brought up to waste things, and that went for wasting time, too.

Mama was always terrible fussy about her kitchen. She was a great woman to clean, and she worked fast and always kept busy with her hands. She'd even knit when she was riding in a wagon, and them Southern women that didn't do their own housework and was used to being waited on bothered her considerable. All the time she was at the boarding house she was turning up her nose at the way they done things. It got so bad she would say things right out at dinner to the landlady about the black, greasy rag that the Negro hired-girl used to wipe off the oilcloth on the table.

Come Saturday, Mama finished laying in her supplies because we knowed we was leaving early on the Monday morning train to live on our plantation that Father had bought sight unseen from that real-estate fellow who was helping the railroad bring new settlers into Virginia. She hunted around until she found a place that carried Leggs' Family Flour because she liked it best for baking. Then she got some Porto Rico sugar, and some corn meal, and a barrel of cut herring, and some soused pig feet, and some Chespeake Bay oysters "packed and sealed special for shipping to the country." Then she got tea, and raisins, and currants and a few other groceries that would keep good and didn't cost too much.

Part of our kettles had been shipped from Pennsylvania, but she bought a bunch of stone jars for storing things, and then some woodenware that was light to ship. Why, them days, we used cedar tubs, buckets, flour pails, butter paddles, spoons, and all sorts of things made of wood. Mama knowed she was going to use a cook stove so she didn't get none of them frying pans on three legs or the iron kettles they hung from cranes or the teakettles that set onto a three-legged bracket, or Dutch ovens. She didn't cook like a Southerner and she wasn't aiming to, neither.

Come Saturday night, Mama had the Negro servants bring in a tub of hot water. She give the girls their baths first because they was the cleanest. Then me and Aaron had ours while she was putting up their hair on rags so we'd be ready to go to church Sunday. Come morning we put on our good clothes and all went to the Methodist church. Us children could hardly keep from laughing at the soft ways of that preacher. Up North, our preacher always pounded on the pulpit and yelled about hell fire and brimstone, but that preacher in Richmond just talked along easy-like and never said nothing about what would happen to us after we was dead. He seemed to be more worried about how folks was going to get along with their fellow men right here on earth.

Father had been talking a lot about our money not going anywhere and that we couldn't spend no more of it or we wouldn't have none left. That's why Mama was fit to be tied, she was so excited, when he drove up with a hired team right after dinner and asked us if we'd like to go for a ride with him to see Richmond. Of course, that was about the only way for her to see things because the city is built on all them hills, but I figgered he wanted to do something nice for her on account of being so short when she wanted to go see the Whitehurst Gallery in Washington. So he decided to cheer her up by taking her to see Libby Prison where her brother starved to death during the Civil War.

Her and Father made a fine-looking pair. He was all of six foot tall; and had long, black hair; and a long, black beard; and the blackest eyes ever I seen. Mama was tall for a woman, and always held herself real straight. Her eyes was dark blue, and her hair was light brown, and all curly around the edges no matter how hard she tried to smooth it down. Mostly she was too tired to do much laughing, but when she did smile, little wrinkles showed up all around her eyes and she had the prettiest teeth you ever seen. Her and Father thought a lot of each other, but it just seemed like they wasn't made to pull real well in double harness no matter how hard they tried. If his brother—who'd been courting her—hadn't died in the Civil War, things might have been different for her. If his first wife hadn't died in childbirth, things might have been different for him. But the way it was they was just good folks doing the best they could for each other and for us children.

Just like that day, you could see Mama was real pleased to think he'd planned this ride for her. Then he begun to act sort of sheepish when he said he had to drive down past the livery stable to pick up a stranger named Jim that he'd got to talking to and had agreed to have come along with us to see the sights. But Jim turned out to be real pleasant and when he wasn't trying to sell Father a corn planter, he told us a lot of things about how the Southerners lived there during the blockade. That was before the Confederate troops burned the supplies that they couldn't take with them and before the Northerners moved in and set a lot more fires. Between them two armies they hadn't left too much for us to see.

Before the Civil War, Richmond had been a planters' city. Mostly they manufactured tobacco, they had some iron foundries where they made farm implements, and a sugar refinery and a woolen mill. But they depended on the North for their goods, and when they was cut off the only way they could get their guns was to run them through the Blockade from Europe, or capture them in battle. Even then they was short of ammunition until they figgered out how to make their own.

Father and Jim got awful interested in talking about how they got along when they was cut off from the Northern factories and munition plants. They had to learn to tan leather and make shoes for their soldiers, and they didn't know how to make good ones. Either them soldiers had to march on sore feet or they had to kill the right-sized Northerner in battle and take his shoes.

And it was even harder when it come to keeping their guns going. They run their own forges with charcoal from the banks of the James River. They made cattridges from copper kettles and old apple-jack stills. They got nitre out of caves in around Richmond; and took dead horses and other animals. They brung in sulphuric acid that they'd learned to make down farther south. Then they mixed it all together to make nitric acid right there in an old building that they'd turned into an arsenal, on the banks of the James River that run through the west end of town.

Mama and the girls got so tired of listening to Jim tell about where all of them different places had stood that they was glad when he decided Father wasn't going to buy nothing from him. He asked us to drive downtown and drop him off on the corner of Broad Street. We come awful close to having a runaway there, when a train come by and scared the horses. But he'd clumb down out of the wagon and was where he could catch hold of our horses' heads and he drug his feet.

Jim got our team stopped but some other folks wasn't so lucky with their runaway. A man and his wife and their part-growed daughter was back of us a piece up the street when the train whistled close to them. It scared their team so bad they laid back their ears, stretched their necks and took out of there on a dead gallop. If you've never seen a team of horses running away down a crowded street, you've missed something. Them horses had a glassy stare in their eyes when they went by us, and their lips was drawed away from their teeth. The driver knowed what he was in for, and he drawed back so hard on the reins trying to stop them, that he broke one right in two. Having just one rein was worse than nothing, 'cause if he pulled on that one, he'd run the horses into the crowds along the sides of the street, so he just had to let them go. Folks ahead had time to get out of their way because the women was hanging on and screaming, the driver was hollering "Whoa!". The clatter of the horses hooves and the rattle of the iron tires on that rough, old street was making a racket you could of heard a mile away. Everybody was shouting, telling the driver what to do. Some fellows run out and tried to catch the horses' heads but they was going too fast. One of them fellows trying to help was knocked flat by the front wheel.

The last I seen of them they was still going down the street lickity split. I never knowed what happened but whatever it was, no good could have come of it. When horses start running they seem to go mad. They'll run over anything in front of them. A team will run straddle of a tree until the wagon tongue either sticks in solid or breaks to pieces. The only man I ever knowed of who stopped his own team when he had one broke rein was a fellow who was moving hay out in the center of a big field, and he pulled hard on that one good rein and run them horses in circles, cutting all sorts of patterns right through a nice stand of hay until they finally run down.

A couple of years after we seen that runaway, folks in Richmond got so tired of having trains going right through their main street, scaring the wits out of their horses, that they held an election and voted to make the Central and Petersburg roads move their tracks. But when we was there, ox carts, wagons, horse-drawed streetcars, and trains was all going along Broad Street together. And we was mighty glad to turn off of it and get onto a quiet, side street.

Aaron and me told Father to drive up past the Capitol. Then we seen the house where Jefferson Davis had lived and a lot more of them big mansion-houses where the folks with money had turned their houses sideways, with two-story porches in front facing a garden, and high iron fences, and gates big enough to drive a carriage through shutting them off from the street. They had a nice, roomy cemetery of their own, too. But the big cemetery was off to itself where there was rows and rows of graves crowded together as close as they could get. Them graves must of belonged to the folks who lived in all them houses that was crowded together, too.

I could see that Father, after he'd got hisself into it, was stalling for time, but finally he turned the horses' heads toward Libby Prison that was sort of off to itself with a canal on one side so it was easy to guard. The Libbys had been a Northern family. When the war started the Confederates took their place away from them before they had a chance to take the sign down that said

LIBBY AND SONS:
SHIPS CHANDLERS AND GROCERS

Nobody else wanted to claim it; so folks fell into the habit of calling it Libby Prison when the Northern soldiers was run in there and corralled up together.

Why Libby Prison was just a big warehouse of nine rooms, built good, with real solid walls. Of course it didn't have no furniture, or water, or toilets. The prisoners just had the clothes they wore when they come in. Most of them had been captured in battle so they didn't have blankets, or nothing to eat out of and nothing to eat. At first the South tried to give them rations, but it got so bad during the Blockade, they didn't have food to spare. Then when they was afraid of a prison break and was running short of men, the orders went out for the guards to shoot at any heads they seen at the bars at the windows. Them poor souls inside didn't have enough good air to go around, and what water they did get wasn't fit to drink. Nights, the prisoners slept on the floor in rows, head to head and foot to foot, spoon fashion. One fellow was elected to be captain for each bunch. There wasn't room for them to lay on their backs, so when it got so they couldn't stand to lay on one side no more, they'd pass the word down to the captain. He'd sing out "Attention! Prepare to spoon!" and then he'd give the signal so's the whole squad could roll over to the other side.

We didn't stay long on account of Mama crying too hard about her brother and them other boys who died there. Father offered to take her up to see Fortress Monroe, that had real nice buildings, but she just shook her head, so we drove back to town to the boarding house.

Mama and us children went inside while Father took the team back to the livery stable. The landlady happened to be in the front hall and when she seen Mama's red eyes, she asked what was the matter. One thing sort of led to another; Mama got a mite peppery about her brother and them other boys that died at Libby Prison and at Andersonville, over to the west of us, where over 12,000 Northern prisoners had died in that open stockade in a little over a year, and the ones that come through it alive wasn't ever the same again. Mama said the Southerners should be ashamed, treating their prisoners like that.

Well, our landlady stiffened right up and she let Mama have it with both barrels. She says: "My husband died of pneumonia right there in Camp Douglas near Chicago because he was run down when he was captured, and he had to sleep on the wet ground with no blankets. My only brother died after the Northerners cut his rations at Elmira Prison, in New York. And you did it just to be mean and to get even with us when you had plenty of food and blankets for yourselves and for them.

"It was the North that stopped the exchange of prisoners. Until you blockaded us in here, so we couldn't get supplies, we did what we could for the boys we'd captured. But at the last we were starving ourselves! Flour cost a thousand dollars a barrel in Confederate money; meal was eighty dollars a pound; and potatoes was thirty dollars a bushel.

"You don't know what it was like to live in Richmond during the Blockade. I sold everything I had to keep alive, and now we're overrun with carpet-baggers swarming down here from up North trying to scrape what they can off the bottom of an empty barrel."

Next thing we knowed our landlady was over in the corner on the settee crying and Mama was there beside her with her arms around her shoulders, talking real friendly-like to her. Aaron and me got out of there.

TWO

OUR PLANTATION

Monday morning we got up real early, packed our stuff, and was on the nine o'clock train when it pulled out of Richmond. The Richmond-Danville railroad had been put out of commission for considerable time after the armies tore it up and burned the bridges at the close of the Civil War. But when our family moved down there in 1870, trains was running regular every day, except Sunday. Father bought our tickets straight through to Keysville so he could see Mr. Thompson, the real-estate fellow, who was to fix up our papers. He said we'd back track from there to Meherrin but that he wanted everything ship-shape before he moved our stuff out to the plantation.

By the time our family got onto them little cars that had been used during that retreat, they'd fixed things up considerable. We used new bridges that had been throwed across the rivers to take the place of the ones the soldiers had burned. We rode on new rails that had been put down on the old roadbed because nobody had ever been able to figger out a way to salvage them old ones without doing more work than they was worth. Every little piece along there we'd come to a big tree that was wearing an iron collar of twisted rails, sometimes three or four foot high, wrapped around its trunk. The Confederate soldiers, retreating from Richmond, wrecked the bridges so they couldn't be followed. But the worst places was farther on, where the northern raiders had come in and tore up the tracks to keep Lee from getting his supplies. The most damage had been done by Wilson and his division of cavalry from the Army of the Potomac. In around Roanoke Bridge, they had tore up twenty-five mile of track in one stretch.

When they tore up the tracks, they done it like this. First, they'd pull the spikes out of several rails together. Then they'd take up the railroad ties and put dry branches with them and build red-hot fires where they'd lay them rails, until they would get so hot in the middle they'd bend real easy.

After that some soldiers would grab each end of a rail and run over to the nearest big tree. They'd walk around toward each other until they met; then they'd change ends and back up to make a complete wrap. Why, when they got done wrapping them rails around them big trees, there wasn't no way of getting them out of there short of cutting down the trees, hauling the rails off to a blast furnace, melting them up, and starting all over again at a rolling mill.

Even if they'd wanted to, they couldn't of got them bent rails out of there because there wasn't no railroad to haul them on. When they did get new rails down on the old roadbed, they was so short of men to work in the fields that they never done nothing with them wrapped-up rails. So, when we went through there, we seen them, and we seen broken down wagons and horses' skeletons, and most everything else that a couple of armies would be leaving around when they'd finally had enough and called it quits. Us children kept gandering around talking about all the things there was to see, but Mama just set there, awful still. Father didn't have nothing to say neither after we passed Meherrin and seen that it wasn't nothing but a wide place in the road.

The train kept taking us right along until we got to Keysville. It was a fair-sized town of about four hundred folks. Mr. Thompson met us and took us up to his house where we stayed all night. Oh, the Thompsons was nice enough folks I guess, only their children was all girls and I wasn't old enough to think much of girls them days. All the time we was eating Mr. Thompson kept going on about how "all this country needs is emigrants with capital and vision, who will work hard," and then he'd keep questioning us about anyone we knowed up North who might be a likely one to come down here and buy a farm. He done a lot of talking about the

advantages of farming, but Aaron and me figgered he looked too
soft to have done any of it hisself. Us children went to bed early and
Aaron and me laid there and listened to them girls all whispering
and giggling in the next room, and them frogs croaking their fool
heads off outside, and we wasn't sure what we thought of the South
ourselves.

Next morning, Mama took Father aside and told him she figgered
we'd been on the way too long to spend time visiting, and she'd
like to get in her new home. So Father and Mr. Thompson quit
beating around the bush and got down to business. Before long
Mr. Thompson had our money and we had a deed, and so we took
the next train back to Meherrin.

Father left us setting right there at the depot while he went
up to Price's store to hire a Negro to haul us, and as much of our
stuff as he could take on the load, out to our plantation. Now Sadie
and Julia had talked all the way from Washington, D.C., about
how we was going to live in a mansion-house. Of course they was
just at the age when they had to be talking about something, but it
got mighty tiresome listening to them. Mama hadn't said hardly a
thing except that she didn't think much of the farms around there.
Her folks was Pennsylvania Dutch and real good farmers. They
raised everything they needed right on their own farm.

If Mama had been a man, she'd of been a blamed-good farmer;
she sure had a feel for the soil.

We all piled in the wagon soon as it got there. When we drove
past the stores, the folks inside all come out to look us over. They
didn't speak first as we figgered they might, but Mama nodded
friendly-like, and us children half waved. They looked sort of seedy
and down-at-the-heel. What bothered me was they didn't smile nor
nothing, they just stared straight at us. I turned around when we
got by; they wasn't talking, they was just standing there looking
after us. Father said the man he hired the team from didn't appear
to like Northerners. Meherrin had three stores, a blacksmith shop,
a school, and several houses.

Our plantation was only two miles from town. Seemed like we'd
no more than got started when we stopped in front of a big, tall,
up-and-down house with a porch sort of falling away from the front
and a bunch of old buildings falling down out in back. Mama just

set there in the wagon and looked at that old house. Then she says to Father, "Is this it, Sam?"

I looked at Father and I could see by the set of his face that he was disappointed, too. Then he turned around to Mama and says, "Yes, Martha, this is it."

The Negro driving the team started to throw back his head and laugh, but he drawed it down between his shoulders just like an old turtle when Father turned around to look at him. Then Father jumped down, and he held out his hand and helped Mama and the girls out of the wagon. Us boys got out by ourselves, and all four of us children followed them up the path real quiet-like. We could see it wasn't no time to be talking.

The inside of that plantation-house beat anything I ever seen. The downstairs was just one big room, with a straight stairway going up from one side. The ceilings was so high I couldn't reach them with a broom, even when I stood on one of them window sills. I know I couldn't because I tried it just as soon as I had a chance. The second floor was just like the first one. On up above was the third floor, made just like the other two. There wasn't a partition in the place. Why, our Southern mansion-house wasn't nothing but three large rooms, built one on top the other, and connected by the steepest stairways you ever seen, and with a big, long porch across the front. A brick chimney run up the wall opposite the stairway, and there was a fireplace on each floor. Downstairs there was a door at the back leading out to the other buildings that clustered around most every which way.

Nearest to the house was the building where we done our eating. Next to it was the outside kitchen. It was empty except for a big, black fireplace, and an old table and bench, and a few shelves along one wall. The other farm buildings and the old slaves' quarters set a piece from the house. Father had a list of things that was supposed to come with the place, but by the time he took over, everything that was loose had been packed off.

After we got unloaded, Mama fixed up the beds the best she could. Her and Father had the second floor, later on they curtained off a corner for the girls to have their bed in, while Aaron and me had the third floor to ourselves. Mama was feeling real bad again. Her ague kept coming and going. First she'd be burning up with fever, then in a little while she'd be chilling so it seemed like her teeth would never stop chattering. Father had her lie down and he went down to the old slaves' quarters where Mr. Thompson had said we'd find Negroes living who'd be glad to work in the field. They was slave families who'd been on the place; after they was freed they didn't have no where else to go, so they just raised a little garden and worked when they had a chance.

Father hired a Negro woman named Sally to help out right along. She said she used to keep house for the widow woman who had owned the place before she had sold it to Bruces, who sold the place through Mr. Thompson to us. That was the first we knowed that they still lived up the road, on the next plantation, and that they had sold their poorest land to us.

Mama stayed in bed that night, so Sally cooked our supper. I couldn't eat the hoecake she'd made. I'd never seen victuals fixed like that, but mostly it was her hands that bothered me. The palms was about five shades lighter than the backs. Sally was the first Negro I'd ever noticed up real close. I didn't know they was all made like that and I figgered she hadn't washed her hands clean or they'd be the same shade all over.

I liked most of them Negroes first rate. The folks worried considerable at the way they sort of felt what was ours was theirs. But Sally seemed to have been waiting for some white folks to come and live in that empty old house so's she could take care of them her way. She done our cooking and a lot of the other housework whenever Mama would let her. She tried her best to make Mama think she was doing things the way she told her to, when she really wasn't. Mama and Sally was both old enough to be set in their ways, and their ways wasn't one bit alike.

Down South, before the Civil War, them folks that lived in big mansion-houses had their cooking done off in an outside kitchen and slaves would be running back and forth so's the food would be served hot to the white folks eating it in the big house. We never could figger out why they done it like that, unless they didn't like the smell of dinner cooking or was afraid of fire. Mama was always tasting and sniffing, and stirring things in kettles. She said that having your food clean and being clean yourself when you was handling it was the most important thing about housekeeping, and the only way to have things done right was to do them yourself.

Up where she come from, the Pennsylvania-Dutch women kept the front parlor shut up tighter than a drum. Her folks always had the shades drawed and nobody went in the front parlor, excepting to clean, unless they had a wedding, or a funeral, or company from a distance. Nobody used the front door, and they sure didn't waste their time setting on no big front porch. Why Mama's folks done their cooking, and their eating, and most of their living in a long kitchen that run clean across the back of their big stone house. That kitchen was used more than all of the rest of the house put together, and she sure didn't think much of living in a place where the kitchen wasn't even a part of the house.

But nothing ever kept her down for long. Come morning she was up for breakfast, and while Father and us boys went out to look the plantation over, Mama put on a big bib apron that covered all the front of her Mother Hubbard. She tied a cloth around her head, and took the girls with her and started out to check on the kitchen before she unpacked her stuff. Sally was out there moving around sort of slow-like, sweeping the floor with a homemade broom. Mama had the first bought-broom Sally ever seen. Folks around there just gathered a bunch of broomgrass—it growed about three-foot high, and they tied it about two thirds of the way up with a piece of twine—and done all of their sweeping with it. Sally just couldn't get over our bought broom, but Mama figgered she was always a lot more interested in looking at it or showing it to folks than she was in using it in the corners and around the edges.

Sally said she'd been looking after the big iron kettle that belonged on the iron crane in our fireplace. She brung it back when we moved in, and Mama had her fill it with water and stir up the fire. Then she sent the girls up to the house to fetch down some bars of home-made soap that she'd brung from Pennsylvania. Mama always saved all the extra drippings and meat fryings and made the nicest, whitest soap you ever seen. It sudsed up good, and she cut the bars big enough so you had something decent-sized to hold in your hand when you was washing. It wasn't no time after Mama got there until she had the table and benches out in the yard, and her and Sally had the inside walls all scrubbed down and everything as clean as a whistle.

When Father and Aaron and me come back for lunch, she set some cold victuals on the table outside for us, then Mama said, "Sam, you and the boys are helping me this afternoon."

Father started right in to tell her about how he needed to get the tobacco seed planted and the fields in shape, but she cut him off so short he changed his mind. It wasn't no time to say nothing about how bad the fields was looking. She'd made up her mind that she was going to cook supper on her new cook stove, and nothing was going to change it, come hell or high water.

By the time we was through eating lunch, all the Negroes in the place was hanging around outside. They'd heard of the goings on in the kitchen and wanted to see Mama. That give Father some help getting the stove uncrated and moved in. He'd bought enough stovepipe so they could set it up right along the empty wall on the side that run at an angle to the fireplace. That was the first stove them darkies had ever seen and they couldn't figger out how it worked. But they didn't have much time to find out then, because Father put them right to work cleaning up around them old buildings.

Then he had us boys bring in the best boards we could find, and he got some shelves up in the kitchen. Mama and the girls got our stuff unpacked and set out just where she wanted it. Mama was used to hired girls up North, and she didn't have no trouble at all keeping Sally busy, but you could see Sally wasn't used to Pennsylvania-Dutch housekeeping. She figgered Mama belonged in the house instead of out there in the outside kitchen bossing her around.

That night, after they knocked off work and was heading back for their cabins, the Negroes helping Father asked if they could come in and see Mama's stove het up. They just couldn't understand how the heat was brung up from underneath, or how the firebox would heat the whole top of it and all around the oven. Because Mama had saucepans, she could cook things in ways they'd never heard of, like stewing cherries up with a little sweetening and thickening to make a pudding, or cooking fruit down and making it into jam. Them days the folks in around Meherrin figgered you

picked your fruit off the trees and either et it right on the spot or
served it raw at the table, just like it had growed.

As soon as Father had a little time, he started in studying the
buildings, figgering out where he'd keep his farming equipment and
his horses and wagon when he got them. The old carriage house had
give up completely. The roof had fallen in and it was in such bad
shape it couldn't be used for nothing but firewood. So he decided
to fix up another building that was about twenty-foot long and
sixteen-foot wide, with a small door in the front, and benches around
the three sides. A big piece of a tree had been hewed out about ten
inches square and was sunk solid in the center of the floor so that
it stood about six-foot high. On each side of that big headpost, there
was another one about the same height and about six inches square.
Them posts was set close to seven and a half foot apart. When us
boys had been looking for lumber to make shelves, Father had said
for us to use them benches. Then he went out with an ax and cut
them three posts down that stood in the way in the middle of the
dirt floor, and he called some darkies to drag them out in the yard and
to help him knock the side out of that building so he could use it
as a carriage house.

I never heard such yelling as when they seen that he had got
them posts out of there. The darkies come running from all over
the place and they begun dancing and singing and carrying on something terrible around them posts laying out in the yard. You see, that
building was their old whipping-house, and until Father put it
out of commission they always figgered things might change back to
the way they was in slave times, and some plantation owner would
start using it again. The widow-woman who had owned the place
during slavery days would make the other darkies bring in two
slaves at a time. She'd have their clothes peeled off and the two of
them was tied with their arms to the middle post and their feet
to them farther posts, real tight, so they couldn't double up. Then
she'd take a big, long whip and beat first one and then the other,
until the sweat would pour off of her and she'd have to set on one of
them benches to rest while the overseer would spell her awhile.
They said she was made so she got more fun out of beating folks
than she did out of anything else. She'd used it so often that them

darkies figgered as long as the whipping-house stood they wasn't really free.

The darkies said that the overseer was meaner than the widow-woman. They told me over and over again about the time when they was slaves and a darky named Old French, who was all crippled up with rheumatism and dreadful slow, couldn't keep up with the rest of them shocking hay down in the south field. A storm was blowing in fast, and the overseer kept getting after him for lagging behind. But Old French couldn't move no faster. The overseer picked up a rock and he throwed it, and it got Old French right in back of the temple and he keeled over, dead. The rest of them darkies had to go on shocking hay until they finished the field. Then about dark the overseer had them pick up Old French and carry him over to the fence corner. They dug a hole and buried him without no funeral, or even letting his wife know that he was dead so's she could be there for the burying. Them darkies on our place talked a lot about how bad things was for them back in the days when Old French was killed. Then they'd get to talking about how bad things had been for them since, and sometimes they figgered they wasn't much better off than they was before.

Back in slave days, they wasn't ever out of work. Why, when there wasn't no railroad through there, the slaves had to roll hogs-heads packed full of tobacco over that plank road from the country way above Meherrin clean down to the ocean. That was all of a hundred mile and it took them almost as long to roll it down there as it did to raise the tobacco in the first place. But they didn't have no other way to get it to the ships that was taking it to England, and tobacco was worth real money, them days.

A short time after we moved South, one of the darky girls on our place up and died. As soon as Mama heard about it, she went down to the cabin to see if there was anything she could do. But she made us children stay home. We was setting there talking, wondering what had made her die, when Julia, who was older than Sadie and me, and awful curious, says, "I wonder if she's turned white yet."

I says, "She ain't white. She's a darky."

Julia says, "No, she's dead, so she's an angel."

And Sadie, who always took Julia's side on everything, says, "Then she's white, because all angels are white."

I says, "I don't believe it. She don't turn color 'til she gets to heaven and goes through them pearly gates."

Just about then, Mama come back and said the funeral wasn't until the next day and we could go if we behaved ourselves and stood by her. They had figgered on having it the same day but the two Negroes who had been sent to dig the grave had loafed along until there wasn't time. It was quite a piece out to the cemetery on our plantation, so they had asked Father if they could keep the corpse in our granary 'til time for the burying. They had made a strong coffin out of some pretty good lumber. After they had laid her out, they nailed the lid on solid and put it up on a couple of boxes so the rats couldn't get at it.

We'd heard quite a bit about that part of it from hearing Mama and Sally talk. But Mama had gotten after us before about asking personal questions so we waited until Aaron come in from the field. Then the girls run out and asked him if he thought the dead Negro girl's corpse had turned white yet. He just says, "No, and it ain't likely to." And he went on in to eat his supper.

But Julia got to thinking about it again in the night. Next morning, when the older folks was busy, she come around with the screwdriver under her apron. She figgered we'd better look inside that coffin while we had the chance. Sadie was egging her on because she wanted to see a Negro angel. And I didn't have to be coaxed, neither.

Well, we done it. It took quite a bit of prying to get one of them boards up. Then when we got it loose, it was so dark in there we couldn't see nothing. The only thing we could do was lift the coffin off them boxes and drag it over to the light that come in from the granary door. We looked out first to see that no one was around. Then when we got it down and sort of bumped it along the floor over to where we could look inside good, there she was—just like I'd figgered —sleeping away and as black as ever.

By that time we was afraid someone would catch us, so we got the lid on and drug the coffin back again. But try as hard as we could the three of us couldn't lift it up on them boxes again. We seen we had to have help. Aaron was off in a far field. Father was working in the carriage house. He was the nearest, but we all figgered we'd better by-pass him.

When we got to the house, Mama was baking bread. We talked all around what we wanted to say, but it was getting late, so finally Julia up and asked her, real polite, if she wouldn't like to see a dead darky. Mama said, no, she had seen one, and even if she hadn't she wouldn't be caring about it. We finally told her what had happened. It was plain she didn't think it was a good plan for Father to know, because she led off on the path that didn't go past the carriage house where we could hear him pounding away.

Mama helped us get the coffin back on the boxes and we sort of figgered she'd forgive us by then. But when she said to come over to the house, I could tell from her shoulders as she stalked off ahead of us, that we was in for it. She licked all three of us as hard as she could. But we had sense enough not to cry real loud. We didn't want Father to find out and give us a worse one.

When we got down to the cemetery that afternoon the darkies was all standing around. They had carried the coffin out and laid it up close to the side of the hole that them lazy fellows had finally got dug. Old William, who lived on our place and was quite a preacher, stood at the head of the grave. Another darky, who was sort of his echo, was at the foot. The girl's relatives and our family lined up on the casket side.

After they sung some hymns, old William started in. That sermon beat anything I ever heard. He never did get around to saying a thing about the dead girl. He just went on and on about the tearing down of them whipping posts. He'd say, "God bless Massa' Sam Hawthorne and Mrs. Sam Hawthorne and all their chillun. I was nothing but a slave, just like an ox. I had a yoke on my neck. When Massa' Sam Hawthorne took his ax, he done knocked out the old bow key around my neck. The yoke fell down and I was a free nigger. God bless Massa' Sam Hawthorne and all of his chillun."

All the time he was talking, the one down at the end was yelling, "Amen, Lord. Amen, Lord."

That went on with them two leading off, and pretty soon they was all yelling, "Come down—Come down—Lord. Come down, Lord, and give us a real big name. A real big name. Come down, Lord!"

And that's only a little bit of what happened. I'll tell you a man could of heard that darky funeral if he'd been setting indoors with his windows shut two miles away from there. Father was so bothered about all that celebrating and mixing him into it when he figgered they should have been talking about that dead girl, that he went on up to the house and set on the porch and read until it was so dark he couldn't see and he had to go into the house and go to bed.

Father was a great fellow to read the paper. While we was still in Richmond he had looked around and checked prices. The daily come too dear, so he ordered the semi-weekly *Richmond-Dispatch*. It cost three dollars a year but it give all the news about everything. Nights he could set and read and wish for things like money to buy lime from the steamer *Hardscrabble* when it come in with a load that was sold right from the dock in Richmond.

Just about the time we was settled, Father read in the paper that the trial for them fellows we seen doing all the rioting in Richmond was coming up. He allowed he'd like to go to Richmond and set in on that trial, but of course he didn't have the time, or the money, or any encouragement from Mama.

It's a good thing he didn't because so many folks crowded in at the trial that the whole center of the floor of the upstairs hall where it was held give way. The floors and everybody there dropped clean down into the basement, excepting the judges who was setting up in front on a separate platform. That was a terrible thing! More than fifty folks got mashed to death, and a lot more than that got hurt bad. We read about it in the papers or heard about it from the neighbors. Why, nobody ever talked about nothing else but that accident when we went into Price's Store in Meherrin.

Of course, having that floor give way like that was hard on the ones that got killed or hurt bad, but all the rest of them folks that had been arguing about who was going to run Richmond got so busy helping out that they quit fighting among theirselves and all pitched right in taking care of burying the dead and patching up the living. The newspapers spread the story all over, and folks up North started taking collections. All together more than eighty thousand dollars was sent in to help them folks in Richmond. Then the governor set aside a "day of humiliation and prayer." It was meant to show that they was sorry they had acted like that, and from then on they aimed to bury the hatchet.

At first they thought they'd have to wreck the building on account of its insides dropping down like that, but instead some fellows that knowed their business figgered out a way to fix it up again. But out at our plantation every time us children got to fighting among ourselves, Mama reminded us about what happened to them folks in Richmond when they didn't get along, and then she'd talk to us about how you was supposed to love your neighbor as yourself. But that was a blamed hard thing to do with some of the neighbors that we had.

Why, one of our neighbors like to scared us to death right after we got there. One night, way after midnight, he come yelling and crashing through the brush, screaming: "For God's sake, don't kill me. I want to see my father and my mother again."

Father pulled his breeches on fast, and went out and fetched him in from the barnyard where he was in the fence corner, moaning and taking on. Him and Mama hurried around, stirred up the fire, brewed him a pot a sassafras tea, and tried to get him quieted down so he'd talk more rational, but he kept right on raving. I went down in my nightshirt to listen, but when Mama seen me she sent me skeedaddling straight up to bed again.

I found out afterward that this fellow, who lived neighbor to us, had them spells quite often at night. During the Civi War, he was told after one of the battles that he was to walk a captured Northern soldier from up above Meherrin on down to Farmville where they was to take him to Andersonville Prison. They had better than a day's walk going through the woods. It was hard traveling and this neighbor of ours was in an old wore-out Confederate uniform and his shoes had wore through so bad that he was leaving blood stains here and there on the ground where the blisters had broke open.

Every step he took made him hate this dressed-up Northern soldier ahead of him just that much more. Finally he decided to kill him, roll his body off into the woods, and wear them good boots hisself. The first time he raised his gun to fire the man ahead of him must of felt him looking at him clean through his back, or maybe he heard the hammer click when he cocked it, because he

turned around quick, and when he seen the gun pointed right between his shoulder blades, he dropped down quick on his knees,
and begun to say over and over again, "For God's sake, don't shoot
me. I want to see my mother and my father again."

It wasn't that he was yellow, but this Northerner was just a real
young boy, and he probably figgered he had most of his living to do
yet. So our neighbor didn't have the guts to shoot him right in the
face. He told him to get up and start walking for Farmville—that
he wouldn't shoot him after all. But every little while he'd change his
mind. That must of been a terrible day. They was both about half
crazy. The Northern boy kept pleading for his life, and the Southerner, bad as he wanted them boots, just didn't have the heart to
shoot him right in the face. So whenever the boy in front would hear
that hammer click, he'd turn around real quick and start begging for
his life. Finally along about sundown, when they was nearing Farmville, the boy ahead was sort of off his guard, and the man behind
knowed it had to be soon if he was going to have them boots. So he
put his gun up to his shoulder and aimed, and fired real quick. It
was a clean shot, and it didn't take him no time to haul the remains
off into the woods and get into them good heavy wool socks and nice,
soft leather boots. He took the things that was in the boy's pockets
and turned around and went on back to his regiment. During the
rest of the war, when he was in the fighting, he never thought nothing
more about it, but after peace come and him and his wife moved out
on a plantation not far from ours, he begun to have these night-
mares.

It got so bad she couldn't stand it, so she just up and left his
bed and board. After that he lived on there alone. The darkies was
afraid of him, and most of them moved off of his place. Everybody
around knowed that he'd get these spells when he'd think that
Yankee boy had come back for his boots, and then he'd start running
to get away from him, and he'd run through the brush and trees
so's it would be harder for the boy to follow him and he'd keep
yelling, over and over again, "For God's sake, don't shoot." Seemed
like he paid an awful big price for them boots.

But we had one family of real good neighbors between our place
and town. Their name was Williams. Old Stitch Williams, the
father, was over one hundred years old. He'd been a tailor; that's

why they called him Stitch. He'd fought all during the War of 1812, but he was still so spry that when his wife died of old age he up and married a younger one and when we moved there he had another set of children about our ages. Sue was the one our girls liked best.

Old Stitch always carried his firewood in from the woods on his back. One time Father let me drive our team all one day to help Stitch haul in some pitch bark. Stitch had a son in his first family who had fought all during the Civil War. When he finally come home, his brothers all thought he was their father. Yep, Stitch was still a mighty good man, even if he was over a hundred years old, and his neck was all withered and skinny and his Adam's apple walked up and down when he talked. He'd seen so much and knowed so much to talk about that Father got to spending hours listening to Stitch tell him how to farm; Mama thought he should have been spending that time working on our plantation. But before midsummer Father was terrible discouraged about our crop.

I just ain't sure whether tobacco or the Civil War was hardest on that country down there. Now you take that plantation of ours. After we moved down and sorted out the lies them real estate fellows had told us and got down to the bare facts, we seen Father'd bought something no one with two holes in his head would touch with a ten-foot pole. It was sort of red ground that had been used for raising tobacco for so long nothing would grow. They'd took everything out of the soil without putting nothing back in until it was so poor it wouldn't of sprouted black-eyed peas. It would dry out and bake and crack open until it was like brick. Or, if it did rain, it would turn into a red mud that stuck to everything, the hardest stuff to try to work and get into shape that I ever seen any place.

All around that part of the country there was fields nobody was even trying to farm, where little scrub-pine trees was beginning to grow, and a few cornstalks was sprouting here and there. Folks who didn't know where to turn for their next dime or their next meal was living in old, tumble-down houses, and hating to show theirselves in their ragged clothes. Us children would hear Father and Mother talking together way into the night trying to figger out what to do, and then next day they'd talk to us children about how we had to all pitch in and help to do the best we could to raise a tobacco crop so we'd have something to sell for cash, and how we'd have to raise all we could to eat, there on the place.

As soon as we had moved South, Father hurried around and got our tobacco seed planted right off. He picked a sheltered place in the woods and piled a lot of brush on a little clearing he made there. Then he burned it to get rid of the weeds and to have the ashes to turn under for fertilizer. After the ground was dug up good, the seed was planted thick and then brush was cut and stuck into the ground, slanting, to hold it off the seedlings but to give them some shade while they was sprouting. Meantime, him and the darkies got the ground worked and hilled up as good as they could so we could get the plants in when they got to be about the size of cabbage plants and could be transplanted. Up until then I'd been helping Mama get in her garden of sweet potatoes, corn, cabbages, and turnips for greens. She'd got ahold of some regular eggs and was trying to raise baby chicks. She never thought much of them guinea hens like the darkies had. But as soon as them tobacco plants was ready to transplant, Father called me to help him and from then on from daylight till dark I was stuck working with them blamed tobacco plants. I just never have believed that the fellows smoking that stuff get enough good out of it to make up for all the hard labor somebody has got to put into it.

When we started transplanting them seedlings from the place where they'd growed, Father had me go along with a big can full of guano, and an old tablespoon. At every hill I had to kneel down and put a tablespoonful of that fertilizer in the hole just before he put in the plant. Them hills was about three foot apart. I never could see what good it done to plant them in hills instead of on the level ground, but that's the way we done it anyhow. Father and them darkies kept scratching away at the ground trying to keep it from baking too hard. My job was to go around to each plant every day and pick off all them big tobacco worms I could find and drop them in the can, and take them over to Hector so he could mash them good and get rid of them.

As soon as the plants started growing good and looked like they was getting ready to flower, all the centers had to be broke out of them. Then the suckers around the bottoms all had to be broke off, until just enough leaves was left to grow good. Only ours didn't grow like we hoped they would. They took a spell in late summer of just setting there, getting drier and drier-looking, when they wasn't even half growed.

Father thought maybe he didn't know how to handle that kind of soil so he started inquiring around to see if there was anyone who could give him some pointers. That's when he heard about a fellow named Joe Axton, who'd worked for the government in England building up the soil until he'd met up with one of them fast-talking real estate fellows and quit his good job and come over to America to start raising tobacco and other crops on a big plantation he'd bought sight unseen. They didn't know that them days it was easier to get land and skim off the cream, and after the good was all gone from it then get virgin soil on farther west. They'd sell their old, wore-out farms to folks like Axton and us and a slough of others that didn't know no better.

Well, Father chanced to run into Joe Axton one day at Price's store when he was doing some trading there at Meherrin. That was how he come to ask us out to their place for Sunday dinner. We got all slickered up and took off early.

When we got to Axtons, her and Mama hit it off right from the start. Next thing we knowed us children was setting in the front room holding our heads real still so we wouldn't mess up the tidies on the backs of the chairs, and her and Mama was just going lickity-cut about making Yorkshire pudding in England and scrapple in Pennsylvania. As soon as Joe Axton, who was a real quick-moving, chipper little fellow, asked Father if he'd like to see his crop of oats, Aaron and me slid off our chairs and started out too so we could get away from all that woman talk. Of course, we never got out of the house because Mrs. Axton said she had dinner ready and in just a jiffy she had it dished up and we was setting down to the table. We got filled up on beef and Yorkshire pudding. Golly, it was good.

Right after dinner, while the women was doing the dishes, we went out to see them oats that Joe had been bragging about. I could see Father studying that field all the time Joe was talking about the things he'd done to build up the soil before he'd planted it. Them oats was only about six inches high and terrible sparse, and all headed out and yellow. In between the stalks we could see places with cracks wide enough so a man could shove his hand down in them. No matter how hard you tried, them fields was dried out all of the time. The humus was burned out and we didn't have no way to put it back in. We didn't even have weeds in our fields; they couldn't grow there neither.

Going home from Axtons, Mother and Father talked it over with us children plainer than they had before. They said we'd all have to scratch around and work harder than ever to get enough to keep us and the Negroes alive during the winter. By then, we knowed our tobacco crop wouldn't amount to much, and the garden stuff we'd planted wasn't turning out much better. Our corn never filled out at all; it just growed a little nubbin here and there. The worms got most of the cabbages. The turnips wasn't so bad, but I never could get enthusiastic about being long on them. The sweet potatoes turned out real good. Come fall Aaron and me gathered dry pine needles that had fell off the trees and packed our sweet potatoes down in them. If you don't have pine needles, try packing your sweet potatoes down in oak leaves, but be blamed sure you don't have no rats or mice getting into the bins where they're stored.

I tell you we really worked. Even Sadie, little as she was, pitched in too. We scoured the woods for berries. We brung in all the fruit from them old trees in the orchard. That orchard beat anything I've ever seen. Most of them trees hadn't never been pruned. Aaron and me like to tore our clothes to pieces trying to get through them branches. Come fall, when Father pruned them trees back, the neighbors thought they was ruined.

When Father and the darkies started in to harvest the tobacco we had raised, I was sure glad to know I'd soon be through with carrying that can around to pick off them big green worms. We had a pile of tobacco sticks about four-foot long on hand. The darkies carried them out and piled them here and there around the field. They worked together, and split the stalk of each tobacco plant down from the top nearly to the bottom, being sure to leave a little piece that wasn't split. Then they'd cut the plant off at the bottom, turn it over, put it astraddle of the stick, and go on to the next plant. They'd fix it the same way, until the stick hung full of tobacco plants with their leaves all hanging down.

Then the darkies that was holding the ends of the stick would carry it to the tobacco barn that was made of logs. Beams made of logs run across just far enough apart so them loaded tobacco sticks could be hung across them.

Them plants hung down in there all the time they was drying. We'd been real careful to see that the leaves didn't touch each other, and we allowed plenty of space for the air to circulate. After the leaves got dry we had to wait for rain so the dampness in the air would keep the leaves from crumbling. Then they was taken down real careful and stripped off the main stem and laid in piles kind of like you flatten out clothes when you put them in a basket. When a man would get a bundle about as big as his wrist, he'd carry it over and put it in the press. Big leaves was put underneath and on top, and when they had enough for a bale, it was pressed down. Then ropes was tied around it and it was ready to haul to market. Only we didn't have very much tobacco to show for all our hard work.

Father got pretty short tempered before that crop was ready for market. He wasn't used to the way the Negroes took their time about doing everything. One day he got so mad at Hector for spitting into the tobacco to "make it supple" and easier to handle them leaves when they started drying out, that he almost hit him. Mama said he was getting so he acted like one of them overseers that you read about in the slave days. Of course she was tired when she said it, but he flared right back and told her she acted like a general herself.

She started to answer back quick and then she just tossed her head and said, "I am a general, Sam, and just look at what my forces have been doing." She took him by the arm, and said she knowed they was both cross because they was too tired and she wanted him to see what her and the girls and old Sally had been doing to get ready for winter.

Mama didn't have no glass jars to use them days. But she had stood over that hot stove boiling and stirring and cooking fruit down, and keeping everything real clean, and she'd filled every crock she could lay her hands on with apple butter, and cooked berries, and all sorts of stuff we'd drug in from here and there. She used heavy, stone crocks, with stone lids that fit down inside the top flange, and had a little sort of a button right smack in the top. And she'd packed her stuff clean and hot. She had a sort of a baby teakettle with a spout, and she'd fill it full of hot rosin or wax tallow, and pour it into the crack where the lid fit into the crock. She always watched real careful to see that every bit of it was sealed. Anything Mama put down kept good. Them days nobody ever opened nothing until after Thanksgiving. They knowed they'd better tighten up their belts rather than to dip into the winter's provisions.

The only canned goods we seen in the stores was oysters. Meherrin Depot wasn't terrible far from Chesapeake Bay, where they put up big cans of oysters and shipped them all over. Why, they just come in big tin cans. I've seen some with the lids soldered on, but mostly they was sealed with beeswax or tallow. They kept good, too. Of course, we had to put out money for oysters, so we mostly et what we had put down ourselves. Mama had some chickens, and we kept a cow. Then in the fall, we'd butcher a hog and smoke part of it, and make lard, and headcheese, and scrapple. But I liked the sausage patties that Mama fried up just like they do hamburgers in a restaurant. Only she would put them cooked sausage patties down in a stone jar and pour their own fat around them, and keep adding sausages and fat until she got the crock full. As long as the lard covered them they'd keep like that all winter.

Mama had been staying close to home that first summer we lived on our plantation and she hadn't met hardly any of the neighbor women. Then one day Captain Billy Pettius come over to see Father about borrowing our plough. Mama asked him to stay for dinner. and we had applesauce in bowls along with our corn pone. He went home and told his wife he'd had something brand new to eat. Next time they went to town they drove over past our place because her curiosity got the best of her. Of course, we'd been living there all summer and this happened in apple time—but Mama figgered it was a lucky chance that brung company inside her door that soon. Them folks down there just didn't take to Northerners.

At first Mrs. Pettius was sort of stiff, but before long she come right out and asked Mama about what her husband had et at our house that day. So Mama told her and then they went out to the kitchen to see the stove, and her stew kettles. She seen all the stuff Mama had been putting down, and before long they forgot all about the Civil War and was swapping recipes; and she was telling Mama about how to make lickin'er out of molasses, and how to use drippings when you didn't have no butter, and how if you hadn't an

oven and had to make hoecakes you could keep them real clean
and nice by wrapping a cabbage leaf around them before you put
them on the hoe and held them over the open fire.

Mrs. Pettius passed the word around too about Mama having a
Singer sewing machine and sets of them heavy cardboard curves
that they used instead of dress patterns. Why, Mama was so handy
she could take them curves and lay them out on a length of calico
and start drawing lines and pinning here and there and then measur-
ing, and blamed if she couldn't cut out a Mother Hubbard to fit
anybody. She'd done a lot of free cutting for the neighbors up North,
and she hadn't been in the South many months before she had her
hand into it again.

Most of them women dropping in for Mama to help them with
their dressmaking acted like they figgered on paying her back with
a hunk of sowbelly or some other victuals later on. They never got
around to it because they never had none to spare. The picking at
all of our tables was mighty slim, them days. Course we wasn't
really poor folks like some of them around there, but times we come
close to being downright hungry ourselves.

Mama was so pleased to have them women coming in and neighboring with her that she was glad to show them anything she knowed.
I tell you, a person had to go down there and live neighbor to them
folks in out-of-the-way places after the Civil War to see what it
really done to them. It was hard on the men who went off into
battle, but when they was gone—and the horses with them—our
neighbor women had been left alone unless they had darkies loyal
enough to stay on and help them scratch around for something to
eat. Both armies come through there foraging. Bands of darkies got
all stirred up when they found out they was free, and they run
wild, robbing helpless women and children, and doing all sorts of
terrible things to them. I don't know what things was like on them
big plantations like you read about or see in the pitchers. We didn't
see none like that in around Meherrin, them days. Why, we had
neighbor women who'd lived just as nice as anybody before the
war and the armies come through there. They was living in old
shacks, and sleeping on mattresses stuffed with leaves and cattails, and
burning cottonseed oil mixed with lard in lamps they'd made out
of gourds, and drying chicory to make a sort of coffee out of it. No-

body in their right minds would want to see times like them again.

Even when we was running short of victuals ourselves, Mama liked to share what she could with folks stopping by, but many's the time she give us children orders to go light on the doughnuts. Sugar was high and hard to get and sorghum was almost as scarce, but Mama got our sweetening for us by trading some of our provisions to a queer fellow named Andy Beeswax, who come around with some honey he'd got from a bee tree on his place. I guess that wasn't his right name but everyone called him that. It fit him good because that stuff was lots more beeswax than it was honey. He was what you'd call superstitious, but I just figgered he was afraid of his wife. You see they didn't have no children and they'd got in the habit of doing considerable arguing back and forth and one day she wished he was dead, right out loud. Well, it wasn't no time until he took sick and like to died. He figgered she'd hexed him and had got someone to help her cast a spell. No, he didn't move out of their cabin. He said he didn't have no place else to go, and anyway he had as much right to live there as she did. But from the time he got out of bed, he never walked through a door again. He said spirits could only follow you through open doors, so from then on he come and he went through windows, no matter whose house it was.

The first time he come over to dicker with Mama about the honey, it like to scared her to death having him come sneaking in through an open window, looking around over his shoulder to see no spirit was following him before he shut it tight behind him. But after awhile we didn't think nothing about it. The darkies all claimed that a conjurer had been working on the spring below our place and that anyone drinking out of it would die. So poor old Andy never let his wife give him a drink for fear it come from that spring. When he was at our place he never took a drink out of the dipper that hung by the water bucket in the kitchen. He always had to go to the well with the walled-up curbing and draw his own drinking water. But, other than expecting his wife to make away with him any minute, they got along just fine. They come over together one day to visit Mama and she walked into the front door just as big as you please. You could see they wasn't having no serious trouble except that he still used the window both coming and going.

Soon as we got the tobacco harvested, Father said, "I aim to go up to Richmond to see if I can't beat the price they're offering around here for tobacco."

I could see Mama sort of studying him trying to figger out if he wasn't just wanting the trip more than anything else. But all she said was, "Well, Sam, we've got so little, do the best you can or we'll all be going hungry before spring."

They didn't do much talking but she helped him pack his shirt bosoms and other things in his carpet-bag. Then she cut an ad out of the paper telling where he could buy first-grade linen for thirty-five cents a yard, and she measured real careful for two dress lengths of alpaca for the girls. She said she could get along without a new dress for herself but they had growed so fast they'd have to have a new one for Sunday. Mama had him take in two bags of feathers she'd saved to sell to the Virginia Bedding Warehouse. She'd brung our own featherbeds and pillows from Pennsylvania, and she allowed she needed the money more than she did the feathers.

Father hadn't no more than left for Richmond when we heard from over Lynchburg way that a terrible freshet, on the James River, was taking out bridges and houses and washing everything down-stream ahead of it. Smart folks moved; but the ones who didn't believe the warnings got caught in it. Out where we was we kept hearing about the drownings, and it seemed like a terrible long time before Father got home because the railroad tracks down around Richmond was under five foot of water and he had to wait for it to go down. He couldn't do nothing but stay there and spend his money for food and lodging. When the flood hit Richmond, it was twenty-five foot deep. Main Street was awash; the gas house and the water works was put out of commission. Most of the bridges went, too. The only way they held the Richmond-Danville railroad bridge was by weighting it down with freight cars loaded with iron.

They'd kept records to prove it and that was the worst flood they'd had in there since the real bad one in 1771, and that was ninety-nine years before the one Father got hisself into.

Right when the flood was at its worst, word reached Richmond that General Lee had had a stroke and was dead. Nobody could get up to Lexington on account of the high water. But we heard that his folks and the old soldiers who walked in from all around there and the students at Washington University give him a fine funeral. And his old horse, Traveller, was there and followed right along behind the hearse.

Father said afore he'd left Richmond the women was all dressed in black mourning veils and the men was wearing them black sleeve bands. Even out where we was the neighbors kept digging at us in little ways about the way the North had done. Like with Mrs. Lee, they'd sold Arlington, the place her folks had left to her, for taxes during the Civil War, and then the government in Washington wouldn't give back the personal things that had been left to her by her great-grandmother, Mrs. George Washington, even when she'd asked for them. Folks down south talked an awful lot about that and about how kind she was and how much she suffered because she was all crippled up with arthritis.

Her old place was turned into a cemetery, and now they've built a big bridge across the Potomac and put lights on the house and made it into a regular showplace. She'd left Arlington in such a hurry in 1861 that she never took a thing with her. Before he died, General Lee wrote out a petition asking for her keepsakes but the Committee on Public Buildings said that even asking for them was "an insult to the loyal people of the United States." Things like that come in handy when they need to fix up museums, but down around Meherrin, them days, folks took treating Mrs. Lee like that almost as serious as they did losing the Civil War.

Father was having a real hard time of it. He knowed them carpet-baggers was wrong and he didn't believe in the way they was stirring up the darkies and putting a lot of fool ideas in their heads. But he didn't like the way the Ku Klux Klan went around with their faces hid. He figgered something had to be done down there but he was all for doing it right out in the open. We had a squire and a sheriff, and Father figgered it was their business to settle things and that other folks should work with them. The Klan hadn't been started very long then but it was plain that all the men around belonged. They started hinting at first about Father joining up with them. After awhile they come right out in the open and told him he'd better. He kept stalling for time, and thinking up excuses until the men around got together and decided to make him show his colors.

One night, after us children was in bed, a band of horsemen come riding into the yard. Me and Aaron run to the window and we could see some of them starting to get off their horses.

Then there come a terrible knocking at the door. The men begun yelling, "We want Hawthorne."

It like to scared us to death, so me and Aaron run to the head of the stairs where we could look down and see Father standing in the doorway. Mama was right beside him, holding her wrapper tight around her with one hand, and holding the lamp up high with the other one, as she was trying to glimpse them men who had come to take Father. But their faces was all blacked so she couldn't tell who they was.

Then we heard one of them say, "Hawthorne, we've caught a nigger stealing tobacco and you're riding with us tonight, or else—!"

So Father got his britches on and some of the men come in and they helped him take charcoal and rub it all over his face. Nobody ever had no sheets to waste getting rigged up fancy, them days. It was plain that Father didn't want to go, but they didn't give him no choice because they said they'd take him regardless. We could see how unpopular he was with them fellows. When they started blacking him up he got ready to talk back, but Mama sort of softened things up by telling him maybe it was the neighborly thing for him to do. She was a great one; when them men left she went to the door and said, "Goodnight, Gentlemen," just as nice as you please.

But after Father was gone she broke down and cried, and then Aaron stirred up the fire and we all wrapped up in blankets and set there until almost daylight, just plain scared to death.

Finally we heard them come riding back, but instead of stopping at our place they rode on down to the cabins and made a lot of noise waking up our darkies and hunting around for Hector. Finally I heard Father agree to bring him down to the Squire's as soon as he was located and then they said good-night, pleasant-like.

Course we started firing questions at him as soon as he come into the door but Father said he was swore to secrecy and he had took an oath, and that us children was to keep our mouths shut from then on about his comings and goings in the night. It was mighty hard on us to be sent off to bed like that while Mama was washing him up to get that black off before she'd let him come to bed. From what we found out from inquiring around and from what we pieced out, guesswork, we learned that the Klan got this darky and they took him out in the woods and tied him to a tree and started whipping him. He kept saying over and over, "You can whip me all you want to, I never stole Mrs. Mohann's tobacco."

Finally they got tired hearing him say that and they listened to him tell what had been going on. They checked up and found he wasn't the one doing it at all.

No, sir, they found out it was Hector who lived right on our place. He knowed he couldn't get away with none of our tobacco because Father kept a close watch and there was so little of it he'd be sure to miss it. But old Mrs. Mohann was easy to steal from, and he was getting it there and taking it down to a place and selling it. Father never knowed Hector prowled around the countryside at night.

Next morning Hector was back, and right after breakfast Father went out and got him to harness up the team. He told him he was taking him in to see the Squire and that the only thing for him to do was to come along peaceable. Hector had been a slave of the Squire's when he was just a boy and you could see, from the way he was rolling his eyes around and begging Father not to take him, that he didn't set much store by the Squire.

But there wasn't nothing for Father to do but take him down and have a trial. Them days we had Squires instead of Justices of the Peace. It was sort of like it is now, only more so. Generally some fellow with time on his hands and no training got to hankering for an office with a title and he'd get hisself elected because nobody no better wanted it anyhow, and then he set back of a table to show his authority. Now this Squire had a son and he'd got hisself elected sheriff and both of them was on hand when Father got there with Hector.

Father said afterwards it wasn't no real trial. Hector admitted he'd stole the tobacco and the Squire said he'd have to give him so many days in jail or so many lashes and since they didn't have no jail and his son, the sheriff, was a husky fellow, the best thing to do was for Hector to get his shirt peeled off and get tied to the whipping post and they'd get the sentence out of the way.

When Hector seen that whipping post, he got down on his knee and he said, "Massa', don't you remember when I was your boy? Massa', I never stole nothing in my life until you sent me over to

Mrs. Mohann's to steal chickens. Massa', I brought Mrs. Mohann's chickens home and we cooked them and you ate them. Massa', I never stole nothing in my life until you tol' me to."

And the Squire said to his son, "Whip this boy as hard as you can —just so you don't kill him."

Father said that was the most terrible thing he ever seen. He tried to make them stop, but they had the law on their side and they almost beat him to death. Father brung Hector back in the wagon and right in to Mother, and she fixed him up the best she could and he laid in his cabin for a long time getting well before he could work again. Father said if that was justice down South, he didn't want no part in it. After that, he got to arguing more with folks and being harder to get along with whenever he stopped to pass the time of day with any of the neighbors.

Soon as our tobacco was harvested, Aaron went into Meherrin and he hunted around until he found a job helping out in Archie Hoskins' store. By then he'd growed into a long, gander-shanks of a boy, and while he wasn't hefty, he figgered it was time for him to start working out to earn his keep. Sometimes he slept down there in the loft above the store, but mostly he walked the two miles home. One day he said a Methodist preacher was coming the next Sunday to hold a meeting in Meherrin. Up until then, they'd had mostly Baptist circuit riders come through there. Mama just didn't go along with them Baptists on this getting immersed. But she didn't say nothing about it when most of the darkies on the place went down to the creek and all got dipped under. She figgered any religion they got done them good, but she said she'd been brung up to be a Methodist and she wasn't going to worship no place where they tried to change her over. We'd gone to a few Baptist meetings in Meherrin, but I could see she was worried for fear what we heard would change us children. Every night we'd read out of the Bible and say prayers. Then after we stopped going to the Baptist meetings she had us sing church songs on Sunday mornings and we'd have our own Sunday school right there at home. We'd always end by singing that one, "Methodist, Methodist, is my name. Methodist 'till I die." She got to being a lot more careful about exposing us to other churches than she did to the measles or the whooping cough. But of course she figgered we had to catch them and the sooner we did and got well again, the better off we'd be.

Them days folks figgered it was a good thing to let their children catch everything they could while it was still summertime. Whooping cough and measles and chicken pox, and all them things, is best to catch in the summer. They don't hang on so long and the children don't miss no school. Folks used to drive around the neighborhood to help their children get measles so's they'd be over them before they was old enough to start school. Sort of like these pre-school clinics they have nowdays. Folks go clean out of their way to take their children to them, too.

So, come Sunday, we got dressed up and went down to hear this Methodist preacher Aaron was telling us about. Golly he was a corker! His name was Preacher Roy, he'd been a preacher before the war and then he went into the army as a soldier when the South was short of men. He was all of six foot and a half tall. He had a deep voice you could hear all over the neighborhood, and he never pulled his punches for nobody. He figgered the world needed reforming and it was up to him to do it by starting at the place nearest at hand. So he started right in after the opening hymn and the scripture to tell what he thought of Prices and their store, and how they sold liquor. He said they wasn't above selling it to the darkies neither. He said he'd been in town long enough to know their place was a den of iniquity, and that God had called him to point out to them and to the world the evil of their ways. Well, none of the Prices was there, but it wasn't long before they heard about it from the folks who was. There was three Price brothers, Jack, and Joe, and another one whose name I don't recollect because he never done much talking around there. But they was all big men and thought well of theirselves and didn't see why this strange preacher had moved into town and started in on them and their business which wasn't run no different than a lot of other places.

Preacher Roy was working for his board, cutting wood out at a farm that was owned by some Methodists a piece from town. The next Sunday he rode in alone ahead of them so he could get the schoolhouse open where they was holding the meetings and so he could talk to anyone private who wanted a little soul-saving done early. He was riding along through the woods singing *Onward*

Chirstian Soldiers and thinking about his sermon, when who should step out and block his path but them three burly Price brothers. The quiet one took his horse by the bit, and Jack and Joe come in on each side, making like they was going to pull him down off his horse.

So Preacher Roy says, "Please let go of my horse's bridle. I am preaching in Meherrin this morning."

Joe spoke up and says, "You're not preaching nowhere until you take back them lies you told about us."

Preacher Roy could feel his dander getting up so he says, "Just a minute until I tie my horse and then we'll see about this."

The three Prices stepped back, watched him tie his horse, and figgered he was going to talk it over from his place on the ground. Instead Preacher Roy pulled off his coat, throwed it over a log, flexed them big muscles of his, and says: "Come ahead. I'll take two of you at a time."

Well, Joe and Jack, who always done the talking, sort of hesitated a minute, but the quiet brother rushed Preacher Roy, thinking he'd be able to take him easy. It wasn't no time until he was knocked out colder than a wedge. That left the other two, and they come in at the preacher together. He had a terrible reach and had done a lot of fighting in the army and had kept in trim with his wood cutting since, while the Prices had let theirselves get a mite soft, drinking up part of the profits at their store. First he'd whack one of them, then he'd whack the other. They never even bloodied him up, and he licked them until they was ready to quit, When he was leaving, he says: "Boys, I am using as my text this morning these lines from the scriptures, *Whatsoever thy hand findeth to do, do it with thy might.*"

Then he told the Prices he knowed they wanted to have a chance to make theirselves neat before coming to church so he'd excuse them for that day, but he'd look forward to seeing them the next Sunday. Word got around about it and a lot of other folks turned out to see if they'd come and what would happen if they did. Sure enough, the next Sunday morning, them three Price brothers filed in for the morning service and set right up in the front row. Preacher Roy give a sermon about scribes and Pharisees that made all the folks so uncomfortable they didn't have much time to judge their neighbors. Afterwards he walked out with the Prices and they had a real friendly visit on the front steps. The folks who'd come to see the fireworks went home, but the Prices got in the habit of attending regular after that.

Preacher Roy was just as good an eater as he was a preacher. After he got to know us and learned about what a good cook Mama was, he got in the habit of coming to our house regular for dinner after every Sunday-morning service. When he used to pile the chicken on his plate, I'd try to remember about how he believed in doing everything with all his might. Only I couldn't figger out why he always picked drumsticks instead of the necks. Maybe he didn't know that we never had chicken excepting when company come.

THREE

BOOK LEARNING

We'd moved so late in the spring, and Mama had been feeling so poorly and working so hard all summer getting enough provisions stored up to keep us over the winter, and Father had been so busy trying to raise a crop, that they hadn't done much planning about our schooling down South. But, come fall, they begun inquiring around. We wasn't in the right district to go to school in Meherrin. Next thing we knowed, we was having to go to school every day to Bruce's plantation, next to ours.

I guess it was what you would call a private school. The Bruces was just a man and a woman who got married, then they had Morgan and Jimmy, and six or eight others. Morgan was older than Julia so it was decided he would be the teacher. Aaron never went to school down South; he was needed to help Father. No, just the children in our two families went to that school.

Bruce's folks and ours had planned to start the school as soon as the fall rains come and us children couldn't work outside. The road from our place to Bruce's had all turned to mud; we had to be scraped good before we went into the outbuilding they'd fixed up with a bench so we could set in a row in front of the table. Morgan Bruce set back of the table because he was chose to be the teacher.

The reason I remember Jimmy Bruce better than the other children is that we got acquainted right off the first day. I can't recollect just what started it but when we went out at noon we got to talking back and forth. It wasn't long before each of us had broke off one of them bushy, little pine trees, and we sopped them good in the mud and begun whacking each other all over with them muddy branches. Why, when Morgan Bruce come to get us to go back to school we was coated so thick with mud he couldn't tell which was which. And from the way he shook us both, he didn't care.

That Morgan Bruce started right in to learn me to talk just like a darky. He'd stand me up and make me say "toe" for *too;* and "gwine" for *going;* and "daw" for *there.* When we come in he'd say, "Howdy," and he'd try to make us "Howdy" right back at him. When we'd leave at night, he'd say "Bydy," and if we didn't "Bydy" to him, he'd make us stay in until we did. He was terrible sot in his ways to begin with. Then when Julia and Sadie started in giggling and whispering about how funny he was, he got more stubborn than ever.

When I wouldn't talk the way he wanted me to, he'd grab me and hold me between his knees and pull my ears and hit me over the head. When I'd go home and talk like he done, Mama would start right in learning me all over again; or she'd cry about how I wasn't getting no education; or she'd get mad and shake me, too, just depending on how she was feeling when I done it. We only went to that school a couple of months. When Mama found out that our teacher couldn't get up to six with the multiplication tables hisself, without bogging down, and I was getting to talk more like a darky every day, she said she'd try to learn us right there at home. Mama was smart; her folks up in Pennsylvania was great ones for schools. She was always talking about how the first meetings to organize Allegheny College was held in her great-aunt's home. Mama never let up on correcting our English and our manners and on trying to keep us in school. She done real well with the girls.

But there wasn't no use talking about the kind of schools they had up in Pennsylvania, because there wasn't none like them down where we was in Virginia. Why, by the time them Southerners went through the Civil War, and lost their men and their horses and their provisions, and then tried to make a living out of that wore-out soil, and them bands of Negroes went through there robbing and stealing and raising Cain generally because they'd been stirred up by a lot of lying promises made to them by cheap carpet-baggers from the North, it wasn't no wonder the schools and everything else was in a bad way. So we just stayed home and helped out all we could and learned some. The trouble was we had so blamed much work to do every day we never did get to holding them regular daily lessons like we talked about when we quit going to school over at Bruce's.

The next year we went to a school over west of our place, near the railroad. It was on a different road from the one we generally took going to Meherrin. About a mile from our plantation, the road we took going to school had a bulge in it—sort of like when a snake swallows a mouse. It was made by a Negro's skeleton laying in the middle of the road.

Quite awhile before we moved South, white men had come across a Negro carrying some chickens that didn't belong to him. They shot him dead, right in the middle of the road, and left his carcass there to discourage other darkies that might be planning to steal chickens. That night the Klan met and give them fellows sort of a vote of confidence; then they rode all over warning folks agin trying to move the body. The children at school told us that the Negro's kin folk had begged to give him a funeral and bury him, but the Klan said no. For awhile, when the smell was bad, some of the white folks thought he ought to be buried, too. But by the time we moved South his bones was all bleached white, and the bullet hole showed real plain in his skull. Folks had drove around him for so long that the road was packed down hard on both sides, while extra-dark, green weeds growed up in the center all around the skeleton. But somehow, us children never got quite used to it being there. When the girls went by they mostly looked the other way, and us boys sort of hurried past there ourselves. After seeing that skeleton night and morning, day after day, I ain't ever hankered to steal no chickens.

The first day we went to our new school, Father drove us over in the wagon; after that we had to get there on shank's ponies. I guess Father figgered we wouldn't know we was there unless he took us the first time. You see we went to the oldest schoolhouse in Lunenburg County, and that old, log building looked like it was ready to fall down and give up the ghost any minute.

Our schoolhouse didn't have no windows. On each side of the room, holes had been bored in a log about three foot off the ground and wooden pins drove in. Then a wide, slanted board had been set on top of them pins and braced from underneath to make a long desk. Right in front of where the desk was, a log had been cut away and a board hung down on the outside over the hole. It was nailed on at the top with a couple of boot soles for hinges. The only way we could get a light on the desk was to go outside and prop the board up with a long stick.

On the other side of the desk was a bench made just as long as the desk was, from a half a log with the flat side turned up and smoothed off. Holes had been bored in the bottom of it, and legs drove in, and sawed off even. Only as many children could go to that school as could set in a row, crowded close together, and facing one of the sidewalls because school was only held in the winter-time and it was blamed cold at the best, setting there with the side of the wall open in front of us.

A desk and a bench just like the other one was along the opposite wall. When the wind would change the teacher would give the signal and we'd shut up the side where we was setting and all move over and set on the other side out of the wind. There was always considerable shoving and pinching going on with us crowded in like that after we got acquainted. But at first we was terrible stand-offish because them Southern children didn't have no use for no one from the North, and they didn't mind showing it neither.

Our teacher's name was Miss Alice Crimes. She always seemed kind of far off and sunk way inside of herself with her own thoughts. I could see Father couldn't figger her out no more than we could when he left us there that first day. It must of been her eyes. You just never knowed whether she was looking right at you or not, but she did have awful pretty hair. I never in all my life seen such a head of brownish-colored hair. It was longer than a horse's tail, and hung down in two thick braids clean to her shoetops.

The teacher's desk was set between them two long benches up at the far end opposite the door, and in front of the fireplace. She kept the only books there was on her desk so's she could read to us and we could say the words after her. She had a can on her desk. It was about the size of an ink bottle and was always kept full of native tobacco, ground fine. Instead of having a pencil, she had an iron-wood stick about the size of a pencil that she kept in her hand nearly all of the time. She'd chawed that stick until it was soft on the end just like a broom. Hour after hour she'd set up there in front of us, talking or reading or listening, and all the time she'd keep dipping that stick brush into this little can of tobacco. Then she'd put it in her mouth and rub her teeth with it, back and forward and back and forward, real good. I heard later that there was a ladies' society of them snuff dippers that met regular, close by. No, I never seen them, just watching that one at work was enough to turn my stomach.

Us boys liked it best when she chewed regular leaf tobacco; it was twisted all up until it looked like one of them twisted doughnuts. We'd set there and watch her munch on it and wonder when she'd spit. Mostly she'd aim at a chink in the wall up near her desk; she'd hit it nearly every time. Sometimes she'd turn sudden and spit in the fireplace, and we never knowed unless we was watching which it would be until we heard the sizzle when she hit the hearth. She was the nicest, kindest, gentlest teacher I ever had. Most of the time she just set there, chewing away quiet-like, and never giving us children no trouble at all unless we done something to get her riled up. But I do seem to remember a lot more about her chewing than I do about her teaching.

That schoolhouse was made of stuff they'd gathered up right there on the ground. The puncheon floor—made from round sticks split in two and laid with the flat side up—was so rough we stumbled around considerable. Even the fireplace was made of sticks built up log-cabin style and plastered over thick with mud. The big boys kept a watch on it in case the mud cracked and it caught fire inside. The rest of us took turns carrying in pitch bark for the fire and keeping the water bucket full so's it would be handy to put it out if it caught. The trouble was it was quite a piece to the creek and them girls was always getting thirsty and emptying our bucket. Mama thought a schoolhouse should have either a spring or a well. When she heard we was drinking water from the creek, she got so upset she was almost ready to make us stay home again.

But I kind of liked that school. Only about a dozen children went there and we got to know each other real well. When I first started they all picked on me because I was the littlest one. But after they had done most everything mean they could think of doing to me, a great, big girl about fifteen years old and full-growed started to school, and that give them somebody newer than me to tease.

The first day she walked in, the teacher says, "What's your name?"
She says, "Emma Jane."
The teacher says louder, "What's your name?"
The big girl yells back still louder, "Emma Jane."
The teacher says, "But who are you?"
The big girl says, "I'm Mr. Epperson's little son."

I laughed so hard I fell backwards right off the bench onto the floor. The teacher run right down and scooped me up and walloped me good.

After that the other children was all nicer to me. It seemed like I belonged more. The big boys got so they'd let me tag down after them to the creek when they et lunch instead of throwing rocks at me like they'd done before. Of course they used to take my good lunch of homemade bread and jam Mama fixed for me and eat it theirselves. But usually they'd give me a hoecake or an ash cake they'd brung. I ain't sure you could call it a trade; them ash cakes wasn't nothing but corn meal mixed up with water into a thick batter and then patted down flat. Folks that didn't have no cook-stove would pull out the ashes onto the hearth and put the ash cake into the hole they'd made and then put them hot ashes back on top. When they figgered the ash cake was cooked, they'd take it out, brush it off and eat it right away or put it aside to eat cold for lunches. Of course, I hated to give up Mama's homemade bread for an ash cake, but I sure got to hear a lot of talk from them bigger boys that I might of missed out on if she hadn't been such a good cook. Yep, Julia and Sadie was there, but they went with the girls. Aaron was working so I was on my own with them boys and it wasn't always so easy to hold it, neither.

Sometimes they'd forget I was from the North and then they'd talk real free. Oh, like telling about the time after peace was declared and the Union soldiers was heading for home from the wars and how one real-fine-looking officer come riding up along the edge of the railroad tracks, not far from where we was setting. He was whistling and singing because he was so happy to be going home to his family, and when he seen some children playing up along the edge of the bank of the railroad cut, he stopped to visit with them while he give his horse a rest. The big boy in the crowd told his sisters to keep the soldier talking and he faded back into the underbrush and run quick to the house and got his father's rifle. When he got back the Union officer was still setting there on his horse telling the boy's two little sisters about how he had three little girls of his own up North. The boy slipped along in the brush until he got close enough to fire, after he looked up and down the track to be sure no other Union soldiers was coming. Then he took aim and fired from where he was laying off to the right of his sisters and the soldier fell dead at the first shot. He'd been screened from the girls by the bushes, and they didn't know for sure what he was doing. They run screaming to the house and their folks come down in a hurry.

The horse had galloped a piece up the cut when he heard the shot and his master fell; so the boy run along the bank above and headed him off. He'd been trained good and wasn't hard to catch. By the time the boy led him down to where the body laid, his folks was there sizing things up. They told the girls to get to the house and to keep still. They seen they'd have to cover their tracks fast or they'd be in real trouble when the next Union soldiers going home come through there. The mother led the officer's horse off into the woods and tied him to a tree out of sight. Then she went back and helped her husband and son move the dead officer's body back into the woods. They took his money and a few little trinkets that couldn't be traced and his shoes and such of his clothes as they could make use of; before they dug a deep grave and buried him in it and piled rocks and brush on top.

That night the father got the officer's horse and he rode into Farmville, where he sold it to a fellow who traded in horses and wasn't no hand to ask questions. I reckon it wouldn't of mattered anyhow—after Sherman and his men had marched through to the sea and both armies had used that country 'round about for a battlefield and soldiers had come foraging at every door—a lot of them Southerners thought no more of shooting a Northerner than of shooting a dog. But them folks who had the boy who killed the officer was sure surprised to find—after they took that horse clean over to Farmville and sold it—that one of their neighbors had gone up to Farmville to buy a horse and just by chance bought that sorrel. That officer's horse hauled truck back and forth for years right along a road that passed real close to his dead master's grave there in the woods. I've rode behind that horse many a time. But

when I started to ask some questions about just where they'd buried
the officer, a couple of the boys held me and one of them twisted my
arm back of me hard and said, "You keep your mouth shut or we'll
be digging your grave there in the woods alongside of his." Everyone
knowed that story in around Meherrin, but it would be more than
your life was worth to start spreading it around among outsiders.

No, I never seen a Negro go to school them days; but I only lived
in the South three years. We left there in 1873 and I didn't get back
again until Margaret and me drove our car there from Oregon in
1939. We went to Meherrin first, and I hunted all over to find some
of the folks I'd knowed. The only one left was old Sue Williams;
her folks had owned a plantation between our place and town. Sue
and Julia and Sadie had been great friends. Sue still had the wedding
skirt with hand-knit lace that Mama had made for her in 1872.

The Negroes I'd knowed when I was a boy was all gone, but I
never will forget how the scars looked on our old Negro washer
woman's arms when she'd stand there rubbing the clothes up and
down on Mama's washboard. She'd been beat all over her back and
shoulders with a whip dipped in hot tar. Of course, she was an
old woman when she worked for us and she'd got her beating when
she was a real young girl, but them scars was deep and had lasted.
When her and Mama got to know each other real well she told Mama
all about how it happened.

She said back in slave days, when she was young and likely-looking,
she'd been a cleaning maid in her master's home. When she'd pick
up the papers and books to dust under, it seemed like she just
couldn't lay them right down without looking at them a little to
see how white folks spelled out the letters so's they could read words.
Several times her mistress had scolded her for looking at the paper
when she should have been dusting. Then the master caught her at
it and he warned her too. For awhile after that she said she'd even try
closing her eyes when she was moving the papers so she wouldn't be
tempted to study the letters. But later on she forgot the warnings because she was so interested trying to figger them out. One day her
mistress snuck right up behind her and grabbed the paper out of
her hand.

Next thing she knowed she'd been stripped of the good clothes
that she wore in the house and was tied to the whipping post out in

the slave's quarters. The overseer give her all them hot-tar lashes that burned so deep she layed on her stomach nights for a long time because she couldn't stand to have nothing touch her back. They couldn't have her around the house scarred up like that so she was sent to a far part of the plantation to work with the fieldhands. That's why she was sold, and when we got there she was just living in one of the cabins on our place because after the slaves was freed she didn't have no place else to go. Mama felt terrible sorry for the poor old soul and she give her a newspaper just so's she could have it to keep but, of course, she was too old then to care about learning to read and write. I guess, back in slave times, it must of been a rule that darkies wasn't to be educated. When we was there they could of learned if anybody had wanted to help them, but shucks, the biggest share of the whites around where we was couldn't read or write theirselves, and Mama didn't think I'd been learning enough from Miss Alice Crimes to pay for the wear and tear on my shoes.

I figgered I was getting along just fine without going to school. Mama didn't like having me hanging around the darkies because I'd begun to talk like one. She kept me busy helping her or Father all she could. So whenever he'd go any place with the team to do his buying or selling, she'd have me go along. The girls was easier to keep busy around the house, but I kept getting into trouble when I wasn't working. That's why I got to traveling around when I was young. Many's the trip I made to Keysville, eight mile south of us. And I've been to Farmville, fifteen mile north of us, more times than I can remember. That's where Lee done his last fighting in the Civil War, and we could pick up all kinds of truck around there them days. Twice Father took me with him on the train to Richmond, because Mama needed to get rid of me. The first time I was so little the conductor let me go free, but the next time he questioned Father and he had to pay part fare on me. I didn't get to ride up to Richmond with him no more.

Along during the summer, the folks drove into Farmville, and they talked to some sort of a school superintendent there who had been a Confederate soldier but had got so hungry he hung his hat on his bayonet in one of the battles and crawled off to the Northern lines where he was fed and treated good and got this office after the war was over. The Southerners around there didn't seem to think much of him. The ones who had been in the Confederate Army couldn't vote so they didn't have nothing to say about him getting into office. He said we was to go to school in Meherrin and come fall Mama got us all slicked up and sent us over there to a Mr. Rowlett. He started right in picking on us and said in front of all the children in the room, "What's your reason for invading the South?"

In all my life I've never seen another person like him. Something awful must have happened to him in the war, and he hadn't had a chance to tell no Northerners about what he thought of them until we come to his school. Going home that night Sadie and Julia and me talked it over. We hated to tell Mama about Mr. Rowlett because she hadn't been feeling like herself. The crops didn't amount to a thing that year, but she'd tried to do her work and keep Father and us children cheered up too.

We didn't feel free to talk to Father about it because he didn't have no idea how hard he'd made it for us children by getting his neck bowed and coming out for Grant in the election of 1872. Up until then him and Mama was getting along fine with the neighbors and she was winning folks over because they liked her ways. But Father was a great hand to take the side where most folks wasn't. It got so every time he'd go to get the mail, he'd get into an argument at Price's store. Mama never said much about it, but we could see she hated to have him go to town. She'd help him into his coat, and sort of pat his collar down and sweeten him up and try to get him to promise not to talk about politics. But nobody talked about nothing else in the fall of 1872.

The Southerners had hated Grant during the war for what his armies done when he was general, but they hated him more for what his officials had done to bleed the country when he was president. Come 1872, the South wanted a change—they figgered any change was better than having Grant president again. But that's where Father differed with them. It wasn't so much that he was for Grant as that he was agin Horace Greeley. He hadn't no use for Greeley or for the things he stood for, and he never went to town without telling everyone so.

When part of the South broke off and nominated O'Conor for president, Mama thought Father would be willing to compromise, too. But he didn't believe in no third party. He said the choice had to be made between Greeley and Grant, and he was for Grant. Then Mama told him if he wanted to vote for Grant the thing to do was to keep still about it and vote quiet-like. But he said, "No!"

He was a man of principle and nobody was going to make him back down.

Then some men in Meherrin said they wasn't going to let him vote, and for him to stay out of town on election day. When that day come he was up real early and rode in heading for the polls. Them fellows was there watching for him and let out a yell and started his way. They figgered on riding him out of town on a rail.

Anything could of happened to him, but Archie Haskins come running out of his store carrying his double-barreled shotgun, and he run just as fast as he could with his peg leg and got beside Father and held them fellows back by aiming his gun at them.

Now this Archie Haskins had been shot in the leg when he was fighting for the South in the Civil War, and they'd had to amputate it up close to his body, and he hadn't died of gangrene like most of them done with that kind of an operation. And he'd had so many other things happen to him and kept right on living that the story got around that he led a charmed life and nothing could kill him. So when that mob seen Archie Haskins standing by Father, them fellows fell back, and Father went right over to the polls and marked his ballot while Archie Haskins stood guard. Then they walked back to Haskins' Store and Archie stood on the porch holding his gun while Father got on his horse and rode out of town heading for home.

Archie Haskins said he done it because in America every citizen had a right to vote—even a blamed fool like Father who didn't know no better than to vote for Grant. That was a funny thing about Father, he always seen the other side best. Why, when he moved out to Nebraska where all the other folks was Republicans, he always voted a straight Democratic ticket. I never heard him let the South down once in them arguments he was always getting into when he went to the store for our groceries. He figgered when no one else was there from the South, it was up to him to tell their side of things.

But all that Mr. Rowlett knowed about us, when we started to his school in the fall of 1873, was that we had come from the North;

that we was the children of the man who had stirred everyone up in the last election by voting for Grant; and that because our mother wouldn't let us go back to Miss Alice Crimes' school another year, the superintendent who stood in good with them carpet-baggers had told him to make room for us in the school at Meherrin. It was a nice building, made of up-and-down boards, and had glass windows. But every time us children would walk in the door, Mr. Rowlett would say something smart about us coming from the North, and then all them children would turn around and stick out their tongues at us. The worst of it was that every once in awhile them big boys would tie my hands and feet together and run a fence rail in between my legs, and jump me up and down around outside the schoolhouse, and that teacher would just stand there in the doorway laughing because I was a "damn, poison little Yank." But I told the girls we'd better not worry the folks about it yet; I figgered they'd let up on me after awhile like they had over at the other school.

Every day us children, big and small, was lined up along one wall for our spelling lesson. We never had no spelling book, or studied the words ahead of time. We never knowed nothing about it until Mr. Rowlett lined us up and opened the dictionary. He'd just start in most anywhere and sound out a word and then we'd keep trying until someone spelled it right, then he'd read the next word and we'd try it. I never got no place because I couldn't figger out what I was supposed to be doing. Then one time it come to me, I started out real slow and said the letters, and I spelled the word right. Next word that come to me I done it the same way. Other children was setting down all around me, and I stayed up until I was the very last; always before I'd been the first one down. I've thought a lot about what happened that day. It must of been one of them visions or something. Because it never happened to me again. Always before that day and always after that day I was the first one to set down, regular.

We never did get to study no arithmetic, because right after spelling come history, and then for the rest of the day Mr. Rowlett would talk about the Civil War, and how if only this or that had happened the South would of won.

I've always figgered he might of been right about that because Lee was a blamed good man, and he hadn't give up yet when he rode out of Petersburg on Traveller during the night of April 2, 1865. The men with him started moving their heavy wagons along one of them plank roads that had been put through that country because of the mud. He'd give orders for them fellows in Richmond to evacuate the city, and to move all of the provisions on hand down to the Amelia Courthouse, while the Cabinet and records was to be loaded into all the empty passenger cars and box cars and run down to the other end of the line. After they'd issued the rest of the rations to the common folks, who didn't get to leave on the train, the soldiers burned the warehouses so the North couldn't use none of their supplies. Then as soon as the Confederate Army crossed the James River bridge, they burned it behind them.

Lee's army was retreating that same way, too, using the wagon roads and the Southside Railroad from Petersburg. It met the railroad we was on about fifty mile southwest, at Burkville. The two railroads made a regular fork there, and Lee figgered on heading out that way after Grant had cut the country off to the south and all he had left was Virginia and North and South Carolina. But Lee still had them tough old troopers of the Army of Northern Virginia and they was ready to die with him if he wanted them to. The Union armies was coming in on both sides. So when Lee give the order to retreat he told his men to see that the bridges wasn't burned until the Confederate troops had passed over, but to be blamed sure they was burned in time so that no Northerners could put out the fires and use them. He took off from Petersburg on his horse, Traveller, with his men and his wagons, but he was counting on his supplies coming down from Richmond on the railroad, and being there at the Amelia Courthouse, that was across both the James and the Appomattox rivers.

Nobody knows just how it happened, but some blamed fool got them orders mixed. When Lee got to Amelia there wasn't no provisions there! He had ammunition but no food. All through the campaign he'd had to depend on that railroad to get supplies for his troops. Men can't fight long with empty bellies, so he sent out begging the farmers for food, but they hadn't none left to give him. Off to the south of them Sherman had burned everything on his march to the sea.

Then word come that Jefferson Davis and his cabinet had got

through at Burkville. But because Lee had lost a day foraging at Amelia, the Northerners had got there ahead of him and had captured the railroad junction, so he had to give up the Richmond-Danville railroad. Because he couldn't move them over muddy roads and swollen streams, and he had to get out of there fast to keep from being surrounded and starved out, Lee give orders to destroy all them caissons and shells that had been made back at that munitions plant in Richmond.

Lee didn't have no choice, he had to head for Farmville up on the Appomattox. When Grant heard that Lee was cut off from the railroad and his supplies, he said to General Sherman, "Lee is caught." So the Northern armies all closed in for the kill.

It was exciting to think all that had happened only ten mile up the railroad track that run right past our schoolhouse. I never cared much about the history that come straight from books myself. Mr. Rowlett didn't see no point in talking about other wars when the only one that really mattered had been lost because we'd got the railroad away from them. When Lee got there with 30,000 men and no food, they had to destroy most of their munitions after leaving broken-down wagons and dead horses and starving men all along both sides of the roads. It must of been terrible for Lee to see them empty wagons coming back after he had sent some of his men out with letters begging the farmers for food. But the farmers was starving theirselves. That country must of looked like they'd gone over it with a fine-toothed comb. The South was doing its best to provision its troops from what was left around there, while the North was using the torch on every house and barn and mill off farther to the south.

After Hood surrendered, the only force the South had left was Lee's Army, and when the North captured the Richmond-Danville railroad at Burkville, Lee knowed he had to get to the nearest provisions at Farmville fast.

Farmville's only about fifteen mile due north of Meherrin; I've rode it many a time in the wagon with Father. But them soldiers of the Army of Northern Virginia had been living on parched corn and mighty little of that ever since they'd left Petersburg. The ones that made it to Farmville et some bread and meat there, and that put new life into them. They formed a line and won their last victory from the North, just four mile west of town. By that time Lee realized he was trapped. Grant had gone into that campaign with 125,000 fresh troops, and they was coming at Lee from both sides as well as from the front.

Lee's men had won a victory but it took the last of their food and ammunition and supplies to do it. Their horses was too weak to pull the wagons or carry a man. Many a man was barefoot. But them old troopers, who'd been together for four years in the Army of Northern Virginia, still wanted to go on fighting.

But Lee knowed there wasn't no sense in letting them all get killed. To stop the bloodshed, he got dressed in his best uniform and met Grant and surrendered. But by that time their losses had been so big, he could only turn in thirty cannon, 350 wagons, and 8,000 muskets, because that was all he had left when he had his men come to the Appomattox Courthouse to stack their arms.

Some of our neighbors, who knowed him well, said that Lee never acted like he was no better than anybody else because he'd had more schooling or because him and his folks had money before the war. He knowed how to do without because he'd lived just like his soldiers, and wouldn't eat good food unless there was enough to go around. That's why he didn't feel the need of taking any of them soft jobs he could have had after the war was over. His soldiers never made nothing out of it; so he figgered he shouldn't neither. Why, when Lee was an old man he picked up a little baby and held it in his arms, then he turned to its mother and he said, *Teach him to deny hisself.*

Lots of times I'd get real interested in what Mr. Rowlett was saying. I could see how them Southerners felt about how brave their soldiers was and how they had give up most everything to fight for what they believed in. But the trouble was Mr. Rowlett took everything personal. Him and them big boys hated all Northerners and I was the only one there to take it out on. One day, when Julia and Sadie stayed home because they had bad colds, some big boys about fourteen years old got me onto a rail during the noon hour. Part of them held me upright so I couldn't turn over after they tied my hands and feet together, and they jumped me up and down on that rail until I was almost dead. I never had nothing hurt me so bad in all my life as that did. Then they throwed me down and went back to school for the afternoon and never paid no more attention to me. I laid there on the ground for awhile and then I crawled on my hands and knees up the hill a little ways so I wouldn't be so easy to find, and I laid down in a little patch of bushes and I hated them folks setting inside that schoolhouse down below. I wished it would storm and the lightning would come and strike them all dead—but it didn't. When school was out I watched them come out of the door, laughing and talking like they'd never done nothing to me. Sick as I was, I rolled over sideways and I picked up a little straight stick, and I held it to my shoulder and I aimed out through them weeds and made believe that we was having another war and I was holding a rifle and that I'd shot every one of them boys and that teacher dead.

About dark, Mama got frightened when I didn't come home from school, and she sent Aaron on a horse to find me. When I heard him hallooing and recognized his voice, I answered. He come up to where I was laying there in the bushes, and when he seen what they had done to me, he picked me up like I was a baby. I couldn't ride, so he led the horse and carried me home to Mama. It took considerable nursing to get me back on my feet again. I never went to school another day in Virginia.

FOUR

PANIC IN '73

Pickings was slim enough our first year down South; they was slimmer the second; come spring the third year everything had gone to rick and ruin. The drought had got our tobacco during the second summer so we was short of money to lay in our bought provisions and we hadn't raised near enough to last us over. Mama was a great hand at stretching, when she had anything to stretch, but she wasn't fooling nobody with some of the meals she set on the table, them days. Of course, we didn't mind a meal of thickened milk once in awhile. Oh, if you're lucky enough to have a fresh cow, you let the cream raise on a pan of milk and you skim it into a pitcher to use later on and you put the milk in a kettle and mix some flour or cornstarch with water to make a thickening and stir it into the milk while it's heating. You've got to watch for scorching or lumping. After it cooks up good and you've added a pinch of salt, you serve it in bowls with sorghum or any other sweetening you've got and some of that cream on top. But the trouble about thickened milk is that when you're short enough of grub to be eating it yourself, you usually ain't got enough feed to keep the cow milking.

It was bad enough at our house but we knowed it was a blamed sight worse at some of the neighbors. We done what we could for the Negroes on our place but they was half starved all the time. Mama hated to see them little pickaninnies standing around the edge of the yard looking big-eyed and hopeful. When their stomachs was full, they was buzzing around the place like bees. Folks raised more pickaninnies on their plantations than they did anything else. It was hard on their folks having them all get thin and drawed-out looking.

The Klan was riding regular making examples to show the other Negroes that nobody could get away with stealing more than once. The white women kept their provisions under lock and key and just measured out enough for the next meal for theirselves to the darkies who was doing the cooking. But even when they looked them over careful of a night before they went to their quarters, it just seemed like them darky cooks would work out a way to get food for their hungry little pickaninnies. Why, one woman in Meherrin sneaked into the kitchen around the back way because she figgered something was going on there that shouldn't be. She kept back out of sight in a sort of an entrance way, and she watched.

By and by, she seen her darky cook peer around to see no one was looking. Then she pinched a little piece of dough off of each biscuit that was in a pan setting there ready for the oven. She pulled her skirt up real quick and popped that dough right into the top of her stocking so's she could take it home and bake it for her children at night.

Our family had never been around hungry folks like that before; they'd always set a good table and they'd always had hay in the barn for the cattle too. But, of course, they'd never had a couple of armies running through their fields up in Pennsylvania, and until they went there and lived like other farm folks down South, they didn't know what things was like first-hand. But because they wasn't used to it to begin with and hadn't seen nothing like it before, they figgered that as long as we had anything to eat ourselves we had to feed the darkies on our place. So, when we run out, we all run out together.

By spring, folks was gathering the first greens that showed. Aaron had rigged up some snares and went regular of a morning, soon as it was daylight, to see if he'd caught a rabbit. Mostly they was smarter than he was. The darkies had cleaned out the 'possums and most everything else around there except snakes. We was always long on them, and a fellow had to be careful if he did any hunting. Copperheads was the worst, but them black or blue racers scared us the most, they went so fast.

I ain't sure about them cow-sucker snakes. Some mornings our cow's udder was as limp as a rag and the darkies all claimed that it was cow-sucker snakes getting the milk. But Father always figgered it was cow-milking darkies. He said she never milked short at night when he was working in the field close to where she was pastured, and that snakes wasn't like owls, doing their dirty work at night. We told the darkies that Aaron and me was going to stay in the barn nights to see them cow-milker snakes at work. We never done it but they thought we did. Our cow milked just fine for a couple of weeks until they seen the candlelight up in our room.

Aaron didn't have no job. Archie Haskins couldn't use him no more at the store. Nobody had the money to buy what he had to sell and he was having such tough sledding he was beginning to pick the stuff off the shelves for his own meals. It seemed too bad for him to be eating hisself out of business; but grocers are lucky; if everybody was starving to death, they'd be the last to go.

The only trouble was, he couldn't get no more groceries unless he paid for them first. He wasn't getting to buy goods on time because them big businesses he bought from was having to pay cash to the bigger businesses they bought their goods from. It made everybody short of money and no matter how hard you figger it's blamed hard for folks to keep going without money.

We tried to get by with using mighty little of it. When the hens was laying, Mama would send eggs to the store. She traded butter, too, but when she did we'd run short of it and of cream at home. Mama made awful good butter and storekeepers was always glad to get it because it never got rancid. She was terrible fussy about it and kept all the milk things clean and scalded. I had to help her and she'd make me churn hard at first and then slower after awhile so's it would come better and gather in bigger chunks. Mama always washed the edges of the churn down careful with cold water, and then she gathered every bit of the butter up with a wooden ladle made with holes in it so the buttermilk would drain off. She'd keep working the butter in a big wooden bowl with a wooden paddle, and she'd slap it and score it and wash it with cold water until every bit of buttermilk was out. Then she'd pack it into a square mold that was hinged on one corner and that had been scalded good and dipped in cold water so the butter wouldn't stick to it. And it would come out in the nicest, hardest bricks you ever seen. Them rolls weighed two pound and she'd wrap them in muslin and tie them with a string, and mostly send them along with Father to trade for our other provisions. But whenever Mama could, she'd hold one out and put it down for winter in a crock that was full of brine made of salt strong enough to float an egg.

Farm folks done what trading they could to get their groceries. But they always had to buy more than they had to sell. Since they only raised one main crop a year, they got to expecting the storekeeper to give them credit until their tobacco was raised and sold, and they got their money. Archie Haskins had trusted quite a few of them, then when they didn't have no tobacco to sell, they didn't pay him back and he got hisself in debt, and the fellows he was owing cut off his credit. Why, by the spring of '73, there wasn't nobody to buy mortgages and the stores couldn't give credit because they didn't have none theirselves. Money was tight.

Father figgered we'd have to get out of there. Mama said she'd never go back to Pennsylvania until she had money and good clothes and could go on a visit with her head held high. She said if she was going to be poor she wasn't going to have her folks and all of her old friends feeling sorry for her. Her and Father never let on to their folks in their letters home about how bad off we was.

So then Father talked about leaving us, where we had a place to live, while he went out West and earned some money on the railroad to tide us over. We knowed there wasn't no use counting on raising a crop that year; the worms, the drought, the firing was earlier than usual. But word come back that they had more men than they could use out West and nobody but homesteaders was wanted. Two and a half million men was throwed out of work when the Civil War ended. Some had places to go home to, but a big share of the single ones had headed west to work on the railroads.

The railroads had been give big land grants by the government, but they had to lay tracks so's they could get settlers out there to buy land from them before they had any real income. So they had been paying their men's wages with money that come from selling bonds in Europe, but come spring in 1873 folks over there had hard times theirselves. When the railroads couldn't sell their bonds, and couldn't pay their men that was working out West, they laid a lot of them off. Some of them fellows they laid off was men from Meherrin who was sending money home regular to their folks, so they could pay their grocery bills. Archie Haskins couldn't let them have groceries unless they had money to pay for them. Aaron didn't have nobody to wait on, so he didn't have no job.

I always figgered that's what saved my life. One morning, about daylight, I woke up when Aaron throwed me on the floor, and then grabbed me up, and shook me hard. He was yelling at me to get out of there, that the house was on fire. Aaron didn't need to tell me that, the room was so full of smoke we could hardly breathe, and pieces of burning shakes and sheeting was falling down into the room from where the roof was burning up around the chimney. Them old dry shakes was going like kindlings; we could hear them snapping and cracking overhead. I grabbed my pants and Aaron grabbed up an armful of bedding and we made a beeline for the stairway.

By that time Father was there. He just took one look at the roof and said, "She's a goner!"

He yelled at us children, "Get out of here."

Then he pulled the door to the third floor shut after him.

The girls never waited to dress. They grabbed what clothes they could carry and run screaming down the stairway. Sadie tripped on her long nightgown and rolled clean down to the bottom. She got bruised up considerable. Julia half drug and half carried her the rest of the way.

We was so panicky we all run outside but when we got clean away from the house and stopped to look back we seen that Father and Mama was still up on the second floor pitching bedding and everything else they could lay a hand on out of the windows. So Aaron told the girls to drag the things the folks had throwed on the ground back a piece so's they'd be out of danger.

Mama grabbed up two real pretty quilt tops she'd pieced out of dress scraps she'd brung from Pennsylvania, and that she hadn't made up because she hadn't no material to put on the backs or stuffing for the inside. We had our fire just before she had Myra, and she used them quilt tops to tie around the baby clothes she'd been working so hard to make. She was leaning out of the window screaming to the girls to catch that bundle and take care of it. But before they could grab it from where it fell, some of them burning shakes come tumbling down on it. Julia shook them off so the baby clothes inside didn't get scorched but them quilt tops got burned so bad they couldn't never be quilted. The only reason we've kept them around all these years is that they come in handy to wrap stuff when we're moving.

Now, of course, it never took as long for that old house to burn down as it's took for me to tell you about it. Why, it wasn't no time until the folks had to get out of the second floor. But they stayed long enough to save the featherbeds and most of the bedding. Mama figgered there wasn't no point in saving herself unless she saved her bedding. Father finally got so mad at her that he grabbed her arm and ordered her down the stairs just like he had us children. He said afterwards that he could see the flames licking around the door to the third floor before he got the one closed to the second floor.

By then he knowed the roof would fall in any minute. Aaron and me was dragging what we could out of the downstairs. The girls begun screaming for us to use the back door because the front porch roof had caught from one of them falling shakes and the darkies begun to yell that the kitchen was on fire. We didn't get much of anything out of the downstairs, but it was furnished sparse anyhow. Mama felt the worst about us saving them old chairs and not getting her sewing machine out.

We was all so scared about the fire in the kitchen where what food we had was stored that we wasn't even looking at the house. All that I remember was hearing a big crash when the roof fell in because right then Aaron and me was running to the spring to fill some wooden buckets with water. Father and Hector clumb up onto the roof and we got water to them in time. They got the fire out after only about a three-foot square of the kitchen roof had burned.

In half an hour our house was burned to the ground. Nothing was left but that old brick chimney and them three fireplaces, one on top of the other, standing there just like a big, black finger pointing at the sky.

We hadn't thought much of that old house the first time we seen it. For a long time it never seemed like it was ours. We used to think we heard steps up on the other floors. Nights when the wind blowed it sort of moaned and groaned, and I used to lie awake and think of that widow woman who'd lived there, and of that big whip she used when she beat them slaves. I didn't like living in that house at all. But after we'd lived there three years it was our home. When it was gone, we didn't have none. And we didn't have money to build another one. We kept wishing for the stuff that had burned up inside. We was starting at taw again, and we had to get set and make our next move fast. Father knowed the land wasn't no good, but he had allowed we could keep a roof over our heads while he went out scouting around so's he could figger out what to do next.

After the house fell in, Mama just set on a box out beside the carriage house for a long time, not doing a thing but just staring at the bed of coals where our mansion-house had stood. She was sort of hunched over and she had that burned quilt top that was knotted around the baby clothes on her lap. Every once in a while her teeth would chatter like they done when she had the ague the worst. Father looked over her way a couple of times, then he picked up the red, white, and blue coverlid and walked over and wrapped it around her shoulders.

He sort of bent over and put his arm around her, and he said, "You know, Martha, I meant well when I moved us down here on account of your health."

She kind of choked up and didn't answer back. Her face was so still and quiet as she set there studying the holes burned all along one edge of her coverlid that us smaller children hung around close to her while Father and Aaron went back to gathering up what they could and moving it into the little house next to the kitchen where we had been doing our eating.

Mama set a great store by that coverlid. It was made real fancy and wove double by her folks in Pennsylvania. They had growed, and carded, and dyed the wool right there on her grandfather's land-grant claim. He had been a real young boy when he fought in the Revolution and so the women who had stayed home decided to make two coverlids for him in red, white, and blue. Lots of folks was weaving blue and white ones, 'cause them dyes was easy to make. But they wanted to use all three of our colors. Mama said they found some folks who had a bed of madder plants that had been brung over from England and they traded carded wool for madder roots. They made some dye from them and the wool come out a real turkey red, and it hasn't faded a bit to this day. But, of course, the kin folks who live in Pennsylvania don't have no holes in their coverlid. They've always kept it in a chest and they only bring it out to show to company. But Mama didn't have no chest to keep hers in so she had to use it as a bed-spread. Nobody ever dared to set on it with dirty clothes on. Having them big holes burned all along one side of her Revolutionary coverlid like that hit her terrible hard.

From then on we done our eating as well as our cooking in the kitchen. Father and Mother and the girls fixed up the little house where we'd been doing our eating so they could live in it. Aaron and me lived there too, only nights we slept in another little building that Father said we'd have to make do.

Oh, there was plenty of room, I guess, if you don't mind being crowded. The thing we didn't like about living there was the danger of fire. Up until then Father had been with us for most of the meals and he always had watched that fireplace close while we was eating, but after we had to move in there to live he said we'd all have to help watch that fireplace. We had a regular fire drill. He had us keep buckets full of water right there on the hearth. That was because our chimney was made of tobacco sticks built up log-cabin style, and then caked over with mud. We had to keep a bunch of long sticks handy to pry the chimney loose from the house and throw it on the ground. It was the only way to put out a fire once one of them stick chimneys caught on fire inside. Of course, we kept watching close and plastering mud on any places that showed a crack. I used to get awful black when I was told to get inside the fireplace and see if there was any place showing that was likely to break through.

We still had part of a good tanned hide over at Farmville, so because us children had forgot to get our shoes when the house was burning, Father loaded the whole family into the wagon and drove us over to the shoemaker's to see about having us shod. Why every town down South had its shoemaker who made up shoes from your own leather on order. We'd killed that beef, and took the hide in and left it with a tag fastened to it that said, Hawthorne. Then after they'd had time to get it tanned we could go to town and he'd measure our feet and make up what we needed, and he'd keep the rest of the leather there until we come for shoes again. We was lucky to have that leather on hand there when we lost our shoes in the fire.

Rich men, who had money to go to the barber, done the same thing

with their shaving mugs. The barber kept their mugs for them all in
a row; they didn't use nobody else's shaving brush and soap. We
never used nobody else's leather in our shoes. The only trouble about
having shoes made to order was that sometimes the shoemaker would
measure your foot and he wouldn't have a last to fit. Then you'd
have to wait while he made one up in your size and that meant considerable delay. Lots of times the shoemaker was a carpenter, too.

Them shoes that shoemaker made for me hurt my feet. Mostly I
went barefoot. Winters we had to wear them shoes and us children
was always complaining about the seams inside and how they wore
blisters. Mama knit real heavy wool socks for us to save our feet all
she could. Them shoes never had no metal grommets, but the holes
was punched far enough back so they didn't tear out bad. Father
made our own leather laces right at home. The leather wasn't split,
and them laces was so blamed thick they didn't break no matter how
hard we pulled on them. But I never could figger out no way to make
them stay tied no matter how hard I tried. They was always getting
loose and tripping me and slowing me down. It ain't no wonder folks
went barefoot, them days.

We didn't have no house. We didn't have no crop. We couldn't
toughy it out there no more. None of us wanted to go back to Pennsylvania broke. Anyhow, letters from our kin folks there was full of
news of banks failing and small businesses going under. Jobs was
scarce all over; money was getting tighter every day. Father figgered
the only thing for him to do was to head west and file on a homestead.

Congress had passed the Homestead Act in 1862, but it took the
hard times of '73 to settle the plains. Just like with us, free land or
anything else free looked good. Under the Homestead Act, Father,
as a citizen who was over twenty-one and the head of a family, could
go out there and take his pick of any public land. He could stake a
whole quarter section before he went into the land office to swear
that him and his family would live on that land and cultivate it for
the next five years. Then the clerk would take his ten dollars and
we could move right onto our new farm. Of course, we couldn't have
the patent until we'd lived there them five years.

We could see that Father was just itching to get out West and get
located, and the best time to leave would of been right then when it

was mid-summer. We knowed for sure we didn't have a tobacco crop worth harvesting, but he figgered he shouldn't leave until after the baby was born.

Right after the fire he wrote to the Union Pacific Railroad telling them we wanted to move west and asking for information about a place to locate where they had a real good climate with an even temperature. He wasn't taking no chances this time about getting us the wrong kind of a place. He figgered if he picked a place with a healthy climate year around, he could go out there and see for hisself that he had the right kind of soil. And, of course, he asked what it would cost for him to get out there by hisself and what it would cost for him to take his whole family.

Well, they wrote right back and sent prices. It would cost about thirty dollars for him to go out alone. But they had a reduced rate for parties. A Mr. D. B. Cady was making up trainloads of emigrants in Richmond and going out with them to Nebraska. They was sending him Father's name; when the time come for us all to go we could take one of them trains. But the first thing for Father to do was to come right on and get located. If he'd come clean to Grand Island, Nebraska, they'd bed and board him for a little while so he could take his pick of one of their good farms.

And they sent Father a book. Now we never did have much to read, but what few books we did have got burned in the fire, and all summer long Julia read to Sadie and me from that book and we went around saying the words over after her. Like them lines near the front,

> I hear the tread of pioneers
> Of nations yet to be
> The first low wash of waves, where soon
> Shall roll a human sea.

You could see from that they figgered on us having lots of neighbors!

That book said the Union Pacific Railroad was opening up 12,-000,000 acres of the best farming, grazing, and mineral lands in America in the State of Nebraska, and the territories of Colorado, Wyoming, and Utah.

Father was bothered by it saying that the land was for sale at low prices, but he figgered the government had only give them every other section, so he could locate on one of them sections that was public domain in between theirs. He could get 160 acres free under the Homestead Law, and with such good land that would give us a living and be all him and Aaron could handle anyhow.

Everybody in America knowed them railroad maps and terminals. The Union Pacific had got 1,037 miles of track laid out to Grand Island, Nebraska. It went right into the heart of the best land in America, right into the valley of the Platte River. From there on to Ogden, Utah, was a "belt of Orange." Things was bad every place else, but when them bankers couldn't get money to pay the men building track farther west, they kept right on saying that the only thing wrong was money tightening up in Europe and in Wall Street. Father said with money being like it was, all that a man could do was get out on a good quarter section where him and his family could get along without it.

All we needed to do was to get Father out there soon enough to stake our claim right in the heart of the Platte Valley. That was where the book said, "The traveler beholds, stretching away to the distant horizon, the undulating prairie, a flowering meadow of great fertility, clothed in grasses, and watered by numerous streams, the margins of which was skirted with timber."

Golly, we wished Mama would hurry up and have the baby so he could get out there before all that land along the Platte River was took.

Myra wasn't born until mid-August. I don't know much about it because Mama farmed us children out over at Williams for several days then. Aunt Fanny, who wasn't no blood kin, moved in to take care of her while the baby was being born. But things didn't go right. Mama had a terrible carbuncle on her breast and a doctor had to come clean from Farmville to lance it. Myra was a nice enough baby, but we needed a lot of things more than we needed a baby sister, right then. And Mama had such a hard time having her that Father stayed around home longer than he'd figgered on. But he said he didn't have to worry about the time of year we moved on account of the good weather they had year around out in Nebraska. That was the part of that railroad book Mama liked best, where it told about the climate in the Platte Valley. It wouldn't be the way it was when we moved from Pennsylvania in that snowstorm; with weather like they had in Nebraska we could move any time of the year.

The book said, "During Fall and Winter the weather is usually dry. The heat of Summer is tempered by the prairie winds, and the nights are cool and comfortable. The Autumns are like a long Indian Summer, extending into the latter part of December. The Winters are short, dry and invigorating, with but little snow. Cold weather seldom lasts beyond three months, with frequent intervals of mild, pleasant days. The roads in Winter are usually hard, smooth, and excellent."

What we couldn't figger out was how them covered-wagon pioneers had missed finding that valley. They'd kept on going clean to the West coast, when right out there in the middle was the best country in the world. Of course, everybody in America knew about how Leland Stanford of the Central Pacific and them other fellows from the Union Pacific had raced across the country, building the transcontinental railroad until they met out near Salt Lake in 1869. The whole country had helped celebrate when they drove that golden spike. By then the East coast was pretty well built up, and the West coast was getting settled too. But, except for the railroad and them covered-wagon roads, nobody knowed much about the country in between. That must of been how they'd left that Great Platte Valley empty all this time. Father had always been a great believer in settlers going out there and filling in them blank places on the map. He didn't take no stock in that True American Society that said "every man was entitled by nature to a portion of the soil of the country." They'd been going around for years talking about how everyone should be give a piece of land excepting the Indians. But Father said land was meant to be farmed, that Lincoln had been right when he signed that Homestead Act fixing it so any man who went out there and done the work and took the risks should be give his quarter section because he'd earned it.

Only half of the land along the tracks had been granted to the railroads. They had been give every other section of land in alternate sections in a wide strip clean across the country. If they got 12,400 acres for each mile of track they laid, that meant settlers could have what was left of that strip. Their 16,000,000 acres had been put in at a value of $2.50 an acre. They got that because they done the work

and built the road. We was to get our farms in between their sections because we was doing the work and raising the stuff that they
needed to ship to keep their freight cars running. Before he left,
Mama asked Father to be sure and file on a farm in close to the railroad. She didn't want to live right alongside the tracks on account
of the trains being dangerous when the baby started walking. But she
figgered it would be considerable company to see them folks riding
back and forth from coast to coast.

We had enough ready cash for Father's trip and Mama had enough
provisions put down to partly keep us going. Aaron and Billy Elliot
was lucky enough to get a job in Meherrin cutting four-foot lengths
of wood into two-foot lengths so's the railroad could get them into
the firebox on the engine. Some other fellows hauled it in to them
from the woods with oxen and mules. Aaron said for Father not to
worry, that he'd look out for us all and take up the slack until Father
got located and could come back for us. So Mama got him packed
up, and we all went down to the train to see him off to Nebraska,
and it was over three months before he come home again.

It wasn't long though until we was getting letters from him telling about how he'd hit some snags. It seemed like Father always managed to be either too late or too soon to get in on the ground floor.
You see, in 1869 when the railroads met out at Salt Lake, the Union
Pacific passed a ruling that they was only going to open up the first
200 miles of the grant for settlement, and they wouldn't open no more
until what they had was settled because they couldn't be hauling
empty freight trains all along the line. So, as far as the settlers was
concerned, Grand Island was the end of the line.

The trouble was that Grand Island had first been settled in 1866
when the Union Pacific had made it a storage place for supplies
while the men building track moved on ahead. They figgered that it
took over three hundred tons of material for each mile of railroad
that they built. They'd had to have food, too, for their men and
horses. So, farmers had filled in close to town when the railroad
family men started sending back for their folks; and doctors, and
teachers, and preachers and other folks that go to make up a town,
had moved in too. The single fellows working on the railroad had
got tired being out there in front without nothing to come back to;
so them other kind of folks that helped them blow off steam come

out there too. For a while the saloon keepers and dance-hall girls had followed along as close as they could to the track builders. But when Father got there in 1873 the railroad building boom was over. A lot of folks didn't want to go back East, so they had stopped off in Grand Island and had filed on them homesteads around nearer the town.

And another thing; the Homestead Act said that any citizen could file on a hundred and sixty acres of public land but when they give the railroads that forty-mile-wide grant they run a joker in with it. They said nobody but veterans could have a hundred and sixty acres. Everybody else could only file on an eighty. Now Father figgered he was entitled to a hundred and sixty and that's what he allowed he'd have. Anyhow, he would of liked to be a veteran only he wasn't. When the Civil War come along he'd figgered on joining up, but his brothers beat him to it. They went off to the war and left him to take care of their folks and he had to farm their land as well as his own. Most all of the veterans who'd been helping lay tracks for the transcontinental railroad had stopped off at Grand Island before he got there and filed.

So he'd tried to get ahold of some railroad land on time but them land speculators had bought it all up. They was rich fellows from back East who seen what was coming and got out with their money before their businesses went under. Anyhow, they figgered buying railroad land was a blamed sight safer than buying railroad bonds, so they'd come out to Grand Island and bought up that railroad land and they was laying out townships, or holding it as a speculation, or paying men who was stranded there next to nothing for breaking their sod. They never done no work, but every town out West had some of them fellows strutting around the streets or riding around in their buggies looking over the fields and charging high interest rates to the homesteaders who'd been out there long enough to be able to get a mortgage.

Father wrote Mama all about it. He said he figgered on going out beyond the twenty-mile limit and for her not to worry if she didn't hear for awhile. Things was costing him more than he figgered, like the filing fee would be eighteen dollars instead of the ten they'd figgered on, but he only had to pay fourteen of it when he made the application. He said it was good country, and nobody could ask for nicer fall weather. He'd go ahead and locate and she'd better get things packed up and ready because we had to be living on our homestead within six months of the filing date. Since we'd have to be hauling our stuff all of twenty miles by wagon, she shouldn't figger on bringing much besides cooking utensils and bedding, and maybe the fire was a blessing in disguise because she wouldn't have to feel so bad now about leaving things behind since they was all burned up anyhow. He said not to be worried about not hearing again because he couldn't send no letter from where he was going, and that we'd see him when he got home.

But nights, when she didn't think we was watching her, she'd set and stare into the fireplace and watch the flames with such a faraway look in her eyes that we'd have to speak to her several times to get her to answer. That's why us children never told her about Mr. Rowlett and how he was running our school. And she never even knowed that I was being rode on a rail until Aaron carried me home because I couldn't walk no more. It wasn't just that Mama was worried about Father. You see, from the middle of September of 1873 when Jay Cooke, that big Philadelphia banker who was promoting the Northern Pacific, went under and most of the other banks in the country closed their doors too, we hadn't heard nothing but bad news.

Mama's folks was having their troubles, too. Businesses had shut down up there. Nobody was buying farm produce or nothing else. Mama's sister said they'd decided to get out of Pennsylvania and she hoped Mama and Father would help her to locate a good farm where they could live neighbor to us in Virginia. A representative of the Settlers and Immigration Society had been to see them and he'd give her a book. They'd been reading it, and it told how Virginia had the best farming land in the world, and that all it needed was immigration. Well, Mama wrote back that same day and she told her to stay right where she was, but to please send her that book.

The book come just before Father did. He hadn't no more than got in the house when Mama started right in and she read him all about Virginia, "its lands, minerals, forests, fields, and gardens." Why that blamed book told all about the country where we was living. It said, "the railroads of the future must to a great extent depend upon the local freight and travel," and that "this company will use every exertion to facilitate immigration to and settlement in this region of Virginia." And right there in that book we read that the Richmond and Danville System run through a country "blessed with salubrious air, superabundant water, and a capacity second to no other for the production of cereals, grasses, and fruits."

Father was terrible sensitive after Mama read him that railroad book about how nice the country was right down there where we was living. Us children knowed better than to run around asking him a lot of fool questions. The next morning he hitched up the team and drove over to Keysville to see if Mr. Thompson had had any offers on our plantation since he'd listed it for sale. When he come home he never said a word about it, and I've never knowed from that day to this if we really sold that old plantation or if we just snuck off and left it. I figgered if he'd got anything for it, he'd of said so. And I can't ever recollect of no money ever following us out West from Virginia. So I just think he put it up for sale and nobody was fool enough to buy it, and them baby pine trees and the berry vines just clumb over them old rail fences and it turned out to be one more of them abandoned farms like we seen so many of down South.

The folks went right ahead with our packing. We knowed that we had to plan our outfit so's it would all go in one wagon. Father was right about the fire making our packing easier. We thought we'd cut down on our stuff when we moved South, but when we went West we was right down to bedrock. Mama had sold what she could to the neighbors. Then old Stitch Williams come over and loaded up a bunch of stuff that wasn't good enough to sell but was too good to throw away. Mama give what few victuals we had left to old Sally who was crying all over the kitchen on account of us moving.

All the darkies on our place took on when we was leaving. Some of them wanted to go along, but Father had all he could do to raise enough money to get the family to Nebraska. He'd dickered around and got a special rate for us, but we had to take the train from Meherrin to Richmond where we was to get loaded for our trip West. Father had sold the team and wagon, but he got to keep them until we was to the train. Then Hector was to drive them over to the fellow who'd bought them; he'd promised Father to give Hector a job driving for him regular.

Us children could hardly wait to get on the train, but Mama didn't like the idea of moving in February with a six-months-old baby. The worst of it was that on account of having that carbuncle on her breast, Mama didn't have enough milk to nurse her. Myra wasn't old enough to eat packed lunches with the rest of us, but Father said we'd stop regular along the way at railroad eating houses. He said we had to move then because he'd kept going up the valley until he'd found a real good farm. It was close to the Middle Loup River and it had a spring on it. Of course it was the farthest one out beyond the twenty-mile railroad grant, because he'd had to keep going quite a ways until he found land close to the river that wasn't already home-steaded. He didn't have no wood for corner stakes, so he'd gone around on his quarter section and gathered up and piled buffalo skulls on each corner and put his name on them. He said they was as high as he could make them and he'd marked his name real plain on top of each pile, but he wanted to get out there before some squatter moved in and kicked them over so the grass would cover them. Anyhow he'd filed and he'd paid his fee at the land office in Grand Island and if we didn't get out there and settle within six months we'd never have another chance at a free farm as long as we lived.

We shipped our stuff in boxes straight through to Grand Island by freight, and we said goodbye to the folks in the stores at Meher-rin. Then we clumb on that train that took us to the Fourteenth Street Depot in Richmond. We all had something to carry. Mama give me the lunch basket because it was wove good and had a solid handle, and she said it wouldn't be as serious to have something happen to it as it would to any of the other things.

When we got off the train in Richmond, we all followed Father over to where a fast-talking, promoting man, named G. B. Cady, was lining up families from a paper he had in his hand. When he found out we was the Hawthornes from Meherrin he told us to wait for just a few minutes until he checked the rest of his list.

While we was waiting, Aaron and Father and me walked over to the track where we got to see one of them new Pullman cars that was made with berths so that folks could undress and go to bed at night. Them beds folded out of sight every day, but nights they was pulled out and made up with clean sheets, and folks walked on carpets on the floor. But we didn't get to ride in nothing like that. Them railroad companies was using up the last of their oldest cars, with the slat seats and the bare floors, to take emigrant parties out West at a family rate.

Mr. Cady worked full time making up and conducting carloads of folks from Richmond to Grand Island, which was as far as they'd take emigrants right then. I don't know if we had more than one carload of folks when we left Richmond or not. All I seen was the ones we was with. But all along the way the train would stop and another emigrant car would be hooked on behind ours. Most of them folks getting on hadn't never been out there, but they'd read that book and could hardly wait until they got located in that Platte River Valley. When they found Father had been there they all begun firing questions his way and he told them about how pretty the land lay, and how it didn't have to be cleared, and how Nebraska had a herd law that every man must keep his own cattle in so that a man could start farming there without having to build no fences to keep cattle out. We was all so busy hearing about Nebraska that we never paid no attention to the country we was going through. Father really believed in that country up where he had staked his claim. That's why he wrote to his brother, Boone, and to the rest of his kin in Pennsylvania, telling them how to find our place and to get out there quick and get located.

The thing I liked best about that whole trip was crossing the Missouri River on a high bridge from Council Bluff to Omaha. Aaron and me couldn't figger out how they got it up there like that. Omaha was a mighty big place with all kinds of folks crowded in at the depot. Mr. Cady told us we'd have almost a day's layover before our train left for Grand Island. Mama went into the women's room and she was gone a real long time. She sent the girls back to tell Father to call someone in charge there at the depot. The ticket agent went in and talked to Mama, then when he come back out again he said she'd found an old woman who was terrible sick and had told him to send for a doctor quick. After awhile Mama and another woman brung her out and they had the folks all clear away, then they stretched the old lady out on a bench and put her coat under her head. I went over to take a peek at her and I could see that her face was all broke out and that she was more dead than alive. But just then Mama looked up and she told me to please go over and stay with Aaron and to set still and to try to mind my own business.

It wasn't long after that until Father got back with a doctor who looked at the old lady and said she was critically ill with erysipelas and wasn't in no condition to travel; that it was a shame for us to be dragging her around like that when we ought to have her home in bed; that he had an emergency call; that since it was obvious that we was transients going through their city he'd like to have Father pay him his five dollars now so's he could be on his way. Father done it! He said afterward he didn't know how it happened, but that regular doctor was slicker than any of them patent medicine men when it come to out-talking the other fellow. In no time he was gone and so was Father's money. Father went over to the ticket taker and asked him to pay back his five dollars. But that ticket taker got real mean and said he was running a depot and not a charity hospital.

Then Father went back to Mama to talk about what they'd better do. The railroad wouldn't help. The old woman was traveling all alone and she didn't have no money. She'd told Mama that the only kin folks she had was on ahead in a covered wagon. After they had left their home back East she had got to thinking about how she didn't want to die without seeing her daughter again. She knowed they was going to stop in Lincoln to pick up their mail, and she had figgered the train would get her there in time to catch them. But she was sick, her money had run out, and she didn't know what was going to become of her.

We was too short of money ourselves to pay for her ticket, so the only thing we could do would be to take up a collection. The other woman who had helped Mama get the old lady out of the waiting room, agreed to stay right there and watch her. The folks each took a side of the depot and started asking anyone setting there for money. They collected over three dollars but that wasn't enough to buy her ticket. Them folks in the depot was willing but they was even poorer than we was, and you can't squeeze blood out of a turnip.

Then Mama set right down and she wrote out a paper because she said she wasn't going out begging unless folks knowed what it was for. She wrote, "This money is to help an old lady to get to where she ought to be." Then she started up the main street with it, but most folks outside the depot didn't give her a cent when she stopped them and asked if they'd help. She was feeling real bad about it but she wasn't giving up easy, so she kept right on. When Mama stopped two handsome, dressed-up, stylish men who was walking by real fast, one of them says, pointing to the other fellow, "Don't bother this man, he's the Governor of Nebraska, and he's in a hurry."

Mama says, quick, "Well, I've come to live in Nebraska, and I've got a right to know what kind of a governor we have. If he won't take care of his own people, he don't amount to much."

The governor picked up his ears, and got sort of red. Then he laughed and says, "I guess she's right about that." Blamed if them two men didn't turn right around in their tracks and follow Mama back to the depot. She showed the governor the old woman laying there, still as death, and Mama says, "I am a nurse. We haven't any money to spare but I'll take care of her on the train if you will get her passage and telegraph to the police in Lincoln so they will locate her family and meet us there."

Mama bossed that Governor around just like he was one of us children, and she looked so handsome in her black alpaca suit, with her cheeks sort of flushed and her eyes real blue because she was excited and wanting her own way, that the governor, and Father, and everyone else around there was real happy to see she got it. He took time out to tell us his full name. He was Governor Robert W. Furnas, and she took time out to show him her children. Then he went over to the ticket man and he wrote out an order saying that the old lady with erysipelas was to have a free ride to Lincoln.

When he come back, he shook hands with Mama, and he says, "Mrs. Hawthorne, I hope you like our state. Nebraska needs women like you." Then he patted Father on the shoulder and says: "You're a lucky man. Take good care of her."

And Father looked real proud and says, "Most of the time she's taking care of us."

Then the Governor and his friend said goodbye to us and he went back up town, and we got on the train. Us children stayed close to Father until we got to Lincoln. The old lady was pretty weak by then but the police had located her kin folks where they was camped in a covered wagon out on the edge of town, and they had drove down to the depot and had a bed all fixed in the back of their wagon. Father helped lift her off the train, and they put her in the wagon, and she opened her eyes and seen her daughter was there, and she reached out and took her hand and said, "Mary." Then she dozed off again. We never knowed what happened to her. Father said she was too weak to last out the trip in a covered wagon until they found a homestead. But Mama said she was lots better off to be in that wagon with her own kin than she'd be in a hospital bed along the way.

We was tired and glad to get off that train in Grand Island, but the Railroad House was small and the eating part so crowded that we waited a long time to get fed. Myra was crying terrible hard, so Mama talked a waitress into bringing her some warm milk, and she leaned agin the wall and Father sort of helped her steady herself and stood so folks didn't bump her while she was getting the baby fed. Finally a family got up to leave and we slid onto a bench between a table and the wall before some other folks got there. Victuals come high. Mama priced everything first and then talked to Father about it, and they told the girl what we was to eat. While we was eating, her and Father talked about how we'd better get out to our homestead quick.

Soon as we finished eating, we left the girls holding the baby and setting on our bundles in the corner of The Railroad House, and the folks and Aaron and me walked down the street to where Front Street, that run east and west, come into Pine Street, that run north and south; from there we could see the whole town. Every store we had passed had a big sign in the window saying that all storekeepers in Grand Island had signed an agreement in October of 1873 that nothing could leave their premises unless it was paid for in cash. They had wrote out that statement and had run it in the papers and posted it all over town, saying that they was real sorry but that conditions in the East, where Jay Cooke and them other big Wall Street bankers had closed up shop and had cut off all chances for them to get credit, had forced them to take this action. Folks didn't seem to be going in and out of the stores much, but the streets was crowded with men trying to run down leads on where to go to locate a homestead. Some of them looked hungry enough to do anything for a square meal. And all the money we had in the world was right there in Father's pocket; excepting for a few green-backs Mama had tied in a handkerchief and pinned inside of the front of her dress to use in emergencies if he got his pocket picked.

When Father was out there before, he'd stayed his first nights with James Michelson, who owned The Nebraska House. He said rooms was dear, but it was the only safe place he knowed to take us. So we went in, and Mr. Michelson, who was a real friendly fellow, shook hands all around and we agreed to stay there as soon as we went back for the girls and our stuff. Going back up the street, Father told us about how Mr. Michelson had used his head when his wagon broke down when he was trying to ford the Platte River a piece from town. That had happened before the coming of the rail-roads, and he'd had to drop out of his wagon train right there. Be-cause he'd been a blacksmith back East and had brung his tools along, he set up shop beside that ford. It wasn't long until he was sending back East for more equipment. He charged sixteen dollars to shoe a yoke of oxen, and them wagon trains was coming through there so thick that before long he had other men hired to help him.

Some other fellows come along and started farming in along the Platte River. Clean back in 1862, Henry A. Kroenig and Fred Wiebe got tired of folks borrowing when the wagon trains stopped and so they opened the O. K. Store right on their farm. All them fellows made money. When the railroad come they moved up to town. In 1866 James Michelson took the money he'd saved blacksmithing and built The Nebraska House. He done well and he'd added on to it by the time we got there and stayed with him in '73. And Henry Kroenig and Fred Wiebe was doing a lot of business in their O. K. Store where we bought what provisions we had to have. Them boys was smart; besides the store, they'd put in the first mill and they'd opened the State Central Bank of Nebraska in 1871, and because they didn't gamble or make fool loans they was doing business all during that panic when folks back East was going under. Trouble was they was so careful we couldn't get no credit, and we didn't have much to eat along with us when we left town in our new wagon that was drawed by a team of green oxen that was the best Father could get with the money he had to spend. After we got our hand luggage loaded we set in the wagon and rode down to the depot to pick up our freight. Father walked alongside them oxen with his goad stick, but the rest of us got to ride. After we picked up our bedding and them other boxes from Virginia, Aaron and me just walked along in back of the wagon. Then when we rode over to Jim Cleary's store to get Mama's new Charter Oak stove that she'd been down and bargained for, and Father's plow and other farm implements that he just had to have, we seen we was up against it for room in the wagon-box.

So, Father drawed off to the side, and him and Aaron took a lot of the things out of the wagon, and they put the stove in the middle and up toward the front. Then they opened one of the boxes and packed the oven and the firebox as full as they would hold. The plow fit in to one side of it with things packed tight around it, too. Then a few boxes went in on the other side. From then on back it was nip and tuck to make it. We seen we'd be lucky if we got all of our stuff in the wagon, and by then we knowed we'd all have to walk. The baby was too heavy to carry, so Father left a little place for her in back and to the right. He tied the load good so nothing would topple over or slide down and mash her. Mama said she'd walk in the right-hand wagon rut all the way so's she could watch her.

Before we left town we stopped at the bakery and Mama bought a lot of bread and rolls, and fried-cakes and cookies, so's we'd have them to eat on the way. Them oxen of ours wasn't broke enough to pull heavy loads and we hadn't got a mile out of town until Father was having all kinds of trouble with them. Aaron had been walking alongside of one, and Father had the other side. Mama said we'd be lucky if that team got us there. After that nobody talked much, and Father didn't have nothing to say about how far we was to go.

We got to Noland's place about noon. By then we'd walked over six mile and us children figgered we ought to be about to our homestead, so we told Mr. Noland we was going to be his new neighbors. But he just looked at us, sad-like, and shook his head. Then he started talking to Father about the best places for us to make our all-night stops. That's the first time I realized we'd only covered six mile, and our homestead was over sixty miles from Grand Island on up the Middle Loup River. The good land along the Platte River had all been staked before Father got there, although nobody was living on a lot of the places. The Loup River was the largest river running into the Platte. The Middle Loup had looked the likeliest of any of them rivers he come to, so he'd followed up it and staked the first good claim with a spring. He said for us not to worry, that we still had quite a walk ahead but our homestead would raise good crops because the soil wasn't near as sandy there as it was in the other places he seen when he come West scouting around.

Mr. Noland said that the reason we had to go so far out was that way back in 1857 word had got around that the capitol of the United States was being moved to the center of the country. Them days, under the territorial law, a settler could preempt land by swearing he was living on it and by paying a filing fee of fifty cents. Bunches of settlers even had to get together and form claim clubs to protect theirselves from the squatters moving in. According to the law, a man could only preempt land once, but lots of fellows become professionals squatters and just drifted around picking out likely spots that would sell good and lying about living there and starting a house on the land. Why some of them just cut four poles and laid them out in a square—others never even done that much work before they went down to the land office and took an oath that they was going to live on their places and not sell out. One of the worst deals was pulled by a land company right there at Grand Island that loaned settlers money to preempt land that their surveyor had picked out. The settler got to keep half the land, but he turned the other half over to the land company in trade for ten town lots. When they didn't move our capitol from Washington, D.C., the company went broke, but the land lay idle because the title was all mixed up and nobody could homestead land that had been preempted.

After dinner we started out again. Father set a slow pace because of them oxen and us children. By night we had only got as far as Noland's daughter's place. They was pleasant enough folks but I'd never slept in a sod house with a dirt floor before and I figgered they must be awful poor. When we got up the next morning it was snowing, but it let up a little and we made a late start. By keeping right at it, no matter how hard the going was, we made it to Dannebrog before night. Quite a bunch of Danes had come out there and filed on land all together. They called it the Danish Land and Homestead Company; their government and a bunch of their relatives up in Wisconsin had helped them get there. Mostly they lived back from the road in little dugouts, but Nolands had told us to go see Lars Hannibal, who had the postoffice in his house, and to see if he wouldn't put us up. At first he was real short with us and come outside, pulling the door shut back of him. He spoke English some, but it was terrible broken. He said he couldn't put up all the strangers that come through Dannebrog. Father wasn't getting nowhere with him, but Mama come around from her side the wagon, and he seen that the snow was caked thick in agin her hair at the edge of her 'kerchief. She says, "Could I buy some milk from you for my baby?"

He looked us all over standing there with the snow coming down on us and our stuff in that open wagon, and he opened the door for Mama and motioned us children inside. Him and Father put the oxen in with his. Father brung in some of the bakery stuff we had left to sort of pay our way, and we put our victuals in with theirs. His wife and Mama was real smiley with each other even if Mrs. Hannibal couldn't talk to her in English and Mama couldn't speak Danish. Then us children was bedded down with theirs along one wall. I was so tired I could hardly keep my eyes open long enough to see Mr. Hannibal and Father setting over by the fire drinking something steaming out of a couple of them big, tall steins, and Mama shaking her head at Father and wishing that he wouldn't.

Next morning we was snowed in. We stayed over that day, but it was plain to see that we had too many folks in that one cabin. No matter how hard we tried we couldn't keep out of each other's way. The second morning, early, we left. It had quit snowing and a couple of teams had been through and broke the road on ahead. We figgered the storm was over. Of course, it was hard walking under foot, but the folks didn't feel that we had any business staying longer.

We made a good many miles that morning, but about mid-afternoon a blizzard struck. Father said there wasn't nothing to do but keep on going until we reached Loup City where some folks had been laying out a new town when he went through there on his way to locate our homestead. By that time we was all scared. We couldn't see six foot in front of us; the snow was about halfway to my knees. Father and Aaron was taking turns walking ahead, leading the oxen; the rest of us followed single file after one of the wagon wheels. Then the storm really hit us. One of the oxen stumbled and fell. We had trouble getting him up, and Father knowed they was through.

The baby was crying in the wagon. The girls was jumping up and down and blowing on their hands and a-screaming. Aaron run back and pulled me in under his coat to see if he could warm me a little. Father grabbed Mother by the shoulders and yelled, "Martha, can you make out while I try to go back for help?"

She said, "Sam, we'll be all right in under the wagon. Shovel part of the snow away. Get the featherbeds and pile them on the wind side, so we don't get buried by drifts."

Blamed if she didn't go right to work helping him. It wasn't no time until they had a place scooped out for us under the wagon. Mama handed the baby to Julia, because she was the oldest, and sent her in first. Then Sadie and me crawled in after her. Aaron's legs was as long as Father's, so they went back for help together, taking turns breaking trail. Before they left, they tied the oxen on the lee side of the wagon to protect them all they could from the wind.

That just left Mama to come in under the wagon with us. The wind was howling through there as she pulled the last of the feather pillows in after her. Us four children cuddled up to her like a bunch of little puppies, and before long I could feel my feet tingling and sort of coming to life again. Mama started right in talking to us about how we was within twenty-five mile of our new home and how it would soon be springtime out there on the prairie.

"I want you children to remember," says she, "that no matter how bad things may be for you some day, you can always be thankful that it's bound to be better than it was in '73."

FIVE

LIVING IN OUR SODDY

The wind had died down before we heard Aaron and Father coming back alone. Mama told us children to stay right where we was while she crawled out to see if they was all right and to fix the milk they had brung back for Myra. The poor little thing had been crying for hours, and we had to keep her under the wagon with us until Mama held a bottle of milk inside of her dress to warm it enough so's it would be fit for the baby to drink. By then we all knowed that if the folks hadn't throwed them featherbeds out the window when we lost so much of our stuff in the fire in Virginia, we'd of all been froze as stiff as planks in that blizzard.

While Mama was feeding Myra, Sadie asked Father if we was going to stay there. He says, "No, only until morning."

Then he told us that him and Aaron had rough going when they left us. The snow had drifted in and filled up the ruts. They couldn't tell where the road was most of the time. Even when there wasn't no snow it looked more like a trail than a road and they didn't have no fences to guide them. After they lost the road they stumbled around for a long time, keeping ahold of each other so's they wouldn't get separated. Then they seen a dugout off to one side. An old German was living there. It was just by chance that a fellow who knowed the country had stopped there for shelter right when Father and Aaron was lost out in that old German's field. If it hadn't of been for them seeing the stranger's team and wagon, they would of gone right by because the snow had drifted over most of the dugout's entrance. They helped the stranger get his horses into another dugout that was set back in the hill alongside of the first one. It was where the old German kept the team of cows that he drove instead of oxen. Then they all went in to get thawed out by the fire, and they had to stay right there until the storm let up so's they could walk into the wind.

Neither the old German or the stranger would chance going out with their teams or on foot that night. There wasn't another soul to turn to for help. Father couldn't leave us alone all night out on the prairie, so he got some milk for us children and him and Aaron started back as soon as they could. The stranger agreed that if it wasn't storming he'd hitch up early in the morning and come by to give part of us a lift into Loup City.

By the time they got back the storm had died down enough so that Father and Aaron could move and feed the oxen. Then they made a little lean-to shelter out of the canvas wagon-cover, and put it at the side of the wagon after they scraped the snow away. Mama said for us children to lie still so the cold wouldn't get in under our covers. She hunted around in the wagon and found a loaf of bread. She didn't take time to find no knife, she just tore off chunks and handed them to us for our supper, and we took turns drinking milk out of the only cup she could find real quick. Then her and Father and Aaron got us up, and shook the snow out of our featherbeds and blankets, and they made one long bed under the shelter and wagon, where the seven of us bedded down the best we could for the night.

Father said he knowed we wasn't very comfortable right then, but it wouldn't be long before he'd have us settled on one of the best farms in Nebraska and we'd be having a roof over our heads instead of a wagon-box. Just before I dozed off I heard him telling Mama about how he was going to file on the 160 acres next to ours. He could get it under that new Timber Culture Act, and all we'd have to do for that extra land would be to promise to plant one-fourth of it to trees within the next four years. Them tree claims was being passed out so that homesteaders would help grow forests out on the plains. Father liked it because it give him a chance to get ahold of more land.

He said he'd been talking to the stranger while the storm was letting up, and they was warming theirselves by the fire in the old

German's dugout. The stranger had said that the farmers around there had found out they needed more land than 160 acres because they was doing what he called dry-land farming. He was married but him and his wife was acting like they wasn't. They had built two dugouts on separate homesteads but they'd put them right together at the corner stakes. A single woman could file on a separate claim and so his wife had gone down and filed under her maiden name and that way they had got twice as much land in one piece. But, of course, they couldn't of made it work if they was like us and drove up with a whole wagonload of children.

Mama sort of sniffed and said she didn't think much of a man that didn't have more principle than that. She said she thought she'd speak to the stranger and tell him it wasn't right for him to put his wife in a position where all the neighbors would think she was a loose woman and living in sin. Father said a lot of folks figgered Congress was to blame for making a law that a single woman could file on a homestead but that a married woman with children couldn't, and that he was sorry he had told her if she was going to act like that about it. He said the stranger was stopping to give her and the children a lift into Loup City, and with roads like they was and our oxen played out she'd just better let him and his wife live as they pleased. "It's none of our business," says Father. "He may be a slicker, but he's sure used his head. With their two homesteads and two tree claims, they've got a whole section of the public domain, and if he'd filed inside the limits of railroad grant, the best he could of got in the way of free land would of been eighty acres."

By morning the storm had blowed itself out; we had a meal of cold victuals because we didn't have no place to build a fire in the snow or nothing to build it with. The stranger come along early and took Mama and the girls and the baby and me in his wagon up to Loup City. Father and Aaron was coming with the ox team and we said we'd wait for them at that new hotel there. It was a long ride. Mama set on the seat with the stranger and held the baby. The girls and me crawled in under some sacks in the back and slept until we got there.

The hotel was just a square, two-story building, with a lean-to kitchen out back. A fellow named Ingram run it, and the place was packed with folks who was stranded there in the storm. The stranger dumped us off and went on to his place that wasn't far from there. It was late afternoon, so we just crowded together and set on a bench and kept still until they brung supper in big bowls and passed it to all the folks who set in rows at a long table. They was a rough bunch and their talk showed it. Mama done her best to act comfortable, but it was plain to us children that nothing but them snowdrifts outside kept her where she was. After we got there, they all started laughing and teasing a big, gangling fellow about how now the last bed was gone and what he was going to do. The beds was on the second floor at the top of the ladder that run up one side of the wall. All they had downstairs was the fireplace, and them tables and benches, excepting for the kitchen out back. A girl named Birdie kept coming back and forth waiting tables. They was all joshing her about this fellow we'll call Slim, 'cause that wasn't his name.

Now Slim had been coming there real often rolling up his eyes at her and mooning around, but he'd always been too bashful to pop the question. It wasn't so easy in a place like that where there was always folks around. He was such a simple-acting fellow that every-body liked to point their jokes at him. That night, Ben Shooter, who had the livery stable, started guying Slim about how he was going to have to sleep on the floor. Some of the others took it up from there and carried the joke a lot farther by telling him he'd have to marry Birdie to make the beds come out even. She was in the kitchen at the time, but just then she come in with a load of victuals. Slim stood right up and says, real loud, in front of us all, "By God, Birdie, let's get hitched. It's now or never!"

I never heard such yelling and laughing, and back-slapping as went on around there. But Birdie wasn't bashful. She allowed she would.

After the crowd quit laughing, they found out that one cf the fellows there was a justice of the peace. So the folks shoved the table back and this fellow said he'd marry them free of charge. Ingram, who run the hotel, said they wouldn't have to pay for their accommodations because she was working there anyhow, and he was real glad to have the beds come out even. We just set and listened until after the fellow stood up with them by the fireplace and they said their promises and he says, "I pronounce you man and wife."

Then while them fellows was all crowding around kissing the bride, Mama slipped over quiet-like to where her warm coat was hanging, drying near the fire. She turned the wet side around so's it would be dry by morning; then she asked Mr. Ingram if he'd show us our room. So he clumb the ladder up the side of the wall, and Mama had me come up last so hers and the girls' legs wouldn't show so bad from down below where all the folks was. Mama didn't find it so easy to go up a ladder and carry a baby at the same time.

The upstairs of that hotel was just one big room. Mr. Ingram said we could have our pick of two beds that was left, so Mama asked for the corner one. Them beds had legs and sides of logs fastened in rows all along the wall. They had smaller, willow poles laid lengthwise for springs, and a straw-filled tick on top. Mama didn't like not having sheets or pillowcases, but she had a few extras of the baby's underwear left clean, so she put them under our heads. She told Julia and Sadie to get in bed first. Then she laid me across the foot with my head back in the corner. That left the baby and her for the outside. Before she crawled in she come down to my part of the bed and listened to me saying my prayers the best she could. It was terrible hard to keep track of where I was because them folks down below had decided to give Slim and Birdie their charivari right after they got done having their wedding. Mama said for us children just to pretend all them folks wasn't there, and she told me to close my eyes and to be sure and keep them closed until morning. When she kissed me good night her face felt all wet and I could taste the salt, but I never heard her crying out loud.

Afterwards them folks all come trooping upstairs together, and there was a lot of loud talk and laughing and horseplay going on around there for hours. But Mama sort of made a wall out of her back, and she kept a real close watch on us children. Every time I'd try to set up and look around she'd catch me at it. Finally I just give up and laid down like she told me to and closed my eyes. With all that wise-cracking going on up there it was a blamed hard place to do any sleeping until Mama spoke up and put a damper on a lot of that rough talk.

Next morning, when we went down for breakfast, Mama's coat was gone! She'd left it right there by the fire. The folks around all allowed they didn't know nothing about it and that someone must

of come in during the night and stole it. So Mama went to the door
and looked for fresh tracks out toward the main road. There wasn't
none. Then she walked back in and stood looking at that bunch of
folks setting there at that big, long table. At first they shrugged it
off and acted like nothing could be done to get it back. Then she
says, "I am going through everything here until I find my coat. It
hasn't left this place yet and I want you to know that I will never
leave here without it."

Well, that put it right straight up to them. Everyone hearing
Mama knowed she meant it. So after breakfast the folks started
hunting around to help find it. Blamed if she didn't just stand there
with her back to the fire watching them. She didn't do a bit of the
hunting herself. Sure enough, in a few minutes, one of the women
came in with it from somewhere out in the lean-to. She said it must
of been picked up by accident and got tucked away back there.

So we gathered up our stuff and set right down in a bunch beside
it, to wait for Father. But he was so long coming that after awhile
folks sort of thawed out toward each other and we heard quite a
bit about Loup City and the country round about there. Nebraska
had been having a regular epidemic of folks laying out townsites and
then selling city lots to them suckers back East that didn't know
no better than to put their money into them paper cities.

Just before we got there the government had sent some scouts
out to check up on the Indians prowling around and see if they was
up to some mischief. But the Indians snuck off and when them
soldiers seen a blizzard coming up they took shelter in a canyon,
where they camped about four miles above Loup City. After they got
in there the snow begun to drift down on them, and it smothered in
so fast that they didn't have a chance to get their horses out.
Twenty-eight of their horses died and the soldiers took about as bad
a licking as they would of if they'd fought a battle with the Indians.
Folks still call that place where they was camped Dead Horse
Canyon, but them days word of things like that happening never
got around very much. Them promotors, who was selling city property
to folks back east, and them railroad writers, who sent books to
folks like us, figgered the truth hurt business; while the rest of us
was too blamed busy trying to keep alive to pay much attention to

what was happening to anybody who wasn't our kin or our close neighbors.

It had been a night and a day since we had left Father and Aaron back on the road in the snow, and we was getting uneasy. They didn't have many windows in that hotel, so we'd been taking turns watching from noon on. Hearing all that talk about them twenty-eight horses dying within four mile of town didn't make us feel no easier. It was dark before we heard them coming. A couple of fellows went out and helped them get the oxen into the shelter. Then Father and Aaron come in, all blue with cold. It took them considerable time to thaw out, eat some hot victuals, and tell us all about their troubles getting there. They bedded down for the night in front of the fireplace, while we went up to our same bed. With Father and Aaron downstairs we didn't feel near as alone up there, in all that crowd, as we had the night before.

Come morning we put our stuff in the wagon and left right after breakfast. The snow was melting fast, and we could follow the ruts plain. The road followed along the bank of the Middle Loup River; the valley wasn't very wide in there and we couldn't tell much about it excepting that sandhills rolled back from each side and there wasn't much to see, no matter how hard we looked. Father said we only had fourteen more miles to go and we'd be home, so Mama and us children kept peering around the sides of the wagon as we went sloshing along through that melting snow trying to see all we could and still keep our feet in the wheel ruts.

When the oxen had to rest or the baby cried too hard, Father would stop long enough for Mama to feed her. Then she'd reach into our provisions and pass something out for us children so we could gnaw on it and half forget how the water felt running between our toes in them hard, old shoes we was wearing.

Father was walking out in front of the oxen, taking real big steps and looking proud of hisself, but us children was walking along in back thinking of how warm we'd been back in Virginia. By and by the going got harder. We didn't have no ruts to follow. The valley widened out until it was about three mile across. Down by the river we seen a log cabin with smoke coming out of it. Then Father stopped the ox team. We looked around the back end of the wagon-box, and there he was—off to one side, scratching around in the snow

—looking at some old buffalo skulls. The girls and me just looked at each other. Why there wasn't a thing to be seen around there but snow, and a clump of cottonwoods off a piece to the right, and we was all of a half mile from the Middle Loup River.

Then Sadie begun to cry about how she wanted a home 'stead of a homestead.

Julia put her arms around Sadie, but Mama waded right out in the snow to stand beside Father. She took a deep breath, and us children seen her shoulders stiffen as she looked out over that big field of snow. Then she says, real slow, "Is this it, Sam?"

And Father stood real straight, and puffed out his chest.

"Yes, Martha, this is it! Yonder is the spring by them cottonwoods," he says pointing at them few trees. "You'll have water handy to your kitchen, and there ain't no better ground outdoors."

He dropped down on his knees to scrape the snow away, then he come up with a double handful of rich soil. Mama pulled off her gloves and squeezed some of it between her fingers. After a minute she looked up, smiled, and says, "Yes, Sam, this is a lot better than we had back in Virginia."

Night was coming on, so Father turned the oxen to the left and we headed for the only shelter we seen. Father said when he'd been out there to stake our claim he'd talked to Old Man McKeller and his son who lived in that cabin, and, while he didn't think much of them, he was sure they'd take us in. Out on the plains folks always felt they had to give shelter to the ones homesteading on beyond, until they got a house built. The McKellers was our nearest neighbors. Nobody had filed beyond us.

Smoke was coming out of the chimney, but the house didn't have no windows and it was shut up so tight nobody could see out, and we didn't have no way of guessing what we'd find inside. Father drove right up in front of the cabin, and then he went over and knocked on the door. Nobody answered so he knocked again. The door opened a little crack and an old woman stuck her nose out. We could see her beady eyes looking Father over first, then when she looked over and seen that he had a woman and children along, she opened the door a mite wider. "What do you want?" she says.

"We're the Hawthornes," he told her. "I talked to your husband

and your son when I was here and filed on the homestead beyond yours."

"The old man's here but George ain't," she says starting to close the door.

Father seen she wasn't what you'd call real hospitable, so he shoved his big, heavy boot into the crack far enough so she couldn't get the door closed. Then he says, "Mrs. McKeller, my wife is not well. We have a small baby and our children with us. We must have shelter until I get a roof over our heads."

She says, "You don't want to stay here. We ain't got room for you, and George don't like strangers. He's real mean with children. If them children stay around my George, they'll be swearing like hell."

Of course, she didn't know Mama. None of us children done no swearing when she was around because if she caught us at it, she'd wash our mouth out with some of her real, strong, home-made soap. Mama was clean, inside and out. We never had none of them dirty stories around where she was.

Mrs. McKeller turned and yelled over her shoulder, "It's that fellow that staked the piece with the spring. Him and his family want to hole up with us."

We never heard his answer, but she yells back inside again and says, "We'll have to. That other outfit's in the old trapper's cabin."

Then she opened the door and says, "Well, come on in—if you can get in. But when George comes home there's bound to be trouble."

So we went inside and stood close by the fire, trying not to take up no space, but with seven of us that wasn't easy. Old Man McKeller had long hair, hangin' down into his eyes, and a tobacco-stained grey beard that hung down over his chest. He just set there on a stool looking at us without having nothing to say. I begun to wish we hadn't come, but Mama talked along real friendly and thanked them for asking us in. She said we'd try not to be no more bother than we could help. She sent Julia out for some dry clothes for the baby and she had us peel off our wet shoes and socks, and rub our feet dry with a towel. Then she fixed up the worst of our blisters with some salve she'd made out of slippery-elm bark before she left Virginia. Mama always kept her medicines and doctor book handy no matter where we was. Then she give us our supper out of things we'd brung in the wagon, and it wasn't long before her and Mrs. McKeller was talking to each other real pleasant.

But the Old Man still hadn't nothing to say until after Father fixed up the oxen and wagon and come in for a bite of supper hisself. Then Old Man McKeller spoke real civil to Father. He says, "I don't care what George thinks. I'm damned glad to have another family between us and them Sioux Indians in the Black Hills."

As soon as the Old Man said "George," Mrs. McKeller started right in stewing again about having us there and wondering what George would think. We wasn't long finding out. No sooner had Father brung in the featherbeds and put them down so we could crawl in along one wall, than we heard George McKeller outside putting up his oxen and yelling about who in the hell had tied that outfit out there. Us children crawled down as out-of-sight as we could get when he come thumping in, shouting that he wanted his supper. He throwed a long shadow up the wall and across the ceiling when he walked over to the fire. We could see he was real big, and hairy, and had a wooden leg. I never knowed how he lost it; he wasn't the kind of a man you felt like asking.

Everything was real quiet in there while he drawed a box right up in the center front of the fireplace. Then his mother give him a big plate of beans that she dished out of the black kettle that hung on the crane. While he spooned them down, Father told him about our plans and how we needed to stay with them until we got our walls up and our roof on. He just grunted once in a while, but he never got up off the box he was setting on by the fire to throw us out. Before he finished eating, us children was so tired we fell asleep.

We only stayed there a week, but Mama said that was the longest week of her life. We was out of that cabin from daylight till dark, helping Father get started with our sod house. Soon as the snow melted we helped Mama get our garden in. We'd rented a half acre of broke ground from George McKeller because his homestead joined onto ours. Both him and his father had filed on claims along the Middle Loup River. They'd turned over a few acres of sod with the breaking-plow soon as they got there, and it had rotted enough to get a garden planted.

About all a farmer can hope to do during his first year on the prairie is get his buildings up, raise a little garden and sod corn, and plow the ground ready for the next year. It takes a year for the sod to rot after it is first turned under. One of the best things about building a sod house is that the women folks can put in a garden where the men skin off the sod to make the walls. Mama was real happy about renting that land from George McKeller. She'd brung her garden seed along and she went right to work getting it planted. Father plowed quite a piece of land to plant sod corn, so it would be growing while we was building our house. Why, after the sod was turned over, he went along with a single-bitted axe and cut a hole down through, in about every third round. He wore an apron Mama made for him. It had pockets and was sort of like the ones carpenters wear for carrying nails, only his was full of seed corn. He'd drop a kernel of corn into each of them holes and then step on it hard so's the birds couldn't get it. Sod corn ain't the best in the world, but it's a crop.

Them days, we had plenty of building material right there on the plains. You never seen two sod houses made alike. After staying at McKellers where they didn't have no windows and the only light come from the fireplace or the open door, Mama said us children would turn out to be as blind as bats if we tried living like they done. So Father said he'd go back to Grand Island before winter and get some glass window-panes, and a cat to do away with them mice that was trying to get into everything we had, and the rest of the things we'd have to lay in for winter.

Our place was level and Father didn't want to build our house dug into the ground because he'd heard about some folks over by Loup City who built theirs like that and a stranger drove his team clean over the top of their roof and never even knowed he was on it until one of his horses like to broke his leg when he come through the ceiling. A dugout is nice if you've got a good side-hill on your place, and they ain't hard to build, but Father said he'd met a fellow who said he even had running water in his. When he built it, he didn't know there was a spring anywere around until it broke right through the back wall, and got to running so lively that he had to move out and build another dugout somewhere else. Mama wanted our house all on top of the ground, too. So the plans was drawed just as easy as that, by word of mouth. Next morning Father started right in working on it.

I liked the way we built our sod house the best of any I ever seen. We started over where we wanted our permanent vegetable garden to be. It wasn't very far from the spring. Father hitched the oxen to the plow that we'd hauled from Grand Island in the wagon and he plowed a long, straight furrow. He was real careful to make all his furrows just a foot wide because that was to be the thickness of our walls. The sod broke off when it turned over so that it was about three inches thick. Aaron followed along after Father, using a sharp spade to cut that sod into three-foot lengths. After we marked the ground off where our house was to stand, Aaron and Father started carrying them three-foot lengths, a foot wide, and three-inches thick, on over to where they belonged in our walls. They laid them pieces of sod on top of each other just like you would for a brick house, filling the cracks with dirt, and overlapping each strip one-half way over the seam in the two pieces that had been laid below it. A place was left in front for the door. When they got the walls up about four-foot high, they left a couple of places for windows. Having thick walls like that would give us nice wide window-ledges inside for setting things or starting plants in the early spring.

The snow had melted; the sky was clear; we figgered the storm had blowed over, and we couldn't stand living down at McKellers no longer. So we told them we was far enough along on our sod house to move up there. No, it wasn't what you'd call finished, but we had about three foot of wall up, and we got along good, living out in the open by the spring without no roof over our heads excepting our wagon-box cover.

Father knowed that he had to get ahold of some strong rafters to put across for support before he put the sod roof on top. He didn't like to use cottonwood to hold up all that weight. There wasn't no other kind of free timber around handy.

By that time Aaron was nineteen years old and trustworthy. He'd split enough wood and fence rails down South to be as good a man with an axe as you'd ever hope to find. When we had enough sod cut ahead so Father could keep on working alone, Aaron went all along the river with the ox team, and he cut our ridgepoles and got back with them several days later.

Them McKellers had talked about the way settlers was moving in on them, and how they didn't like being crowded, all the time we stayed there. Of course, we kept trying to change the subject, so we hadn't found out just who they was or where they lived. We knowed that a man named Brown and his wife, and a little girl had got caught in that April storm and had made a run for the cottonwoods down along the creek. Just by chance they had stumbled onto an old, deserted trapper's cabin where they had holed up until the storm was over. We didn't have no time to visit nobody, but the McKellers said that them Browns had filed on a piece back to the east of us. It was dry land, without no spring or creek, so they was having to dig a well besides building their house and planting their sod corn. Julia and Sadie was all excited when they heard that there was another little girl living right there in our valley.

We hadn't had no chance to meet the neighbors until George McKeller rode over one day with a message. He said that some Indians had showed over to Ming Coombs' place. He was a bachelor who lived in a dugout about two mile east of us. He figgered they was some of them Sioux Indians scouting around getting ready for a raid, trying to find out how best to kill the men before they carried off the women and children. After the settlers started coming, the Indians wasn't getting so many wild animals, so they started capturing women and children and using them for trading-stock with the whites, who would pay real good to get them back again. Men was harder to handle so they didn't bother holding them over in captivity. Young girls, they figgered, was the best, because they could either marry them or trade them back to the whites. Of course if they had long hair their scalps come in handy, too. Them Sioux warriors never felt real dressed up unless they had some blonde or light-brown scalps hanging at their belts. Sadie and Julia had been growing good, and they had awful pretty hair.

Right after we heard about them Indians, an old trapper stopped by to get water at our spring. A regular trail run down through our place. It had been used by game and Indians going down to the mineral springs below us, and trappers going up for furs above us, and them prospectors who was beginning to sneak back into the Black Hills trying to get past the government men who had promised to see that the hills was held for the Sioux Indians. Now this old trapper allowed that them Indians, who like to scared Ming Coombs to death, wasn't Sioux at all, but just some begging Pawnees who wouldn't hurt a flea. But when Father went over to the McKellers to tell about him being there, they figgered that the trapper was probably a squaw man down there studying out the land for them Sioux.

George McKeller had a horse, so he rode right over to see Ming Coombs again. Next thing we knowed, work was stopped on our sod house and we was getting ourselves all slicked up and ready to go to a meeting that had been called to see about protecting the settlement. Mama fixed food for a potluck dinner, and we all got to ride in the wagon going over because we had left our stuff covered over with the wagon-box cover, and piled alongside the walls that was almost up for our new house.

The meeting was held at Fredinburgs' place. The Fredinburgs was two brothers who had filed on adjoining claims in close to the sandhills, and quite a piece from the trail to the Black Hills where we was living. Lou Fredinburg had a whole houseful of children. His brother was a widower, and lived with him. The Browns had come with their little girl. Her name was Gertrude. And Ming Coombs was there. He was an educated bachelor who had tried to raise peach trees in Michigan and went broke there when yellows spoiled all them orchards up where he'd been living. Then there was the McKellers. And then there was us. Our five families was all the folks that lived in the valley until Uncle Boone and his folks come in there, over a year later.

We couldn't rightly count in Peter Morlensen, who had settled there in the county in 1872, and had built the first house. It was half dugout and half logs. Because somebody with a map had drawed a mark and made a county line between his place and Loup City, he'd been made the county treasurer and was told to ride around every year and get what money he could out of the settlers for taxes. But he was a lot closer to settlers over on the Loup than he was to us, and we knowed if Indians come down on us from up-stream, he'd be making a beeline for that settlement.

The men decided we'd better take time out to work on a stockade, so's we'd be ready if an attack come. Widower Fredinburg had the most likely spot for it because there was a little knoll on his place where folks could see out good, with a spring near by. Our place and McKellers was too flat and right on the old Indian Trail. Anyhow, our homestead was the farthest one out of any of them. There wasn't nothing between us and them Sioux Indians up in the Black Hills excepting several hundred miles of sandhills, and they was noted for being able to cover a lot of ground fast.

Father said he hadn't been thinking about nothing but the land and the spring when he filed on that piece. Under the Homestead Law, he couldn't never file again; it was our one chance to own a farm and a home. We had one of the best pieces of land there was, and the Homestead Law said that we couldn't live away from it for six months at a time for any cause whatsoever during the next five years, or we'd lose it. We had to live there and toughy it out, and them other families was all in the same boat.

That whole Platte Valley had been Sioux territory until the railroad started building through there, and government men was sent out to get them to sign treaties to move them away from the railroad grant. In June of 1868 they'd been herded over to Whetstone, where the government had built a new agency for them on the Missouri. Fort Laramie and all the other trading posts along the Platte was closed. But the Sioux still had the right to come into the Platte River Valley and hunt. Why, them Sioux chiefs never even signed the treaty promising to keep out of the Platte Valley until 1874, and that was the year we was there building that blockhouse.

Now them fellows back in Washington, D.C., keeping the books might of figgered that them Sioux Indians was going to stay over where they had been told to go when the treaties was signed, but a lot of them Indians still believed in the treaty that give them all the land between the Big Horn Mountains to the west, the Platte River on the south, and the Missouri River on the east and north. Of course when we promised that no white man would go into their new reservation unless he had business with the Indians and that the treaty would be binding unless three-fourths of the Indian braves wanted to change it, we hadn't figgered on needing a road through their new buffalo hunting grounds to the Montana mines, or that we was giving them land where there might be gold. We had to keep making them new treaties all the time because every time we signed one, we'd find out we'd give them something we

could use ourselves. In 1874 Custer had gone into the Black Hills
to see if it was true that they was full of gold, and prospectors was
slipping through past the government men and getting into that
Indian territory. By that time them Indians was so mad they was
buzzing around like a bunch of hornets whose nest has been tore
up. Things was happening on both sides.

Red Cloud and his men killed eighty of them road builders who
was going through the Powder River Valley. Over on the Dannebrog
side of us, a fellow who'd been sort of touched in the head ever
since he'd come across his brother dead and scalped when he went
home from doing his trading in Grand Island, shot and killed an
old Indian squaw who was riding along the road, peaceful-like on
her pony. Of course he'd said that he was going to kill the next
Indian he seen, but the worst of it was the old woman was the chief's
mother. So many things like that was going on that we begun to
figger we needed protection from them Indians who wouldn't stay
on their side of the Loup River unless the white men stayed on theirs.
Besides, we heard that them cattlemen, who had been running stock
through there and using the Loup rivers for their side-fences, and
riding herd across both ends, was going around saying that they
wasn't going to let a handful of settlers come in there and put them
out of business. The land looked good to us; other things didn't.

So before that first meeting broke up, a petition was drawed.
Ming Coombs wrote it all out by hand because he was real good
with books; but when it come to farming, I ain't sure he knowed
which end of a cow give milk. Our five families all went on record
asking the government to send us protection, and to build a fort
on up above us on the Middle Loup because we was the farthest
families out. All the men signed it, and the next homesteader going
in the sixty miles to Grand Island was supposed to take it and mail
it from the post office there direct to President Grant in Washington,
D.C. Us children knowed he'd growed up on a farm out in Ohio before he got to be a General and a President, so we hoped he'd figger out
about our fort hisself. He'd know more about snowdrifts than them
blamed fool soldiers had, who led them twenty-eight horses into a
canyon where they got buried and smothered to death under the
snow down by Loup City.

The men worked together and they wasn't very many days throwing up that stockade. Then the Fredinburg men rode over to help us with our soddy when it come time to put the ridgepole across and the rafters on. We'd brung in a big load of them round willow-brush poles that growed down along the river and was about the size of a fishing pole. We laid them lengthwise of the house, back and forth, real thick, across the rafters. Then Father and Aaron put two rows of sod on top of that, and so us children figgered we was about ready to move in. Of course we didn't have no doors or windows but the holes was there for them and it didn't matter too much, as long as the weather stayed good. But Mama said she'd been talking to them other women while the men was building the stockade, and they told her sod houses was terrible dirty and the roofs leaked bad. She wanted the ceiling fixed. Lots of times folks had to move outside after a big rain because when it quit raining outside, it begun raining inside. Why a sod roof could turn out to be just like having a bunch of little springs in the ceiling, with dirty water running down into the food and wetting up the bedding. Then if the rain kept up, big chunks of mud would start to fall, and unless a sod house was built with real good rafters that was strong enough to hold up the weight of all that wet dirt, the roof would cave in.

A sod house is warm in winter and cool in summer, but sod ceilings is bad. They wet up when it rains, they dust off when it gets hot. Mama said she wasn't going to have neither, that she had brung a big roll of rag carpet that she had wove herself when she was a girl in Pennsylvania, and that she wanted it used to cover the ceiling so's she could keep the dirt out of our victuals. Father said that was fine with him and that he thought that rag carpet would make a real pretty ceiling and he'd fix it for her as soon as he could. But that before he did, he was going to waterproof our roof so it wouldn't leak.

When we'd first got there and the snow melted, we seen that the whole valley was covered with buffalo wallows. A few years before thousands of buffalo had been slaughtered by the Indians who had sold the robes and tongues to them traders for next to nothing. The meat all went to waste. In the old days, when the Indians roamed the prairies, all they needed was to be near a buffalo herd. They could eat the meat, sleep under the robes, cover their tepees with their hides, and still have plenty left over for trading stock. They never figgered they'd run out of buffalo and then lose their land. But when we got there buffalo bones was laying around on the ground as thick as cones under a big fir tree, and we had to pick them up, and pile them up, and work around them until we was blamed sick of ever hearing the name buffalo, but we never seen a single live one there in our valley.

In the dry summers the buffalo had kicked up soft dirt with their hooves and throwed it on their backs to get rid of the flies. Then when it rained the holes would fill up with water, and them buffalo had wallowed around in them places just like an old hog does in a mud hole. I suppose at first they was just little puddles, but buffalos is big, and after a number of them rolled in the same place, they left considerable of a hole. I never figgered that buffalos wanted to go around with all them chunks of dirt hanging on their sides. They must of rolled in them wallows to get rid of the flies or maybe just to scratch theirselves. But having them do that turned out to be a blamed nuisance for us because the water couldn't run out of them places, and it just evaporated after they went off wearing some of the best topsoil, and down in the bottom of each of them wallows was a thick alkali deposit that we gathered up, mixed with water, and smeared on our roof like plaster.

Excepting for using that stuff out of the bottom of them buffalo wallows on our roof, they turned out to be about the worst nuisance we had. Us children had all helped pick up bones so that Father could plow some sod under for corn and for our house. He told me to go ahead and plow while him and Aaron worked on the house. Why, sure, I was nine years old by then and that team was more broke than it had been to start with.

Father wanted the plowing to go along because it's lots easier to do when the ground ain't dried out, unless you've got buffalo wallows. But the stuff in them wallows, even the ones only eight inches or a foot deep, sticks to your feet when it's wet. It was bad enough for the oxen, but all that bothered them was carrying around that extra weight. But I was barefoot and that moist alkali mud would stick to my feet and they would crack, and the blood would run out. I tell you it was bad. When I went in at night, Mama rubbed linseed oil on them and the next morning I put more on before I went back to plowing again. That's where I made my mistake. That linseed oil that was dried on my feet just seemed to make that mud stick harder than ever. I never knowed nothing could stick and burn like that. Finally I went clumping over to the house with my feet in them big balls of alkali mud, and Mama chiseled them off and fixed me up the best she could, and that's what made Father see how good that stuff would be to put on top of a roof, because I couldn't have been no worse off if I'd put my feet in concrete and then let them dry.

The only way Father could handle them wallows when it come to farming was to haul in wagonloads of sand and dump them in to sort of loosen that ground up and work it. Of course manure would of been better, but we didn't have none. But he figgered on getting a herd of cows just as soon as he could, and when him and Aaron throwed up a shelter of poles, with a brush and a straw roof, for the oxen, they made it big enough for some cows, too.

The folks had heard about a place back in the foothills where there was some real nice white clay. That's a great country in there for chalk cliffs, too. So Father drove over to get some clay and the rest of us stayed home and brushed down the inside walls of our sod house until all the dirt was gone, and about half an inch of grass roots stuck out all around inside. That sod was terrible thick and full of roots. A man could plow a strip a half mile long and a foot wide without having it break once. Them days nobody ever heard of erosion. It was blamed hard to get through that sod down to where the dirt was underneath. After we got the walls swept down clean, we swept and smoothed up the floor. Then after the dust had settled, and Father got back with the load of white clay, we mixed it with water and plastered them walls, leaving places for our window frames to set when we got them, and it made as nice a finish as you'd ever hope to see. Mama's stove was brung in and set up by the chimney. That roll of rag carpet was hung like a canopy to cover the ceiling, and our beds was made along one wall out of round pole legs and sides and real nice springs made from the same kind of willow poles that growed down along the river and come in handy when we went fishing. The fishing there was good. Mama went down whenever she could and brung in real nice messes. Out on the plains, them days, gardening and fishing was generally considered as part of the women's work. Mama always liked to go fishing; it give her and me a chance to do our talking and thinking where it was quiet. Mama sure was glad to get our house finished so's her Charter Oak stove could be moved inside. She give it a real good polishing and checked it careful for rust. Well, sure, it was a lot harder on that stove being outdoors that way than it was on us children.

It ain't no wonder Father bragged about that soil. Before the house was finished, the garden was up. I never seen things pop out of the ground like they done there that spring. Every night, after supper, we'd go past our sod corn to see how it was doing, and then we'd walk over to the garden we'd put in on that piece that was rented on the George McKeller place, just to see how good it had growed that day; and, of course, Mama would have us take a few minutes to pull any weeds that had begun to grow. Father figgered things was doing so well that he could leave long enough to get our window sash and some other things that we was needing, and to find out about how much he'd have to pay for cows, and who'd give him cows on credit since we'd have to go in debt for them. Word got around that he was going and the neighbors give him their lists of what they had to have from Grand Island, and he took in the letters that had to be mailed and promised to pick up the mail that was being held there at the post office. Sixty mile was quite a ways to haul what groceries and other stuff we had to have, but we didn't have much choice about it. There was a store, fourteen mile away at Loup City, but they had to haul stuff by wagon theirselves and after they tied their money up in it and took the risks they sure wasn't giving it away for nothing. Mama studied a long time over her shopping list. She didn't put down much food because we was raising our own and didn't have no money to waste, but she had to figger on what else we'd need for a long time to come because things in Loup City was higher than a kilt, and nobody knowed when Father would ever be getting as far as Grand Island again.

By the time Father got back from that trip we wasn't even sure if it was him coming or not because by then we was used to seeing clouds of dust in the distance. Every day prairie schooners was stopping down by the spring, and women was visiting with Mama and washing out their clothes and talking her into selling them some of her good, homemade bread. And their men folks was inquiring around about the country on beyond. On each side of the railroads, wagonloads of folks was branching out along the streams looking for homesteads. The prairie was filling in. Father'd had enough trouble locating our claim when he was out in 1873, but by the spring of '74 things was getting plumb crowded in Nebraska. But them folks stopping at our place went right on because they was hoping to find springs and creeks and timber, and all them things they'd read about in them wore-out books they was carrying under their wagon seats, because they was in the great Platte Valley, and the book that they read nights by the campfire had told them what they'd find.

Us children was over weeding in the garden—where we had the nicest vegetables I've ever seen anywhere—when I looked up and seen Father driving up to our sod house. I lit out of there lickity-cut, and, because I had a head start and could outrun Julia and Sadie anyhow, I got there first. And when Father seen me he reached right down under the wagon seat, and he picked the blackest little kitten you ever seen right out of a box that was in back of his feet, and he give her to me! By that time the girls was there too, and they begun putting up a terrible holler about wanting to have the kitten. Father figgered for a minute he was in for it, then he says, "I only have one kitten here, and I only have one boy. Mont, the kitten is yours. I expect you to take good care of it and to see that your sisters get to play with it, too."

We took turns holding the kitten and helping Father get unloaded. Father tried the new windows and they fit good. Soon as him and Aaron got the team put up and fed, and he et dinner, he went right to work fastening them in because Mama was complaining about the flies and mosquitoes coming in when she was cooking. He told us all about how we was going to buy fresh cows from a fellow named Stevens who was running a big herd of eighty head on farther down toward Grand Island. He said a good cow brung $16.00, but he was dickering for a special price because we was buying so many to eat up our hay. But when Mama got to asking about that part of it, and how was he figgerin' on taking care of the milk in hot weather, he sort of hemmed and hawed a little bit and I wasn't sure but what the sparks might begin to fly a mite, so I took my kitten away from Sadie who'd been holding her too long anyhow, and went on out to look at the garden again. Golly, it was pretty. I

never seen stuff growing as good as that in all my life. And Mama
had brung some flower seeds along and Julia had planted hers to
the right, and Sadie had planted hers to the left of the door at the
house, and they'd covered some little rocks with that white clay
so folks couldn't walk into our flowerbeds. I felt sorry for them
children that had just pulled out in a covered wagon from down
by the spring. Why, we had as pretty a sod house as you could ever
see, and before long we'd have cows giving milk, right there in our
shed, and we had a garden with potatoes and other stuff just ready
to eat, and sod corn almost growed. Best of all I had a black kitten,
and it was all my own. Right then I decided to name that kitten
Mam Blacky, so's it would turn out to be a mama cat, and it would
have a lot of little kittens, and I'd be able to sell them and we'd
make lots of money that way. I figgered that, excepting for money,
we had just about everything a family could ever hope to have.

But while I was standing there looking over the prairie, I seen a
little fire starting way off to the west. We'd heard enough about
prairie fires to be blamed scared of them and I started to run to the
house to tell the folks about it, when I seen it wasn't a fire but a storm,
because it was off the ground and coming towards us like a big
cloud, and I run fast and started yelling that a snowstorm was going
to hit us. It was a storm all right. In no time grasshoppers begun
raining down on us. The sky was black with them. The air was so
full of them we could hardly see. Mama give me the broom and told
me to run for the garden and to beat them off the cabbage plants. I
tried, but I wasn't making no headway. Mama worked out there
longer than I did, and I never give up until the sharp barbs on their
legs had cut me so bad I was bleeding all over and had to go to the
house. They ate everything and they got into everything. Sadie had
pulled off her apron and throwed it over her little flower garden
before she run out to try to help Mama. When they come back to
the house, they seen that the grasshoppers had et clean through her
apron and that the plants in underneath was gone. Julia and Father
was down by the spring, carrying boards, trying to cover it over and
save our water supply, but thousands of grasshoppers drowned in
there, and before it was fit to use again Father had to take their
bodies out by the bucketful. Aaron had run out to see about the sod
corn, but he come in soon after I got back to the house, and said

that every cornstalk was as thick as a man's upper arm with them grasshoppers.

By then we knowed that we was helpless to fight them, and that all we could do was to hole up in our sod house until the wind changed and they moved on some place else. Grasshoppers is like that. When the wind is blowing from the west, they light, and they don't go on again until the wind changes. They stopped a long spell with us, and we heard afterwards about what had happened to the neighbors, like with old Pete Morlensen, who seen them coming and hauled all the hay and manure out of his barn to cover up his cabbages. He figgered he'd saved them, but when they was gone, he dug down under the hay and manure and his cabbages was gone too. Why them grasshoppers even et the pith inside of them stalks and never left nothing but just a little spear of that hard outer shell of the stalk.

Farmers wasn't the only ones having trouble with them neither. Over at Kearney they stopped the railroad train because them mashed grasshopper-bodies made the tracks so slick and oily that they couldn't get no traction. But, of course, we didn't know nothing about that then. We was all in the house, and outside they kept hitting them new window panes until we figgered they'd break through the glass any minute. And Mama was using the elm bark salve as sparing as she could because she knowed it would never last to fix all them cuts on our faces and hands and feet and legs where them grasshoppers dug their sharp barbs into us.

And those of us that wasn't being doctored had to run around killing the ones that had got in the house and was jumping all over the place, and Father was using the broom and a thin board for a dustpan, scooping them up and dropping them into the fire where we'd hear them sizzle as the flames licked around that oil in their insides. And for days we had nothing to eat, nothing but some boiled wheat and boiled corn with nothing to put on top. Them was terrible days. I'm glad I'll never be coming over them again.

After the grasshoppers moved on and we opened the door and tried to start living again, we seen long lines of covered wagons coming back. All the canvas was et clean off of them, and them bare bows stuck up just like the ribs on a skeleton. And we could hear little children crying when the families stopped at our spring that

Father and Aaron was cleaning out trying to make the water fit to drink again.

While the men was skimming out the grasshoppers and filling the water jugs before they left—heading back for Grand Island—them poor, thin women would come to our door asking Mama if she had food to spare for their children. And Mama would just have to stand there, shaking her head. Then in the night we'd hear Mama crying because she didn't have no food to share with them children or to give to us. Mama said we couldn't turn back like they was doing. They was still adrift. But we was anchored.

We had to stay right there and toughy it out because there wasn't nothing wrong with our sod house—or with the land we'd built her on.

SIX

YOU CAN'T NEVER TELL

Mama'd kept track the best she could. She figgered that all them homesteaders who'd gone up stream was back out excepting the Andy Woods, who was twenty mile above and off to theirselves, and the blacksmith and his wife and two little boys. The Woods went into Grand Island a different way, but we'd got to know the blacksmith and his family well because they'd camped down by our spring while he was getting located and them two boys helped me work so I could help them play. They stopped in a few times afterwards going to and from town, but, of course, folks didn't see each other much, especially women-folks. We wouldn't of seen nobody neither if it hadn't of been for our spring.

Us children kept wondering what had happened to the black-smith's little boys. Then one night we found out. A couple of trappers stopped in to tell us. They was going by the dugout, and at first they figgered it was deserted. They tried the door. It was tight fastened, and folks wasn't in the habit of locking up. They peered in the window and seen blood inside; so they made a run for the door and broke it in with their shoulders. The whole family was dead, and there wasn't a single speck of food in the place. The blacksmith must of got tired of seeing his wife and them two little boys starving. He'd used that big blacksmith's hammer, that he'd kept from the time he quit his trade to go homesteading, to mash their heads in. They was all three laying there in their beds, dead, and he was dead on the floor beside them, with his throat cut. Them grasshoppers moving in on us got on folks's nerves. In times like that you can't never tell what's going to happen out on the prairie.

Because the grasshoppers had got so bad they stopped the trains, they was news. Word got out about how folks in Nebraska was starving and was needing most everything, and the government voted money to send help, and all over the country folks started packing relief boxes and shipping them in. The boxes got there first. Them days you had to put heavy iron straps around boxes shipped by freight because some fellows dropped them on purpose when they was doing the unloading. Then when they was broke open, stuff would disappear at the different divisions where they changed trains. Sometimes it took boxes a long time to get to where they was shipped because they'd be stored until the railroad had enough freight to make it pay to send a load to the place where a box was going. Lots of stuff that was shipped got lost along the way. But when folks back East heard about how bad off we was, they went through their closets and give away their own clothes to help us folks out in Nebraska. A bunch of them boxes had come straight through from New York, and had been hauled out to Loup City. Waugh, who got hisself elected judge and then was put in charge of grasshopper relief, sent word up that he had appointed Father and Mama and Porter Brown as a committee to open and divide a big box of clothing that was for the settlers in our valley, and would they please come and get it and see that it was distributed.

So Porter come down, and him and the folks went to town and they got the box and met the relief people. They found out that there was a surplus of buckwheat somewhere else and so the government was sending it to Nebraska, and they was shipping in them old Civil War uniforms too that had been stored in warehouses ever since the soldiers had quit fighting. Father said some of them good heavy uniform breeches would of come in handy if he'd only had them when them grasshoppers was running up his pants legs, but they didn't have none of that stuff ready to distribute yet. So, Porter and Father loaded that one big box, and them oxen of ours hauled it back the fourteen mile to our house.

Mama said she didn't want it opened until all the neighbors come, because she wasn't going to get criticized for holding out the best stuff for ourselves. When all the folks had gathered at our house,

Father took his single-bitted ax and he struck right through the lid. He knocked off the iron bands and Mama stood up by the table and started taking the things out from inside. First come a man's suit. It was made of black and white checks, real wide ones, and all the fellows let out a yell when she held it up because they'd never seen nothing as sporty as that. A man couldn't of wore it milking; them blamed checks was so loud they'd of scared the cows so bad they wouldn't give down no milk. Mama kept right on lifting things out of the big box. That one suit was all they'd sent for men. There wasn't a single thing in the box for children. All the rest of the box was packed tight with the fanciest dresses I ever seen. They was made of real heavy silk, with nothing up around the top where a woman's shoulders sunburns bad, and they had all them trailers hanging down in back where she needs her clothes cut off floor length so's to have her legs loose for walking. When Mama got about half done with lifting them dresses out of the box she just quit and set down on a bench and cried like a baby. Porter Brown, trying to cheer her up, grabbed one of them big feathered hats that had been mashed down flat in the packing, and shoved the crown up enough to get his head in and says, "See, Martha, what I've got to wear plowing?"

Blamed if Mama didn't stop crying and start in laughing. Nobody could get her stopped for awhile, neither. But before long she entered into things and was having just as much fun as anybody there. The men and the women and us children got into them fancy dresses and we had a dance. No, Sir, we never had so much fun in our lives as we did that night we unpacked the relief box that had come to us straight from New York, with "Do Not Open Before Reaching Destination" wrote in great big letters across the side. We laughed so hard at how folks looked in them dresses, that nobody minded having to go home without no refreshments. Them days, folks was used to cinching up their belts; and having that party done us all a lot of good.

The buckwheat come; we all got hives. No matter how hungry folks is, they can't get away with eating straight buckwheat.

So we planted most of our buckwheat to get a quick crop, but we kept enough back to keep everyone in the valley scratching all the rest of the summer. Of course, we had more prairie chickens than we could eat. They was in fine shape because they hadn't been eating nothing but grasshoppers. When they didn't have no green feed to eat they got so fat on them grasshoppers that when Mama'd put them in a hot pan the grease would just run out of them. But they made us all feel sick because we figgered they tasted just like grasshoppers. Even the fish we caught in the Middle Loup tasted like them grasshoppers.

Prairie chickens are good eating if you don't overdo it, but they are the blamedest fools I ever seen. Aaron put an old crate, with slats on the sides, down by the creek. He fixed a little trap door in the front. It was hinged at the top, and when the chickens shoved agin the bottom of it, it would swing up and let them walk right in, then it would fall shut behind them so's they couldn't get out. There was a slat on the inside to keep it from swinging out if there was pressure put on the inside. He hung an ear of corn down from the top of the box and scattered a few grains on the bottom. Them prairie chickens would see the corn, and they'd shove agin the little swinging door to get at it. We figgered it out so that the ones inside couldn't reach their necks up high enough to get the corn and they was too close to the top to fly up to it. We couldn't afford to waste no food on them. Every night and morning we'd go down and empty the trap and wring their necks, then we'd take them dead prairie chickens up to Mama and the girls to be dressed and cooked. We'd eat what we could and put the rest down in their own lard for winter.

Having them prairie chickens on the place sure come in handy one day when a rattlesnake bit one of our oxen right on the upper lip when he was eating hay. Mama and me was the only ones around when it happened. While I was getting a shovel and killing the snake, she let out a yell and run just as fast as she could down toward the creek. In a minute she come back, lickity-cut, carrying a live prairie chicken that she had grabbed up out of our trap. She told me to help hold the ox and she tore that live prairie chicken right apart between its legs, and held its hot insides tight agin that snake bite. She talked soothing to the ox and got him to keep his head still until the poison was drawed out of his lip into that prairie chicken's insides. Mama said it wouldn't work unless you had a live chicken. The ox had quite a head on him for a few days, but he got well.

We had considerable deer and elk and antelope along the Middle

Loup back in 1874. The trappers hadn't got quite all of the otter, beaver, badger, and skunks, but they had thinned them out so bad that they was running their lines up to the north of us into the lake country and along the Niobrara River. Sure we'd promised them Sioux not to go up there, but the fur bearers was cleaned out over on our side. While them trappers was slipping on up north, the boys like Jim Mapes—whose folks lived way downstream from us— picked up what money they could trapping in their spare time when they wasn't helping their folks homestead. By the time they got through they'd cleaned out any animals the regular trappers had left. But no matter how hard they worked they never made no real money trapping.

Jim Mapes was running his trap lines farther and farther from home. When it got too hard to get back nights, he fixed up an old, deserted trapper's cabin down on the river not far from our place. When he was camped there he got in the habit of dropping over to visit us of an evening. Sometimes he even pitched in and give Father a hand when we finally got around to making crops. After he was hurt, and Mama nursed him, she got to treating him more like he was one of her own. Jim had one of the blamedest accidents I ever seen. Some folks heading back East in their prairie schooner had left a big, yellow, she-greyhound down by the spring because she was having puppies and nobody had food for their dogs anyhow. When we was cooped up in the cabin we remembered about seeing her and wondered how she was doing out there. Father said that if the grass-hoppers moved on and things picked up again, we might be able to trade them puppies for something we could use, and we could keep her and raise some more.

By the time the wind changed and the grasshoppers left, that dog was hungrier than we was. She seen a jack rabbit running along in a dead furrow that Father had plowed down towards the creek and she lit out after it. Jim Mapes had holed up in his shack down below when the grasshoppers was there. Then, soon as they left, he started out to see how we was making it. Just by chance, him and that jack rabbit was heading towards each other in the same furrow at the same time.

Jim said he seen the jack-rabbit flying his way so he crouched down and got all set to catch it like you've seen fellows do out on the football field. But just as he reached out to scoop up that jack rabbit, the hound hit him in the brisket. From then on neither him nor the hound knowed what hit them. Aaron and me seen them fall. We yelled and run down there. The folks come too. At first we thought both Jim and the greyhound was dead. We carried Jim back to the house first, though, and he stayed in bed real quiet and rested up for several days because his whole front was black and blue. Mama had to bandage him where his ribs was stove in. The yellow dog come out of it just fine excepting for having the breath knocked out of her, but even with Jim helping her, the jack rabbit had got away.

After the grasshoppers left and give it a chance, our hay started coming good. Father said that before long he was going to go down to Stevens' place about forty mile below and start dickering for them cows. Stevens kept his cows on a sort of schedule where they was dried up in the winter, when they didn't have no green feed, and then come fresh in the early spring when the weather was good and the calves done better. Us children sure watched the grass grow after that; we was all wishing for milk, and Mama said it wasn't right to be trying to raise a baby without it. But the neighbors didn't have no milk for their children, neither.

Word come that the government in Washington was going to take the money set aside to help the settlers whose crops had been eat up by grasshoppers, and put it with some other money and build a fort to protect those of us living on the frontier from the Sioux Indians, who was getting out of hand. Them Indians was sore because the goods that had been promised them didn't get there and what come wasn't up to snuff. They figgered if the government didn't keep its promises to them, they wouldn't keep the one they made to stay on the reservation. The Indian Service men wrote out an order telling them all to get back to the reservation at once. But them Indans couldn't read and, since the order was give after they was gone, they didn't have no way of getting it. So the Indian Service men said they was defiant and they asked the army to take over. Well while all that was being hatched up back and forth from Washington, them two problems must of met up with each other on someone's desk back there. We'd sent a petition asking the government to send help and to build a fort to protect us settlers who was the farthest out on the

Middle Loup River. The Army was asking for money to build forts while money had been set aside to help the settlers who was eat out by the grasshoppers. Of course, we could of used seed potatoes and seed corn, and all the help we could get to raise a quick crop before the winter storms come. But somebody back in Washington, who didn't know what time means to a farmer with fields to replant, said we needed our self respect, and that the army could build a fort and the farmers could all work on it and get paid, instead of being handed that help straight out. You know, it was one of them W.P.A. deals, only they never called it that, them days.

Word come that plans was being drawed and, come fall there would be employment for all of the men and their teams. We didn't hear nothing more about grasshopper relief or what them Sioux might be doing in the meantime.

Mam Blacky was the only one in the family that had enough to eat to grow good that summer. The mice all come hunting too. I never did see a cat as much at home with folks as she was. She'd come right into the house and scramble up the wall and lay on that rag carpet canopy that covered the ceiling, just like she figgered it was her hammock. She was so blamed heavy she was always pulling it loose. Aaron was the one who kept trying to fix it back up, and, of course, that was hard to do with them plastered sod walls. Finally he got so tired of her hanging down there in a big bunch in the middle of our ceiling that he reached up one day and hit the carpet a whack under where she was laying. Mam Blacky come fogging out of there with her fur all up on end, and her back arched high. She was spitting and glaring at everybody. Sadie reached out and picked her up to see if she could talk her out of her mad, but that cat wasn't going to make up. Why Mam Blacky was so mad she run her claws clean the length of Sadie's arm, so she just let go and dropped her. By then, Mam Blacky figgered everyone was agin her and went high-tailing out the door, and didn't come back again. Aaron felt awful bad about it. We all hunted every place but she never showed. Cats was worth lots more money than dogs, them days, so we figgered some of the strangers around had stole her.

Father and Mama said we'd have to save money every way we could if we was going to get them cows. One day when Father was in Loup City a fellow offered to trade him for our yoke of oxen, and still give him some money to boot. Now this fellow was driving the biggest pair of Texas longhorn steers ever I seen. They didn't look too good, but we knowed our oxen wasn't the best in the world and Father needed money bad, so he made the trade right there in the street. Then he went over to the blacksmith shop where Porter Brown was having his horses shod, and he asked Porter if he could ride one of his horses home. They turned them longhorns loose and started for our place. Father and Porter had to try to keep up with them steers to keep them from getting lost and they run every step of that fourteen mile to our place. When they got there, the steers was as fresh as daisies, but the horses was covered with lather and clean wore out.

Shorthorns is easy to drive. You walk on the left-hand side of them with your whip, and if you want to turn left, you tap the near one on the head to slow him up and you tap the far one on the rump to speed him up, so he walks around the nigh one to turn left. If you want them to go right, you holler *Gee*. If you want them to go left, you holler *Haw*. But them longhorns hadn't learned no rules. Father couldn't use a whip because they'd turn and take a swipe at him with them horns. He tried using a long goad-stick, but that wasn't much better. He seen that he'd bit off more that time than he could chew.

We had to keep them longhorns and try to work them. The story had got around. Nobody would trade. Them days, if you couldn't get rid of what you had, you just used it, no matter how bad it was. Our clothes wore out, but not them steers. That team was so tough to handle that Father put each of them on a pole. No, the way to handle one of them steers is to take a pole about sixteen foot long, then bore a hole through one end of the pole, and tie it to the steer's neck with a stout rope. Then when he tries to hook you— and he sure will—you grab the end of the pole and hold on while he's trying to charge. But we couldn't be dragging a couple of six-teen-foot poles down the road every time we had to go to the store, so Father used the extra money that he'd got for trading our oxen to buy a horse and a pair of saddle-bags, and the rest of us just stayed home.

One day our meanest longhorn was alone in the corral that we'd made of logs. At one place there was about a fifteen-inch space between the lowest log and the ground. I was nine years old, and used to handling oxen so I never thought much about going in to drive him out to water. But he sort of lowered his head and come at me, and I never seen nothing look quite like them horns. A big man couldn't stretch his arms wide enough to reach across. Why, they was so wide they saved my life.

You see, I slipped and fell flat on my face when I was reaching for the pole. And, while I was scrambling up on my hands and knees, he hit me. When he turned his head way over to hook me with the horns on one side, the horn was so long it went past me. He couldn't move his head far enough to one side to reach me with the point of his horn. He bruised my ribs bad though, dragging the horn back across me. Well, I started crawling for that low place I could see clean across the corral—where the opening was. Mama had seen what had happened and she was running that way and screaming. That old steer was bellowing in my ear. Then he swung his head the other way and come down hard again. I don't know why he didn't pierce my lungs . . . them horns was just too long, I guess. He kept swinging back and forth that way, first to one side and then to the other. He was so mad he would roll his head way down, but the horn was always too long to catch me and throw me up so he could finish me off. But he sure blacked me up good. When I finally crawled as far as the log I managed to roll under.

Long after Mama had washed me up and put me to bed, I could hear that old longhorn bellering away and taking on out there in the corral. I've had my share of close calls, but the nearest I ever come to looking Saint Peter in the eye was the day when I had that run-in with him. No. I wouldn't say a Texas longhorn is worse that a grizzly bear, but I'd just as soon tangle with one as the other. And the cows was just about as mean as the steers. Father and me seen a wild Texas longhorn cow up by the ford, and we drove her home, but she didn't like it a bit there, and she went right to work goring our horse. Father couldn't do nothing with her, so he had to draw his pistol and shoot her. Then he found out that the horse was gored so bad he had to shoot him, too. After that happened, Father bought a mule.

Them days the cattle men was driving hundreds of longhorns through from Texas over a trail that crossed the Middle Loup about six miles above our place. They was to feed all of them Sioux Indians at the new Red Cloud Agency on the south bank of White River, right in close to where Fort Robinson is now. When they moved them Indians away from the old Red Cloud Agency on the Platte River in August of 1873, they done it real peaceful like by starving them out and cutting off all their rations and shutting all the trading posts so's they couldn't neither buy or sell. Then they opened this new Red Cloud Agency seventy-five miles north of where they had been and off to the west of where we was. They'd give them their rations every five days by turning a bunch of longhorns out of the corral and letting them kill their own meat. Even though they wasn't satisfied with the other rations the government sent them, the Sioux sort of got used to that place. Then when Custer found gold in the Black Hills, they had to be got out of there, too, but they wasn't so easy to get moved up into the Bad Lands, come 1877. When we seen the cattle men driving them longhorns through in '74, our government was holding out longhorns as bait so's they'd behave theirselves and quit killing whites.

The Texans, who had the contract to furnish meat to the Red Cloud Agency, always stopped to camp and rest before making the ford on the Middle Loup, six miles above our place. The pasture was better on our side, so they'd look the longhorns over there, and the ones that was too footsore from rocks and stubble to make the rest of the trip was cut out at the meadow and left. Them steers was wild enough to start with, and they got a blamed sight worse. But it didn't take them long to fatten up and they made fair beef. The women and children was all afraid of them. The men went armed.

Just like with that fellow Oames and his wife who come in and filed on a homestead up close to the ford. They got their log cabin up, and she went out in the yard to fetch in an armload of wood from the leavings he'd piled out there. When she heard a noise in the brush, she looked around, and coming right at her was a big, Texas longhorn bull. She let out a scream and run for the house. Oames was inside. When he heard her yell he reached for his gun, figgering the Indians had got her. But she come charging right through the door with that big bull at her heels. Oames fired over her shoulder, but before his bullet stopped that bull, he was halfway through the front of the cabin, wearing their new doorframe just like it was a collar. I never heard of a man getting his meat as easy as that. Why that old bull delivered hisself right to the pot. But do you know it like to scared Mrs. Oames to death. After that she was real skittish and wouldn't go out of the house alone and would beg him not to leave her. Maybe that's why their baby come and was dead and buried right there on their place before any of the neighbors even knowed she'd had it.

Women was alone lots more than the men, them days. Homesteaders had to work out, every time they could, to keep their families from starving. Of course women was safe enough as long as they had a good fire in the stove and a teakettle of boiling water handy. Many's the time I've seen Mama stir up the fire and heft the teakettle and set the bailer handy when she seen a stranger coming up the trail. A bailer is a kettle made with a long handle. It ain't a dipper because it's too big. When Mama had her head up and her eyes flashing, and that bailerful of boiling water in her hand, she was just as safe as if she had a gun, loaded and cocked. Julia wasn't her blood daughter but she was the same kind of woman. One day a fellow grabbed her, and she reached around back of her on the kitchen table and snatched up the case knife that we'd used so much and sharpened so many times that it was all wore down to a long thin blade, and she whirled around and slashed him across the arm that was holding her, and she left him there spouting blood all over the kitchen while she run for help. On up above us there was a woman living in a sod house who saved herself from a terrible attack when her husband was away working on the fort because she had her big kettle of hot water handy. A band of about seventy-five elk come down to feed on their meadow. It was summertime. The flies was bad, so them elk started looking around for some soft dirt to hook their horns into and throw over their backs to drive them blamed flies away. Well, they come right over and started hooking onto her sod house, with her alone inside. She didn't have a gun. Hollering at them didn't do no good. They was hooking her house to pieces, and she figgered if she did try to make a run for it through the door they'd probably finish her off just that much sooner. So she filled her bailer with boiling water and the first old bull that hooked his head through the corner of her house and poked his nose inside got a face full of boiling water. He let out a beller, backed up, clamped his tail down tight and went out of there full speed making a run for the upper Niobrara country. He made so much noise them other elk took out after him and she never seen one of them on her homestead again.

More folks was coming and going. Nights down at the spring we'd hear news, firsthand, from the upper country.

Homesteaders was told to keep together and to locate in close to the forts. Sioux, wearing fresh scalps, was slipping around in their old hunting grounds to the north of the Platte River and they wasn't wanting no prospectors up in them Black Hills. The army was heading folks off from going in there, too. Only they kept looking for them prospectors on the main trails from Pierre to the west; and Sidney and Cheyenne to the north, and Bismarck off to the southwest. Them guards didn't know that the trail past our place was turning into the back door to the Black Hills.

And many a man starting up that long old trail for gold was carrying in his pack some of Mama's bread that she'd baked real good—and then put back in the oven to dry hard so's it wouldn't mold. We got to know men who wouldn't never have showed at a door if it wasn't that word got around that a man could get spring water and oven-baked bread on the Hawthorne homestead.

Sixty miles above us was the Cedar Canyons, where there was a big stand of tall, red cedars that the railroad needed bad for making trestles. The law said that only homesteaders could cut cedar there and it had to be used in the construction of their own buildings. But the freighters knowed that if they brung cedar logs down to sell at Kearney, no questions would be asked. A bunch of them fellows got to hauling back and forth regular and traveling together in a wagon train so they could be ready if the Sioux got out of hand. They always stopped at our place and camped down by the spring. Nights, when the weather was bad, they brung their blankets in and slept on our floor. We didn't like their business and we didn't like seeing them big loads of cedar—that was needed at home—hauled down to be sold to the railroad. But a rancher would of been a fool to get a bunch like that down on him; anyhow, you couldn't turn folks away from your door if they was needing food or shelter.

One night some homesteaders down by Loup City had a fellow come to their door and they was afraid to open up and let him in, so he went on to the next place. By that time his feet was froze so bad the folks there cut his boots off and wrapped his legs in sacks and hauled him in a wagon to Kearney to see if the doctor there could amputate his legs and save his life. But he'd gone too long. Gangrene set in and he up and died. Them days, you done your neighboring with all kinds of folks and you got to know them all because you wasn't just picking out the ones that was like you to start with.

So we seen them all, coming and going. But the one Mama never got over wondering about was the woman, weighing about one hundred and ten pounds, and all of sixty years old, who come walking down the trail without no pack on her back and wearing regular shoes. She said she was hungry, so Mama filled a plate for her. Then Mama asked her about her wagon but she said she didn't have no outfit, that she was just traveling through there alone. Mama was frightened. She figgered the woman might be living with the Indians and had been sent by them to do their scouting. So Mama started asking her more questions about where she come from and how she lived. She said she got along just fine eating berries and fish. Mama asked her how she caught the fish and she said in her shoe. After that Mama just give up trying to talk to her. She fed her good and watched her going down the trail until she was clean out of sight. We kept a close watch for several days but nothing special happened. From that day to this our family has wondered about her, off and on. There was something mighty curious about that woman dropping in on us that way.

By midsummer the grass was growing good and Father was getting ready to go down to see if he could buy them cows. He didn't have money to pay for them, so we knowed he'd have to run his face and we wasn't sure how good that would be. Mama said she wanted flour and some other provisions for us children. We'd been eating a lot better since she'd been baking and selling bread. She had been wanting to go to town and sort of jumped at the chance when the McKellers asked her and Father to ride in to Loup City with them so's she could lay in our supplies before he left. Of course, she should of smelled a mouse because the McKellers never done nothing without an axe to grind. But Mama had been wanting to see them because she had one that needed sharpening, herself.

Mama was real worried about us children not getting no schooling in Nebraska. She had wrote to the new capitol at Lincoln to get the law on how a new school district in a new county could be started. They wrote back:

> All unorganized sub-districts shall be organized by holding a school meeting of the legal voters of said sub-district on the first Monday of March, who, when assembled shall organize by the appointment of a chairman and secretary, and proceed to elect by ballot three school directors for such sub-district.

The one with the highest number of votes was elected for three years, the next one for two, the next one for just one. After that they could elect one each year. They could levy bonds, build a school, or do most anything they pleased in their district, just so's they let the precinct clerk know who was elected and that they took an oath to support the Constitution of the United States and the laws of Nebraska.

Mama figgered she'd have a good chance while they was riding to town to talk to the McKellers about having a school. It was plain that nothing could be done until the first Monday of March, but she had laid the groundwork with the Fredinsburgs and Browns, who was the only ones with children, and Ming Coombs, who was the only one who'd been to college. Mama had tried to talk to Mrs. McKeller once before, but the old lady was a real ripsnorter if she figgered someone was trying to show up her George, and she says, "My George was as highly edificated as anyone until one day when he was walking along and suddenly he lost it." He'd lost one leg, too.

Going to town that day, George McKeller brung up the subject of school hisself. He says, "Hawthorne, there's a contractor in Loup City I'd like to have you meet. He'll sell the bonds and build us a fine big schoolhouse. All we'll need to do is vote for it at a special election."

Father couldn't figger out what it was all about, so he went on over with George McKeller to talk to this fellow and he turned out to be a regular slicker. Because they was together he figgered that Father and George was birds of a feather. He said that a couple of men like them was all that he needed on that school board. Father said he didn't want no part in their plans. He told them that his wife was calling a meeting in March when the law said they could, and that he was more interested in what his children was learning than he was in where they was setting. Anyhow, he didn't see no sense in putting all that money into a building and all that debt agin the land, and he was going to fight it every inch of the way.

When George McKeller and Father got back to the wagon, they wasn't speaking to each other. Mama said she'd never had a cooler ride in spite of the heat. They was surprised, though, when George McKeller drove up in front of his place and says, "This is as far as we're going, Hawthorne. If you ain't doing nothing for me, I ain't hauling you out of my way."

Father says, "I can't see why a bachelor like you is mixing up in school affairs unless it's to feather your own nest."

By that time, they'd all clumb out of the wagon. Old Man Mc-Keller showed he was nervous because he went right over to the log sticking out of the end of the cabin where he kept his used chaws of tobacco and traded the one he'd been working on all the way from Loup City for one laid out on the log that didn't look as tired as the others.

But George went right ahead taking the harness off his horses and never went near his tobacco log to trade his quid. Him and his mother was just as cool as cucumbers, but by that time Father was plenty hot under the collar. Mama and Father gathered up as much stuff as they could carry the half mile to our house, and then Father says, "I'll be back in a little while for the rest of our stuff."

George never even turned around. He just went right on unhooking the tugs from the singletrees, and says, "Suit yourself."

Well, the folks come up to the house and they got me to lead the mule to bring back the sack of flour. Mama went along too, because she didn't trust them McKellers and she wanted to be sure she had all of her stuff. When she got there and lifted her box out of the back of the wagon, she seen that her ham was gone. In its place was a little ham-hock, all rolled up, that wasn't a third as big as the one she'd bought in Loup City. Now we hadn't had a whole ham in our house since goodness knows when, and Mama had figgered and counted and planned a long time about buying a ham before she went to Loup City. And she'd kept the clerk waiting a long time after she got there while she studied and priced to be sure she'd picked the one with the most meat and the least bone. She knowed what she bought. And she knowed what Mrs. McKeller had bought.

Mama wasn't a woman to give up easy any time. But that night, after her and Mrs. McKeller got to exchanging words, she was the maddest I've ever seen her. The only reason she carried that little nubbin home with her was that George McKeller drawed his gun and ordered us off his place. Before she got to our house she was talking to herself and answering back, too.

Of course, she had Father ride over to Loup City and check with the storekeeper about the weights. That was all the good it done her. His record showed she'd bought the big one and that Mrs. McKeller had bought the little one. But she knowed that all the time anyhow. We said we'd never have nothing more to do with McKellers, and that when the time come we'd hold a school election at our place.

But Father hadn't no more than left to see about buying them cows than who should come riding into our yard but that mealy-mouthed contractor, named Ingersoll, from Loup City. Why that fellow was oilier than them grasshoppers. He started right in talking to Mama about how he knowed she had the good of her children at heart, and that he realized Mr. Hawthorne had a hasty temper and seemed to have taken an unwarranted dislike to him. So he was asking Mrs. Hawthorne to talk with her husband to see if she couldn't get him to vote for the proposed bond issue to build the new schoolhouse. He said he had talked to others in the community and they all seemed favorable to the plan, but it was his sincere desire for the election to be unanimous when it was held . . . he would like to give Mrs. Hawthorne a twenty-dollar gold piece as a mark of his appreciation for her help . . . she was such a comely woman that he would personally consider it a pleasure to buy a dress length for her in pure silk, of any color she would choose, but that his own preference would be for the shade of blue to match her eyes.

Well, by that time Mama was over by the stove. She filled her bailer and started his way, saying, "You get out of here and don't you ever come back again."

He left in a hurry, looking over his shoulder as he went to see if she was letting fly with her bailer. When we started checking around, we found he'd come to our place last. The only one he'd missed was

Ming Coombs, and he'd left a twenty-dollar gold piece at each house as a mark of friendship and to show that his interest in the valley was sincere. We was worried about it but we was trying to make a crop and we didn't have no way of knowing what was going on until Aaron chanced to hear from the neighbors that the special school meeting was being held the next night at George McKeller's place.

By then Father had got home with the cows, all twelve of them that he had bought on time because Stevens, who owned them, was running short of hay and he'd rather have what money we had and a mortgage, than to have them starve over the winter. Most of them had real big udders. Father hadn't got a cut price because he had taken them at sixteen dollars a head in order to have his pick of the herd. Even when they wasn't milking and their bags was soft, they hung way down. Mama said he'd done a good job of picking, but how was she going to take care of the milk and make butter that was fit to eat from twelve cows when they all started milking and the weather got hot? He told her she was the best butter maker in the world and by spring, when they freshened, she'd have it figgered out, so he wasn't going to worry about that part of it. He figgered his big job was to get the hay made and into stacks so's they'd have feed to winter over. But when he heard about the school meeting, he took time out and rode around that very night to see what had been going on while he was away buying them cows.

Father found out that everyone except Ming Coombs knowed about the meeting and planned on attending. They'd all heard the McKeller side of the ham story and it wasn't the same as ours. So they had talked it over among theirselves and decided that the ham was at the bottom of the whole trouble and that we was agin that nice Mr. Ingersoll and the new schoolhouse because the McKellers had told around about us trying to get away with their ham. Of course, they never come right out with that story but Father said that the whole bunch of them wasn't near as friendly as they'd been before. He figgered there wasn't no other way of getting the straight of things, so Father rode right down to McKellers and knocked on the door. George come and stuck his nose out through a little crack and Father seen that he was having a meeting already. He wasn't asked in, so all he could do was say, "George McKeller, you can't hold a school meeting tomorrow night. It's the wrong date and you haven't posted a notice."

George says, "I'm holding it, ain't I?"

Father shouted, "The meeting ain't legal, but if you have it, I'll be here."

George says, "Don't bother, Hawthorne, we don't need you."

And then he laughed and them fellows inside laughed. He slammed the door and barred it right in Father's face, so Father took the hint and come home. He was so mad he could hardly talk.

The next evening Father went to the meeting, but Mama stayed home. She'd figgered on going but he told her the other neighbor women wasn't planning on it and that attending public meetings was a man's job. Sure enough, when he got there the McKellers had run in a whole bunch of strangers who had filed on claims in the valley just to get the twenty dollars, or probably more, that was being handed out to pay for votes. Two strangers set at the table with George. One was called the moderator; the other was the secretary-treasurer. That contractor was there and made a big speech about how we could have a new schoolhouse without it costing us nothing, right now.

But Father and Ming Coombs, when they seen how things was going and that a bond issue for four thousand dollars at eight per cent interest was being put over, got to taking turns, spelling each other, and talking agin it. Ming said it was just like putting a mortgage agin our few homesteads and that he favored education but not spending all the money on a school and leaving nothing for the folks to improve their homes. Father got so mad when he told about the meeting not being legal because a notice wasn't posted and it had to be held in March, that George McKeller told him to shut his mouth and set down. Then, from where I was listening outside, I could hear that George McKeller had quit talking and that him and Father was slugging it out. Things was crowded enough in there with everyone setting still, so them other fellows pulled them apart and begun shouting, "Let's go outside and finish the fight."

I could hear Mrs. McKeller yelling about how they was wrecking everything in the cabin, and George bellering at her to bring his gun so's he could shoot Father and finish the fight right off.

When I heard that, I legged it for home. Father hadn't wore his revolver. The men had all left their guns at home because Ming Coombs had said that they wasn't supposed to go armed to a district school meeting. So I knowed if George McKeller started shooting, it was up to me to take a hand in it, too. I got to our house all right where I grabbed up the Long Tom shotgun, loaded it with a heavy charge of buckshot and powder, and rammed in a big wad of paper. The gun was longer than I was but I managed to get it out of the house and down under the bank of the creek that run through the corner of our place and come out real close to McKeller's house. I knowed I could get a shot in from there. I was getting along just fine and was almost out of sight when Mama seen me ducking under that bank. She let out a yell and took after me. I had quite a lead on her, but it was blamed hard going down there in the bushes while she was running along on the level ground. I acted deaf and didn't answer until she got right above me. When I seen she had me headed off, and she says, "Mont Hawthorne, you come right up the bank and give me that gun," I done it.

While Mama was running me down and I was trying to tell her what I was doing with the gun, Father and George McKeller had bloodied each other up good. Finally, the men got them separated. George kept saying over and over again that he was going to kill Father. But the meeting had broke up and nobody figgered he really meant it until they was leaving. Father was setting in Ming Coomb's wagon with his back to McKeller's house, and they was driving out of the yard when George up and took a pot shot at his back and blowed a hole right through the top of Father's hat.

Being shot at from the back like that made Father sort of nervous, so him and Ming Coombs kept right on going until they got to Pete Morlensen's dugout, where Father swore out a warrant and George McKeller was hauled up for trial in the first assault and battery case ever to be tried in Valley County, Nebraska. Ming Coombs helped Pete make out the papers, with Father as the plaintiff and George as the defendant. Ming was sent to serve George with a warrant and all the men knocked off work the day of the trial.

Pete and Ming had worked terrible hard over that trial. Ming wanted everything done up right. When they was making out the warrant, he kept calling Pete "Judge Morlensen." Finally Pete got mad and says, "I ain't Judge Morlensen, I'm just old Pete." And he worked things around so that Orson S. Haskell was there that day, with the regular law book of the State of Nebraska, and they'd studied it and they knowed just what they could do because the law said:

> If any person shall be guilty of an assault and battery or of an affray by fighting or beating at fisticuffs, such person shall, upon conviction before any justice of the peace of the county in which the offense may be committed be fined in any sum not more than one hundred dollars or imprisoned in the county jail of the county not exceeding three months, or both fined and imprisoned as aforesaid.

Well, that was the law, and they read it out loud, right there in Pete's dugout. Then they swore in the witnesses, and everybody there told what he'd seen. Father couldn't tell as much as the others on account of having his back turned at the time George took the shot at him. George allowed it wasn't assault and battery because they was all through fighting and he was just shooting. So they read the law again, and then set around talking it over trying to figger out what to do. George admitted he'd shot at Father. He said he was blamed sorry he'd missed him, and next time he hoped he'd do better. But the warrant said "assault and battery" and the law said the most they could do was fine him up to one hundred dollars and/or put him in the county jail for three months. But we didn't have no jail and George didn't have no hundred dollars. So finally George Haskell says: "George McKeller, you stand right here by the table and empty your pockets of every cent you've got, and then you get the hell out of here and try to behave yourself for a change. If you don't quit going around shooting off your face and your gun, you won't have a friend in the world. Court is adjourned."

But shucks, it takes more than a trial to change a fellow like George. In just a few days, he seen Mama over working in the garden plot he'd rented to us and he come rushing over, waving his gun, and threatening to shoot her if she didn't get off his property. Now Mama had worked blamed hard on that garden. She'd re-planted what she could after the grasshoppers was gone, and she wasn't going to lose it the second time if she could help herself. So she straightened right up and says: "You try to shoot me and see how soon you'll get your neck stretched. This is my garden. You rented this half-acre to us. You go on home. I'm not afraid of you. A barking dog never bites!" And she turned her back on him and went right on hoeing the beans.

About that time Uncle Boone and Aunt Sarah, and her mother, and their children come out from Pennsylvania to homestead in our valley. They staked a claim right next to ours on the Loup City side, and while Father was busy helping them get their place registered at the land office in Grand Island and their dugout built, Mama was busy with the cooking. While both families was crowded in at our place, George McKeller pulled a fast one.

Yes, sir, that George McKeller called a special election that was legal because the notice was posted. The only trouble was he'd posted it on a tree down by the river and nobody seen it there. So they held the meeting by special invitation and we never even knowed they was having it until it was over, and three thousand dollars worth of bonds, carrying eight per cent interest, to be paid off in ten years, was voted and sold to folks back East. No, the schoolhouse never got built, but the farmers there had to pay for it anyhow. One load of lumber was hauled to the location on the McKeller farm that George had sold to the district because he'd got to be chairman of the board, and then some man come along with a paper and attached the lumber for the contractor's debts and another man with a team come along and hauled it away before that lumber had a chance to weather from being out in the open.

They never seen that contractor, Ingersoll, again. I tell you that fellow was a cutthroat of a skinner. Why folks was years paying for a schoolhouse that wasn't ever built. Having that debt agin the land, while us children was having to grow up without no schooling, hit the folks terrible hard. Seemed like Father sort of give up then. He wasn't ever quite the same after that happened.

The worst of it was, some of that riff-raff that come in there for the twenty dollars and the school election liked it just fine and settled down neighbor to us. Buckskin Bill had been a horse thief and was knowed far and wide as a tough nut to crack. He sure must of knowed his business. I've heard tell that he could go out and rustle a hundred head of cattle and drive them across a field and through a canyon and never leave a trace behind. Most cattle rustlers wasn't near as good as him; he must of been about the best there was.

Another fellow, named Bodie, and his wife and child had come in there and filed on a claim close in to ours. One night during a bad rain storm, Bodie come to our house, yelling, "My God, Sam, get up. We'll all be murdered in our beds."

Before Father could get his pants on, Bodie had broke the door in. Father reached for his gun thinking he'd gone crazy. Looking into that barrel calmed Bodie down considerable and he says, "Hawthorne, I need help. Buckskin Bill and Stringer has took my pigs."

Father and me and Aaron, and Jim Mapes, who'd been caught by the storm and was sleeping over night at our house, dressed and went back with him. By the time we got over to Bodie's, daylight was beginning to show around the edges of the sky, and we could see tracks plain in the mud. Them fellows had left all sorts of big footprints around Bodie's pigpen that was made by digging a pit and piling the sod solid around the edge. Them same footprints led over to Buckskin Bill's sod house that had a lot of fresh dirt around it, too.

After we'd followed them tracks between the two places, we went on back to Bodie's and we helped him hitch up his team and then drove over to our place so that Mrs. Bodie and the baby could stay with Mama while Bodie and Father drove over to Loup City to see Judge Waugh. Father said that after the way things had turned out in the McKeller trial he wasn't going to give no more of his business to Pete Morlensen and George Haskell. But when they got to Judge Waugh's he told them he couldn't come over to investigate because we was living in Valley County, but that if we swore it was an emergency, he thought he could act and send out a deputy and have Buckskin Bill brought in to stand trial. He said Bodie couldn't take no hand in it because he was the one who owned the pigs and was signing the complaint. The Judge couldn't take no part because he would be the one trying the case. So all he could do was to deputize Father. Next thing Father knowed he was a deputy, and he had a paper that said he was to bring Buckskin Bill in "Dead or Alive."

At first Father felt real proud about being a deputy sheriff, but the nearer he got to Buckskin Bill's place, the more he wished he wasn't. The worst of it was that when he went up to the door, Bill's wife opened it just as soon as he knocked, and he could see that the Stringers was all there too, setting on the edge of a bench, looking

like they was crouched and ready to spring. But Father had the law
on his side, so he says, "Bill, I have a warrant for your arrest."

And Bill says, "You won't take me."

And his wife says, "Go ahead, Bill, and mash the son of a bitch's
face in."

And Stringer begun lipping in too, shooting off his mouth.

But Father had used his head that time. Aaron and Jim, who had
come up with him, showed at the window and let out a yell, after
they had drawed and covered them folks inside. Then Father says,
"Bill, this warrant calls for you dead or alive."

Father stood there in the doorway and he read the warrant out
loud, just the way Judge Waugh had wrote it. But Buckskin Bill
spoke up and says, "My name's Martin Luther Diamond, and I ain't
going to jail under no other name but the right one."

Father had the boys keep him covered and he made him come
along anyhow, but by the time they got to our house, it was so late
we had to keep him there all night. The men took turns guarding
him. Along toward daylight, on Father's shift, Bill had to go outside.
Father was along, watching him close, and he seen he was moving
away from where he was supposed to be. Father let out a yell at him
that woke me up, and I heard Bill say, outside the window, "I'm
just going up home for a little while, Sam."

And Father says, "You try that again, Bill, and you'll be going
home feet first."

Come morning, Bodie hitched up his team to take Bill down to
Judge Waugh's for the trial. Mrs. Bodie went along, too. A lot of the
women as well as the men was wearing them old Civil War uniforms
that the government had sent out for grasshopper relief, so Mama
had loaned Mrs. Bodie her good dress to wear to town for the trial.
The Bodies was awful fine folks and they felt bad enough about losing their pigs without having Buckskin Bill act like he done that
morning. You see, they was setting on the front seat of the wagon
while Father and Jim was on each side of Buckskin Bill in the back
seat so's they could guard him, and Aaron was riding the mule and
covering him from the rear. Buckskin Bill kept making fun of Mrs.
Bodie and laughing and yelling, "Lot's of style up there in borrowed
clothes."

Of course we figgered Judge Waugh would take him off our hands and put him in jail. But all he done was to fine him and pocket the fine. Then after Buckskin Bill had swore to keep the peace, he turned him loose, and he come out and clumb right into the wagon alongside of Father and Jim and rode home again, pleasant as you please. Bodies was out their pigs; we was out our time.

But what I can't figger out is that whether you call him Buckskin Bill or Martin Luther Diamond, he's still the same fellow that moved in neighbor to us on the Middle Loup, and, if he was such a good horse thief as some of them storytellers claimed he was, then how come he left all them tracks so plain in the mud between Bodie's pigpen and his own cabin?

By September Father had made what hay he could, and Mama and us children had harvested all the wild plums and choke cherries and berries we could find, but we knowed that there wasn't near enough to carry us through the winter. The other families was all in the same boat, and we was real pleased to hear that the army had finished them plans for the fort, and that settlers with teams and wagons was to get the preference on jobs, and that work was starting right away on Fort Hartsuff. Blamed if the government wasn't building our fort clean over on the Loup River, seventy-six miles above Grand Island and eighteen miles northeast of us, and across the river. That's figgering as the crow flies and we wasn't crows. Them Sioux Indians was out to the west of us, and when them Indians showed, we'd have a blamed hard trip going up and down over them sandhills clean over to where we could ford the river, and then we'd have to go on up to the fort. No matter how you figgered it, we had quite a piece to go to get to that fort. Yes, sir, even if there wasn't no Indians around to slow us down it was quite a ways.

The worst of it was the army said that they didn't have no place to house women and children. Anyhow, the homestead law said we couldn't move off for six months at a time for no cause whatsoever. And with cattlemen moving in and burning settlers places, and claim-jumpers snooping around, moving into empty houses, anyone would of been a blamed fool to move out of a house if he ever figgered on moving back into it again. But we had to have the money, so the men took the teams and went over to work on Fort Hartsuff, and that give Father a chance to go in debt for a team of horses. We figgered if there was an Indian attack, we could drive them steers over to the fort, although I knowed they'd be about as dangerous on the road as the Indians was.

Golly, Fort Hartsuff was built good. It cost over a hundred and ten thousand dollars, and they used it from the time they finished it in 1875 until 1881. Then somebody got to figgering around and decided there wasn't no sense in having all them soldiers and buildings over there so far from the Indians. The army pulled up stakes and moved out, but they couldn't take them buildings, so the Union Pacific Railroad bought the fort for five thousand dollars. Then something went wrong with their plans about running a railroad through there. Nowdays, Fort Hartsuff comes in handy for cattle that go in them big buildings for shelter out of the storms. Them days, building that big fort did give our men a chance to earn some money and to get back to where it was more settled while the rest of us stayed where we was, holding down the fort on our own homesteads.

Of course, none of the men got to bring home much of the money they made on account of them spending so much time at the saloon at Calamus, right across the road from where they was building the fort. Mama and Father come to out-and-out words about it, but he said a man had to stand his turn, and then if he didn't step up to the bar when the other boys treated, they got real surly. Mama said she figgered they didn't have to waste much time coaxing him.

Big wagon trains was hauling gravel four mile; and timber eight mile; and lime from kilns on the Beebe ranch forty mile away. The cement come seventy-six mile from Grand Island. The stockade, built of up-and-down logs, covered better than a half an acre. Fort Hartsuff had two real long barracks, and a mess hall and a hospital, and a big horse-barn, on the river side. Them buildings was in a sort of a hollow square, with a parade grounds in the center. The officers homes was big and solid. Masons come a long way to make real fancy fireplaces with arched tops. Trees and flowers was planted in the yards. Why, Fort Hartsuff was made more like a town than any other place out there on the frontier. It had a post office, a jail, a reading room, and a barber shop. But the fortifications and the water supply, and the place where they stored the ammunition, was what the settlers wondered about the most, because if trouble come that was the only part we'd be using.

After they had built most every kind of a quarters there was at Fort

Hartsuff, they moved in General E. O. C. Ord to run the whole out-fit, and they made our own cousin, Lee Heron, chief engineer. No, I never heard tell of him doing no engineering before that, but he risked his life getting some white women away from the Indians, and he done all right for hisself after he got knowed far and wide as an Indian scout. Why, when Lee Heron was an old man he got a free trip clean from Nebraska to New York just because Eddie Ricken-backer wanted him to tell about how he won the Congressional Medal of Honor.

When I was a little boy, I liked to hear them stories, too, because I figgered on getting away from the homestead and hitting the trail, just as soon as I could. Many's the time I went over to the fort, when it was being built and afterwards, and I'd set there listening to them old Indian scouts talking, while I'd have to wait for Father to get done visiting with the boys.

The scout I liked best was old Happy Jack. He was just a little fellow, bent over and twisted, and he hadn't been able to talk quite right since he come home one night and found his wife and the children scalped and his cabin burned. After that he always had to double up his fist, and hit hisself several times on the right-hand side of his head, and whistle three times before he could get words out at all. Folks who didn't know him or his story used to laugh at him, but Happy Jack liked me because he'd had a boy about my size. That's why he'd let me set beside him and count the seventy-three notches in the handle of his knife, and when he'd run his hand back and forth across my hair, I knowed he was thinking of his own boy they'd scalped, and of how he'd swore to God that he'd go on killing Indians until he died hisself or run out of Indians.

When old Happy Jack would come to the fort for provisions, Lee Heron and some of the other old-time frontiersmen was real good to him. Happy Jack and Lee had hunted buffalo together for the rail-road, and they'd been friends ever since. But the officers who'd come out there from the East didn't like having old Happy Jack around because they figgered he was dirty on account of his tobacco-stained beard and wore-out buckskin clothes and moccasins.

Then Doc Middleton, the best horse thief that ever lived, stole a team of government horses and took the wheel of the wagon along that they was chained to with a padlock, while a bunch of soldiers was sleeping right alongside. The soldiers couldn't track him, so old Happy Jack trailed him for them, and they seen where he'd headed into the Cedar Canyons. Sheriff Ben Halliday and the officer from the fort wanted to put men at each end of the canyon where he was hiding and make a drive on Doc like he was a herd of elk. But old Happy Jack started knocking on the side of his head and whistling. Finally he got the words out to tell them that if they'd leave it to him he'd bring Doc out of there without a bunch of soldiers getting shot.

So they give him a half hour, and old Happy Jack got down on his belly and crawled along with his rifle until he got to where he knowed Doc Middleton was hiding. Then he whistled to let Doc know who it was before he begun shooting first to the right of him, then to the left of him. Only each time he burnt the grass a little closer with his bullet. Doc could see that Jack could pick him off any time he had a mind to. So he jumps up with his hands up over his head, and says, "Damn you, Happy Jack. You're the only man in the world that could take me alive."

The soldiers come and made a big to-do about capturing Doc Middleton. They took him back to the fort for his trial and locked him up for a spell. But after they got tired of keeping him and turned him loose, he went right back to stealing horses again and drifted over into the Niobrara country.

After General Ord got there, he decided they needed another town. So it was laid out and named for him. The county seat was there, lots was sold around the courthouse, businesses went in, and it got to be quite a place. It put all of them folks in Calamus right out of business. Developing town sites paid better than farming, them days. Locating county seats got to be such a good way to pick up easy money that folks had to watch their records or they'd be kidnapped and moved to a new location.

When the fort was finished in December of 1874, General Ord sent out invitations to folks all over saying that him and Company C of the 9th U.S. Infantry was entertaining at a Grand Ball. Most everyone went but us. We couldn't on account of being Methodists. Father would of weakened if Mama had give him half a chance, but by that time old Mr. Huntington was coming to our place regular of a Sunday. He was a widower who lived way off on a homestead that drained to the North Loup, but he'd felt the call, and he never took a dime for saving souls. After plowing all week with his oxen, he'd feed and stable them to give them their day of rest, and then he'd walk most the night to get to our place early of a Sunday morning. Mama always set a lunch out for him before the rest of us went to bed, and he'd come in and eat and catch a cat nap so's he'd be ready for Sunday school at ten and preaching at eleven. Then he'd eat dinner with us and stay through the day so he could preach again at night before he had another lunch and walked home during that night to start his work again on Monday. He said that the Lord had called him to come and minister to the folks in our valley. He kept it up too until the next year when the Hawley's come in there and homesteaded up on the bluff while Mr. Hawley rode circuit. They had a boy, D.O., who was about my age. He just went by them initials and he always come with his father. We got to know each other well because the Methodists held all their meetings at our house. But Mr. Huntington was our preacher when the invitation come for us to go to the dance at the fort, and the Sunday before that grand ball he talked for over three hours about the evils of the flesh and how Christians must be strong to withstand temptation. No, you couldn't count that time as dancing when the relief box come. Because that just happened. It was sort of like spontaneous combustion. We didn't have no music, or practiced steps, or nothing like that. We just hopped around, holding hands.

During the late fall, when the weather was too bad to work out in the fields, Charley Matthews got up gumption enough to ride all over with a petition for the government to establish a mail route up through our part of the state. It would run from Kearney on up to Loup City and then to where we was. That was about half way. Then he wanted it to go from there on up to a little settlement where he lived, sixty mile north of us. Him and a fellow named Oscar Smith had filed on some real fine mineral springs that bubbled up in Victoria Creek, close to where it run into the Middle Loup River. It was right at the edge of them Cedar Canyons, and they'd throwed up a store on Smith's place and put some sleeping rooms in above it. But they was a hundred and twenty mile from the nearest post office and he wanted to see if something couldn't be done about it. He stayed at our place overnight, and the folks told him they liked the idea fine, only they didn't figger we had no more chance of getting that petition answered straight than we had of getting a fort built between us and them Sioux Indians. But when he asked right out if Mama would be willing to have the post office at our house, she was real glad to sign the paper saying she would. We never got our mail, them days, unless someone was going to Grand Island, and we couldn't hope for that more than maybe once a month. Then Mr. Matthews said they needed a trustworthy single man to ride horseback over the upper sixty mile of the route, and that folks figgered Aaron should apply for the job. Aaron was real pleased at the chance because he had heard that the government paid their help regular. Mama didn't like having him do it on account of them Indians, but finally she give in and he signed his paper to send along with hers. Don Hulse had already wrote in for the route between Kearney and our place.

We didn't have no name for our valley; up until then nobody had thought about needing one. But the paper had a place to fill a name in, so Mr. Matthews stayed around and him and Father rode all over to get the names on the petition and ask folks what they thought of Brownsville for a name. Rightly, the place should of been named for the McKellers, who was the first settlers, but they was so mean, nobody would have it. The Browns come next, so we sent in their name. After a long time a letter come back saying Nebraska already had a Brownsville, and it was up to us to pick another name. By that time Uncle Boone and his family was pretty well settled in their dugout. His wife, Aunt Sadie, was real fanciful and hadn't seen no grasshoppers nor nothing like that yet, so she says, "Why not call it Arcadia?"

It sounded real pretty, and it suited our valley, too. You couldn't ask for a better place to live when things was going good. We was just a piece from the river, where we could catch bass and catfish, while wild plums, gooseberries, grapes, chokecherries, and blackberries growed thick along the banks of the creeks and up in the draws. And that ground in there can't be beat. Yes, sir, we figgered she was right, and that was the name we sent in, and that's what they call the town and the post office today. Them folks that bought Uncle Boone out, cut his homestead up into city lots, and then they subdivided our old place next. When I went back in 1924, after being away for forty-three years, I seen a big sign saying *Hawthorne's addition to Arcadia,* and I was real glad that Aunt Sadie, after looking out across that bare field where there wasn't another house in sight, says: "Let's call it Arcadia."

Them folks back in Washington must of liked the name, too, for they let us keep it. They have got a terrible lot to say when places get named. Just like when they opened up a place above Arcadia several years later. The folks there got so tired of having the names they wanted turned down back in Washington that they finally wrote in Broken Bow because they figgered no one had thought of that one. They'd found some old Indian relics up there or they wouldn't of thought of it theirselves. Nobody had. That's still its name.

It took a lot of time and a lot of writing around before Mama got to be postmistress of Arcadia, Nebraska, on February 9, 1875. They sent her a real fancy commission that she put right up on the wall of our sod house, and Father took a packing box and made cubbyholes for the six regular families who was living in the valley and then he left a bigger place for the extras that just come by once in awhile to pick up theirs, and he left the biggest place of all for the mail that was to be sent away.

But it took so long for us to get set up for business, that it wasn't until the fifteenth of April, 1875, that our own Aaron Crouch, who didn't have no other real home and had come to live with us when he was just a little boy, carried the mail to the other end of that long route alone. After that, come rain, shine, or Indians, he carried it regular once a week over one hundred and twenty mile, round trip, on horseback. Every Saturday night he stayed overnight up at the other end of the line. There was a girl up there growing up by the name of Amanda Higgins, and he courted her regular Saturday nights until she was old enough to get married. Then when they did, that give him a home at both ends of his route until we moved West. Aaron didn't leave with us. He had a good job, so he just stayed put all the rest of his life.

When Aaron first started to carry the mail, he said it was terrible hard to tear hisself away from some of the folks living along the route who never got to see nobody but him. Having him get that job helped us children to learn a lot about the neighbors and the country on up above. Just like with old Mrs. Woods. She claimed that the Hawthornes was her nearest neighbors, although we never seen her. After Mama found out what a store she set by just knowing we was only twenty mile away, she got to writing her notes, and Aaron dropped them off, free of charge. I guess there wasn't nothing Mrs. Woods wasn't willing to tackle or that she couldn't figger out a way to get through. Just like when the grasshoppers come, Mrs. Woods grabbed up a bushel basket and throwed it over her head and run for her chicken house. When she got there she took the basket off her head, filled it full of chickens and made a run for the house. Her husband was working in Grand Island and couldn't get home. From then on, until the grasshoppers left, Mrs. Woods and them chickens lived cooped up in there together. When she figgered they was hungry, she would open the door a little, just to let in enough grasshoppers for them to eat right then. She figgered them fool chickens would bust their insides if she didn't cut down on their diet. The way she managed, they come through just fine. When she was hungry, she ate chicken.

I kept telling Mama that I didn't need no schooling and that folks with horse sense got along a lot better on the prairie than ones that just had book learning. But she kept throwing it up to me that I didn't talk like Ming Coombs. One day Ming come driving into our yard and says to Father, "What do you think of my new team of young oxen?"

Father sort of grinned and says, "Young oxen? Why I'll bet them old fellows hasn't got a tooth in their upper jaw."

Ming says, "I'll bet they have."

And he run around in front and lifted up the lip on the near one, and then on the far one. Then he stepped back and says, "Hawthorne, I can sue the fellow that sold me this team as three-year-olds."

Then Father looked in their mouths and says, "Ming, them old fellows has lost their teeth for so long that the holes are all healed up where their teeth come out."

By that time Ming was fit to be tied. He turned around and was all for heading back for Loup City where he bought that team until Father told him to hold on a minute, and then he says, "Ming, you blamed fool, didn't they learn you that a cow critter never has teeth in its upper jaw in front?"

Ming Coombs was really an awful nice fellow, excepting for being uneducated in the things he needed to know most, so the men held a meeting and figgered that since he wasn't making it farming they'd ought to elect him county school superintendent and give him a part-time job teaching us children. We knowed by then our new school-house had turned into nothing but a big debt agin our farms, but the women-folks kept on saying that we should have school, regardless. And Mama had put Father up to offering to let them use our sod house daytimes, as soon as we got our log house finished, because nights they wouldn't be holding school anyway. Having two houses, we figgered, would give us a chance to spread out more.

Father went over to Ming's place for the meeting. Ming had asked him to come early to look at his cow. When Father got there he found that the cow was giving just as much milk as ever but for several weeks there wasn't no cream raised on the top of it. Father couldn't figger it out, and neither could the other men when they got there, so they went on in and started the meeting. Ming lived in a dugout that had just one window with the pane broke out. I ain't sure, maybe he couldn't stand it without some fresh air in there. He'd waited to milk until Father got there, so when they got inside Ming set the bucket of warm milk on the table, long enough to light a little kerosene lamp with a wick about as wide as his thumb nail. Ming was real proud of that lamp and said it didn't burn a teacupful of kerosene in a week. Father held the lamp close while Ming poured the milk in a pan and it looked as rich as any he ever seen, but when he carried the lamp back for Ming to set it on the shelf, the other pans of milk standing there was as blue as any skim milk that run out of a separator, and not one single speck of cream showed.

Well, they give up trying to figger it out and took the lamp and went back to the table and started right in talking about them school bonds and us children getting our book learning. Ever once in awhile they'd take time out to damn George McKeller for his part in the whole thing. You see, George had got hisself elected chairman of that school board, and that give him the three-year term in office. On account of the notice being posted down on a tree by the river, that turned out to be a regular meeting where he was elected and them bonds was voted. The contractor had got the money when the bonds had been sold; so the 8 per cent interest and all the principal was piling up agin our homesteads right along.

The meeting run on real late. Father chanced to glance up and he seen a black shadow move across that broken window-pane. He knowed it was George McKeller come to get him, so he slid his hand down and reached for his revolver that was inside the belt of his pants. Then he realized that the other men was reaching for their belts, figgering he was trying to get the drop on them. So he whispers, "He's at the window."

By that time they figgered out what was up, and they drawed, and cocked, and turned real easy to look—while the shadow moved right through that broken window-pane and across onto the shelf near by. Father grabbed up the lamp and held it high above his head so's he could see. And there on the shelf set Mam Blacky. She was as sleek and fat as a well-fed rat, and she was lapping away at the cream that had just riz to the top of Ming's last pan of milk. Father was so surprised that he let out a yell and she sailed right out of there like a streak. Ming nailed a board over the place in the window where she'd been coming through, and when she couldn't get no more cream at his place, she moved right back with us and never even acted sorry she'd been away for all that time. Ming was sure pleased to have cream on top of his milk again.

We was real glad to have Mam Blacky home but we didn't think much of our other visitors. One night during the dead of winter, we was just about ready for bed when we heard a lot of horses being drove into the yard, and some fellows was yelling around out there. One of them says, "Yep, this is Hawthorne's hay, all right."

Father got into his shoes and went to the door, and three big fellows come in and the first one says, "I'm Enoch Berry. This is my brother Jim, and this fellow helping drive our horses is Charley Webster. We've run out of hay down at Lone Tree, so we've come up to finish out the winter with you."

I could see Father studying them and I knowed he didn't like their looks. They was all wearing two guns in their belts, and was swaggering around like they figgered they was tough, and that's just what they was. Finally Father says, "I'm feeding twelve head of cows, a team of longhorns, and my own horses. You'll have to go on somewhere else. I'll be needing all the hay in our stacks."

I figgered Enoch Berry would get mad, but he was real soft-spoken. All he says was, "Sorry, Hawthorne, but we don't have no choice. I can't let my horses starve. You're the only man we've found with hay. If you'll let them stay while my brother and I ride around and locate a place where we can drive them to, we'll pay you well."

Charley Webster moved right in to look out for them and to drive them down through the snow to water. Enoch and Jim come twice and took some of the horses away each time. Father got suspicious when over half of our hay had been et and three quarters of the horses had been drove away. So he went out and picked out the best one of them horses that was left and fastened it to our mule with a chain and two real good padlocks and drove them both down into a piece he'd fenced off for spring calving down in the cottonwoods along the creek. He'd heard that Enoch was driving them horses that he'd fattened up on our hay down to Grand Island and selling them.

Sure enough, he come back for the rest of them one night, and Charley Webster, who'd been sleeping out in the hay, had saddled up and gone with them off down the road. Come daylight, Enoch seen that the roan was missing so he sent Jim and Charley on with the rest of the horses and he come back to get him. He swaggered up to Father who was working on a neckyoke there in the yard and he says, "Hawthorne, I've come for my horse, but I don't see it around."

Father says, "Oh, do you mean the roan you left as part pay on your feed bill?"

Enoch got mad and yells, "Damn it, Hawthorne, that's my best horse and you're not going to keep him."

Father wasn't armed, so he turned around and started into the house where he'd left his revolver. Mama and Mrs. Brown and Mrs. Fredinsburg was in there finishing a quilt. I heard Enoch say he was going to kill Father if he didn't get his horse, so I took out of there and I run for over a mile to get a fellow named Jerry Hayes, who was plowing, to come and help us. By the time I got to him I was so out of breath I couldn't talk, but he could tell something was wrong at our house and he took off for there lickity-split. When I got my breath I run back too.

Them women heard all the noise and it scared Mrs. Brown and Mrs. Fredinsburg so bad because they knowed that Father wasn't armed that they run and hid their heads in the featherbed so's they wouldn't have to hear Father being shot. But Mama had filled her bailer with boiling water, and when Enoch come through the door on Father's heels, holding that gun between his shoulders, she stepped right out from in back of the door, and Enoch seen that she was armed and ready to let fly with her bailer. She says, "Enoch Berry, you put that revolver in your holster, or I'll throw this right in your face."

That give Father time to get his gun and he says, "You get off this place, Berry, and don't you dare show around here again."

That's the last we seen of any of them fellows. Later on Enoch went to the Black Hills, and he started following Wild Bill Hickock around because he'd heard about the reward that the gamblers in Deadwood had put on Bill's head. After Enoch had spent considerable time tailing Wild Bill and was about ready to shoot him in the back and get the reward, what did Wild Bill do but swing around and get the drop on him first. Then he says, "Enoch, I'd of thought you'd have knowed better than to try to get that reward." Then Wild Bill shot him right in the belly, throwed him across his horse, and started back with him for Deadwood. When they got there he seen that Enoch still had considerable life in him yet. He looked through his pockets and Enoch had enough money on him to buy a one-way ticket to where his folks lived at Lone Tree Station on the old overland stage route. So he says, "Enoch, you won't live long, but I think you'll make it home with time to spare." Wild Bill patted him on the shoulder and told the driver to go as easy as he could. It was all of seven hundred miles to Enoch's folks' place, but they made it just fine and he lived for two whole days after he got there.

His brother, Jim, got killed in a bad accident too, right there at his own home. He'd been down to the railroad station one real hot day, and he seen that the mail clerk had left both doors of the mailcar open to get a little air inside. When the clerk throwed a big mail sack in one door, Jim reached through on the other side, snaggled it out, and rode down with it to a bunch of bushes on Wood River where he cut the mail sack open, took what money there was in the letters, and throwed the rest away. Just by chance some Pawnee Indians was down that way hunting. They knowed there was a law agin robbing the mail and they figgered they might get a reward, so they went up and tattled.

Early one morning, soon after that, a government inspector drove up to Enoch and Jim's folks' house in a buggy. Jim come to the door, got the drop on him, took away his revolver, and ordered him off the place. That inspector acted like he was scared to death of Jim and seemed real glad to leave there alive. He'd been walking away from the house with his hands held high over his head, but when he got down to where he'd left the buggy standing, he reached in the back and brung out a double-barrel shotgun loaded with buckshot and got Jim with both barrels right through the chest. Then that detective dumped his carcass into the back of his buggy and drove into the courthouse with him and collected the reward just as easy as you've seen the fellows come in from the hills around here and turn in coyote scalps for bounty. No, I don't think he give them Pawnee Indians a cut. They just told him who done it and where he was. They didn't get in on the kill.

Of course Mama didn't have no way of knowing when she run Enoch out of our house with a bailer full of boiling water that him and his brother, who lived down below us at Lone Tree Station, was going to turn out to be famous badmen of the old West. But Mama never was a woman to get impressed with folks easy, no matter who they was.

After the Berry boys was gone and the weather faired up, it appeared like we'd come through the winter just fine. Of course Uncle Boone's family had hard luck when their dugout got flooded during the spring thaw. A lot of their stuff was ruined and they all got pretty well waterlogged when about three foot of water run in on them, but the only one in the family hurt bad was their old tomcat. When the water first come in, he clumb on a stool, then when it come up around his feet on the stool, he jumped to the top of the hot stove, where he burned his feet terrible before he dove into the water and swum out the door.

Uncle Boone wasn't too strong; he had one crippled hand. Because he wasn't full growed when he run off and enlisted in the Civil War and got shot through that hand, it never got to be as big as the other one. But he got a pension and that give him a little money regular, every month. But with a family the size of his, he was always needing more money than he had. Him and Aunt Sadie had awful nice children, all nine of them. After the high water run in and spoiled their dugout, Father and him decided to haul enough logs down from Cedar Canyon, sixty mile above us, to build a real good house for Uncle Boone's family before winter. The rest of us had cleaned out all the cottonwoods that was the right size for house logs before he got there.

Uncle Boone and Father hustled around to get the crops in, and as soon as the prairie grass was up high enough they made our firebreaks. Us settlers in the valley was lucky; we had the Middle Loup River for one side of our firebreak. Then we plowed and burned about three firebreaks to each section, crisscrossing them so it looked like a big checkerboard when we was coming down over the sandhills on the road from Ord. We made our firebreaks by plowing three furrows, then leaving a space fifty-foot wide between, and plowing three more furrows. When we was ready for the burning, all the folks in our two families that was big enough to walk would go out along the line and hold wet sacks to beat out any little fires that might jump over and start in the hayfields, while the men would light the dry grass in them fifty-foot strips between the turned furrows. We'd be real careful to see that the fires didn't jump over into our fields; we stayed there until they'd all died down. Nobody ever burned their firebreaks on a windy day.

There ain't nothing worse than fire on the prairie, and I've seen many a one in Nebraska. When you're way out without no river or trees close by, and nothing but sky above and dry prairie grass around, you can't tell how near you are to a fire. And if the wind is blowing, the fire will run along ahead of it faster than a train. One day Father and me had forded the Middle Loup and drove across the prairie to the west to see if we could find timber to build Uncle Boone's house closer than having to haul it sixty mile from the north. We drove clean over to the South Loup, over thirty mile away, and seen there wasn't no timber that we could use. Coming home we had the hot sun on our backs. We was tired; so was the horses. I was setting there on the wagon seat, alongside of Father, just about asleep, when he says: "God, Mont, look!"

I turned around to where he was pointing and I seen a prairie fire rolling along and spreading out red, all underneath the sunset. It was right in back of us and coming closer every minute. Father says, "Hold the horses, Mont, and don't let them get away."

Then he handed me the lines and jumped down out of the wagon, jerking his block matches out of his pocket before he hit the ground

and he begun lighting little fires all along in the grass in front
of us. I had a terrible time holding them horses until he got back
in the wagon. Why, he even throwed one match right in at their
feet, and before I could hand him the reins them flames was licking
up and singeing their bellies. Then he told me to lay down flat in
the bottom of the wagon when the time come for us to make a run
for it. He spread his feet wide and braced hisself solid between the
end gate and the wagon seat, and set there tense and ready, holding
them horses that was trembling and scared to death as they seen
the flames in front of them and smelled the smoke at their backs.

But we had to wait until the embers died out in the fire that
Father had set on ahead of us, so that the horses' hoofs wouldn't
get burned. And I knowed from the way Father looked as he
watched the fire ahead and then kept turning to look at the one
behind that we didn't have no time to spare, and I figgered it
would be awful hard on Mama to lose the team and wagon as well
as Father and me. Then he says, "Mont, keep your head down in
that blanket. We've got to move along even if there is some fire in
the ashes ahead."

Of course we was real lucky because the fire we started that day
burned a nice, wide path for us right to the Middle Loup River,
and when it died down we forded across to our place on the other
side. Sure it was a good thing for us and for them that nobody
had got around to building a house on the west side of the Middle
Loup, but if there'd been a house there, they'd of had a firebreak.
The worst thing about having to keep plowing and burning them
in the the same places over and over again, was that the sand and
dirt begun to blow away. After a few years, them places where folks
made their firebreaks begun to look like railroad cuts all through
the prairie.

The second year we was on the prairie, folks had a terrible time
fighting fires that had been started here and there in the sandhills
to burn the grass where them blamed grasshoppers laid their eggs.
That didn't stop them though, because they moved in on us again
just as soon as our garden was up and they cleaned us out the same
way they had before. Maybe lightning don't strike twice in the
same place, but grasshoppers do. But the second time they come
to our place they left more of our hay, and by then the cows was

milking and Father butchered a veal, so we didn't go near as hungry as we did the year before. We still wasn't doing no neighboring with McKellers, but they must of got along better, too, because our biggest bull calf that Father was saving—figgering on using him for a herd sire—was bawling down in the fenced pasture toward their place. We knowed he was there, but come morning he wasn't, and we never seen hide nor hair of him again.

It took more than grasshoppers to keep the settlers from moving in on us; blamed if a bunch of them didn't turn out to be them Seven Day Baptists. It got so mixed up with some folks holding Saturday holy, and the rest of us keeping the regular Sunday, that old Pete Morlensen, who'd been listening to both circuit riders and had sort of give up when the grasshoppers come two years in a row, said he'd decided to quit working altogether and be a seven-day man and act like every day in the week was Sunday. Of course, he didn't mean it. Why it wasn't no time until he was out there planting his fields again, but this time he was through raising cabbages and potatoes and beans for the grasshoppers. No sir, he sent to Omaha, and had them send him all the pumpkin seed they had because he figgered if the grasshoppers come again they'd never get through them tough hides and pumpkins would be good feed for his cattle. But blamed if them pumpkins didn't all turn out to be watermelons, and he give everybody watermelons and Julia and me got a load of them from him free, and drove clean over to Loup City to peddle them. We done well on the first load, but folks got awful tired of eating straight watermelons. Someways, they're harder on you than buckwheat.

But Pete wasn't the only one having trouble keeping the Sabbath. Mama said that she never knowed what a day of rest was after them twelve cows come fresh. She might of had to stay up most the night working but she never missed having the house or us cleaned up and ready when the neighbors gathered at our place for the Sunday preaching. Golly, them cows kept us busy. We all pitched in and helped milk, night and morning. Then Mama and the girls made butter every day and they drug me in on the churning, when I wasn't out riding herd on the cows.

Them Sioux was getting out of hand; everybody went armed. We kept hearing of settlers getting scalped and cabins being burned.

Mama didn't feel a bit good about me having to take the cattle so far out to graze, but we needed the hay in close for winter. Father told me that whenever I seen something coming toward me out on the prairie to tether my horse and hide. Many's the time I've laid out in the tall grass on my belly and watched to see if it was Indians heading my way, but them bands always turned out to be deer or elk or antelope.

After the weather turned hot, Mama said she knowed, no matter how careful she packed it, the butter would get rancid while it was being hauled over sixty mile to Grand Island. Father said he'd seen butter throwed out along the road because the storekeepers wouldn't take it. And Mama said she wasn't making butter for the coyotes and wolves to clean up, so she had him bring out a big crateful of them heavy crocks that holds six gallon apiece, and she'd make butter, and work it until every drop of buttermilk was out. She'd salt it good and pack it down in one of them crocks. By fall she had a whole row of them buried in a deep trench down by the spring, with the lids fastened down tight to shut out the air, and several inches of dirt piled on top to help keep them cool. We'd bury them crocks just as fast as we filled them and that way the butter never had a chance to get rancid. When cold weather come, Father took them crocks of butter in to Grand Island and Mama went along with her list of what we needed in food and clothing for the winter, and she outfitted and provisioned us because that butter was blamed good and it was sent right out to Leadville and Denver and sold as fresh butter and it brung ten cents a pound, which was considerable above the regular market. But, of course, us children didn't have no way of knowing that our butter-making would pay off so good when we was working with the milk during them hot summer days on our homestead out there at Arcadia.

Mama and me had set ourselves up in the nursery business, too, that spring. By then I was ten years old and had done considerable work helping out around home, but that was the first time I'd ever branched out on my own. You see, a lot of homesteaders had filed on tree claims, just like we had, and the Timber Culture Act of 1873 said that any homesteader could apply "for an additional 160 acres, which would become his, if he planted at least one-fourth to trees within four years." It didn't say what kind of trees or how big, and there ain't nothing in the way of trees as foolproof as cottonwoods. They grow good without water. Even grasshoppers won't eat their leaves if they can find any other kind of provisions. Some folks even raised cottonwood trees by putting cuttings in the ground and keeping them wet until they had rooted good. But Mama and me had a lot better scheme than that.

Cottonwoods had growed thick down along the Middle Loup until the settlers come and begun cutting them. The seed had blowed all over them sand banks and little islands out in the river, and Mama and me found whole beds of little cottonwoods about as big around as a pencil, that we could pull up just like grass and carry up to our place where we had dug a trench along by the spring. We'd bunch and tie them together in lots of a hundred trees and keep them wet and heeled in there until somebody come along to buy them. You'd be surprised how fast the word got around that we had trees for sale. Before long, folks who had to get some kind of trees to prove up on their land, was driving many a mile to buy them little cottonwood seedlings from us. Well, what we charged all depended. If we figgered they was good for it we'd ask three dollars a thousand. But money was terrible scarce and many's the time we've settled for two dollars a thousand. But anybody getting them at that price had to promise to keep their mouths shut about it. We always started selling our trees at three dollars a thousand; then we went on down to what we could get.

Uncle Boone had dickered around and got ahold of two yoke of oxen, on time. It takes a lot of trips to haul enough cedar logs to build a house. Them canyons was sixty mile above our place, and we had to allow time for the cutting and the round trip, too. I'd been begging to go; I sure was getting sick of homesteading, but Father left me right on the cow milking until they begun to dry up, come fall. Then blamed if we didn't hit a blizzard on my first trip to the Canyon. We'd only got as far as The Willows when the storm hit. We had to tip our wagon bed on its side and take shelter because them willows had all burned up in a fire and nothing was left of them but some old black brush. We was snowed in there for three days and while we didn't have much shelter, them oxen didn't have none. Their ears and tails all froze and dropped right off; when Father seen it he said they'd lost a lot of their value as trading stock.

They could hear just as good as ever, even if they didn't have nothing to funnel the sound into their heads. But after they lost their ears and tails they never appeared to be finished off quite right; and they took an awful licking from the flies because they didn't have nothing left for switching.

You'd of thought Father and Uncle Boone had had enough trouble for one trip, but Father got into it again. He was alone in camp one day after we'd made it to Cedar Canyon, and a couple of real pleasant-looking strangers stopped by to pass the time of day. Father was tidying up our camp, getting ready to go up and help Uncle Boone fall timber, but when them fellows come along he set down with them on a log. They got to talking about how we lived in Arcadia, and Mama had the post office there and sold bread, and we knowed all the folks going back and forth along the Middle Loup. Father just thought them fellows was some other homesteaders come up there to haul logs and he talked sort of free. Then one of them hauled out a paper and a badge and he says, "Hawthorne, my name is Ball. I'm the United States Marshal from Omaha. I am subpoenaing you as a witness for the government to appear in Omaha to identify the men we are arresting for stealing timber out of this canyon."

Well, there wasn't a thing Father could do about it except put the paper in his pocket and go about his business. Many's the time I'd heard him say that somebody should stop them fellows from taking the timber out of there and selling it to the railroad when it was supposed to be set aside for the use of homesteaders. But I don't think he was hankering to take a hand in stopping that rough bunch hisself.

We was snowed in for most of the winter; come spring of 1876 the government called Father to come to Omaha as a witness at that trial. He'd been hoping he could go, while he was laying around the house all winter, but they sent for him just as spring work opened up. Mama got his clothes ready and his carpetbag packed, and Uncle Boone drove in with him as far as Grand Island; he took the train from there to Omaha. All his expenses was paid and it would have been a nice trip for him, excepting for the part about having to give testimony against them fellows that had been stopping at our house regular going to and from Cedar Canyon. After he left, Mama and us children was left alone there on the homestead, excepting for the one night a week when Aaron got home from delivering the mail. But with them twelve cows beginning to drop their calves, Mama and the girls and me had plenty of work cut out for us.

Then the paper come that told about the Custer Massacre. Don Hulse brung it along with the rest of the mail as far as our place, and then he turned and hurried right back to be with his family. Mama set there at the table reading it out loud to us, and that's the first we knowed about Custer and them 264 men getting killed out there by the Sioux Indians, and right at a time when we figgered he was keeping them away from us. All the time she was reading, us children set there looking at the windows and thinking we heard noises outside. We figgered them Sioux would be coming after our scalps most anytime.

Aaron come the next night, but he couldn't stay. He was under oath to get the mail through, and anyhow he figgered he owed it to the folks on up above to carry the news about Custer. Everyone was ordered to the forts. Part of the neighbors went to Fort Hartsuff and part of them went on down to Loup City, where there was a good blockhouse, provisioned and ready. Aaron figgered we'd gone to the fort too, and so when he got up above and found out that the Indians was sneaking in around close, he got Amanda Higgins and her folks into a blockhouse and done what he could to help out in the upper country. Everyone along his route went to the forts except the Lawhorns. The old man was terrible stubborn and wouldn't leave, so that night, when he was sleeping, Mrs. Lawhorn packed a little bundle of provisions and run all night and made it into Victoria Creek about daylight. She stayed there for about ten days, and then when he never showed, she legged it back again.

Of course Aaron didn't have no way of finding out that Mama had decided not to go to the fort; but after he was gone she said she'd never go off and leave them cows while Father was away and she was in charge of things at home.

When Lee Heron, who was our cousin and chief engineer at Fort Hartsuff, heard from the neighbors coming into the fort that Mama was still on our homestead, he was terrible worried and went to the commanding officer to get permission to come after us. He didn't want him to leave because some hunters coming into the fort had come across Indians sneaking up toward the open gate through the brush, and they figgered that an attack might come there any time. But Lee finally talked him into letting him take four government mules and a wagon to come for us, but he only give him a forty-eight-hour pass. On the way over, Lee seen Indian sign, and he counted where eleven Indian ponies had forded the river right above our place. But nothing he could say or do would budge Mama—she was going to stay with them cows, and if she wouldn't go us children wouldn't neither.

Lee got more and more excited as his time drawed to a close. He never slept a wink all that night, but just kept right on talking. Next morning when he left, he says, "To the devil with the cattle, Aunt Martha. You've got to save your lives."

"The cattle are all we've got," she says.

By that time he was real disgusted, and he says, "Pack what you need. I am taking you to the fort."

"I am staying right here and taking care of the cows until Sam gets home," she says.

Lee coudn't do no more. While he was pulling on his coat, he says, "I'm sorry to go, Aunt Martha, but I'm under orders."

Mama says, "Well, I'm not." Then she called after him, "Thank you for your trouble, Lee."

After he'd left, John Cook, an old buffalo hunter come. He had two revolvers, a rifle, and two big belts of cattridges. He says, "I'll stay until help comes."

But he didn't like our glass windows, so he got sod and boards and filled them in, excepting for a loophole to shoot through at the top. He said that another bunch of settlers was holed up together at a place above that they used to call Oak Grove, but since then they've changed its name to Comstock. He figgered we might want to go up there, but Mama said we'd toughy it out where we was. She had him stand guard while we went outside and done the milking just like we would on any other summer evening.

Then Scab Faced Charley come by, heading for the fort. But when he seen us there he said he'd just as soon stay with us as go anywhere else. He was one of the nicest fellows I ever knowed; but

I've never seen no other face like his. It was covered solid with small-pox pits.

We afterwards heard that it wasn't because we had them two men guarding us that the Indians left us alone; it was the Wild Irishman who kept them away. He was a trapper and hunter who had managed to make friends with them and with us, and folks claimed that he'd told them Sioux to leave us and our cattle alone. But we never knowed the straight of it for sure.

The Wild Irishman was the fellow who worked so hard to capture Great Horse, the black stallion that ranged back and forth between the Black Hills and Denver. Bon Foreigner, a New York horse-breeder, had offered twenty thousand dollars to anyone who could bring him in. The Wild Irishman had trailed Great Horse for weeks, with horses, carrying a rope. He was a great walker and so he decided to run him down on foot. A man can stand broken rest better than a horse, and he was going to keep him going and never let him lay down and rest. The Wild Irishman was closing in on Great Stallion on foot, when a soldier out there on Indian duty found out about the twenty thousand. He figgered he'd pull a fast one and crease Great Stallion with a bullet through the top of his neck and get him down and put a rope on him; but he miscalculated. He shot too low and broke his neck. The Wild Irishman come up to where Great Stallion was laying dead and he said he never seen nothing so beautiful as that horse in all his life. After that happened the Wild Irishman got wilder—he boasted that he never cared about nobody or what happened to them. But because Mama had took him in and fed him and looked after him when he was sick and out of grub one time down by our spring, he sent word out to the Indians that they'd better leave her alone or else.

It wasn't long after that when Father got home. As soon as he'd heard about the Custer Massacre, he'd asked the judge to let him come back to be with his family. So they called in a court reporter and made a record of what he knowed and he took the train to Grand Island and caught a ride from there to Loup City, and walked the rest of the way home. He sure was glad to see that we was all right, and he throwed Myra up over his head, and dug in his pockets for treats for us children. He told Mama not to worry, they'd figger out something right away.

Then when he seen she wasn't as scared about things as he'd been about us, they set right down and talked it all over, and decided that the only thing to do was to move the cows and us children down to where it was more settled. Somebody had to stay on the homestead, and he figgered it better be him. Julia said she could ride as good as a man, if trouble come; and she'd stay right there with him and look out for all the things she could, and see that he got his meals. Mama says, "That's the best plan, Sam. We can't be taking chances with the cows. If we keep them here, the Indians may run them off before they're even paid for."

SEVEN

BLACK HILLS AHEAD

Old scouts was slipping out along the creeks and across the prairie, checking up on them Sioux. Prospectors was taking their chances with the Indians and heading for the Black Hills. Our government had give up trying to keep the Treaty of 1868, when we promised we'd stay out of their mountains. The land on beyond and up in the Black Hills was wide open. The gold rush was on. Nights I'd lie awake thinking about getting out there and sneaking up on Red Cloud, and Crazy Horse, and Sitting Bull. One night, an old Indian scout, who'd just got back from serving under General Crook in the Battle of the Rosebud, set by our fire and told about how they'd used their heads and got out of the trap the Indians had set to wipe them out. He figgered that Custer hadn't been near as foxy as a fellow had to be, if he was going to keep alive in Indian territory.

We was right on the frontier. I was itching for action. Blamed if Father didn't send me down to Stevens' place below us on the Middle Loup, to ride herd on their cows and ours, for the whole summer.

Stevens only lived twenty-six mile from Grand Island. The folks worked out a deal with him to take our cows and Mama and us children down to their place. Then they'd put in a cheese factory and she'd run it. Stevens was shorthanded, and didn't have no way of using his milk. Both families was to pool what cattle we had and throw in our work and run them two herds on shares. Of course we wasn't to get nothing out of it, but our board and room, until we paid Stevens the balance we owed on them cows.

No, we didn't know nothing about cheese-making. But there was a fellow in Grand Island that did. We got him to come up to Stevens' place for a few days to help Mama get started. The day we went down with the cows, I rode the mule. The rest of the family, excepting Mam Blacky, was in the wagon with Father. They brung what bedding we had to have. Yes, sir, I looked for that cat three days steady after she left that time. She wasn't back at Ming Coombs place because I went over there on purpose to look. Nobody ever seen her in Arcadia again.

Before he went back to the homestead, Father helped fix up a sort of a loft for our living quarters. It was in a building where we was making and installing the cheese vats downstairs. We et in the house with the Stevens. They was real pleasant folks. Clean, too. Mrs. Stevens took to Myra right off and kept her around while she was cooking on account of them not wanting her to get drowned in them big vats of milk.

I spent most of my time that summer out on muleback riding herd on the cows. The Nebraska Herd Law was wrote so that folks could go right to farming without having to build no fences. Nobody had to fence cattle out; it was up to the fellows that owned them to keep them in. We had twelve cows. Stevens had sold part of his herd the year before, but he still had twenty-five head. That wasn't counting the calves, neither. We had too dang many cattle to keep track of.

From sunup on, I'd set out there in the heat watching them cows. Every morning when I'd leave the house, the women would give me a lunch to eat when the sun was straight overhead. After I'd et and some more of the day was through, I'd start looking up to see what the sun was doing. When I could hold two fingers between it and the sky line, it was time to round up them cows, drive them to the barn, and get to milking.

The mule got about as tired as I did. He was just plain cussed, to boot. If I got off his back, even for a minute, he wouldn't let me up again. He was so big that I couldn't get back on, once I got off, unless he put his head down and begun to eat. Then I'd run and jump on and wrap my legs around his neck. When he'd raise his head to shake me off, I'd slide down on his back again. But with my bare feet, and him acting like that, and them snakes here and there in the grass, I never got off, unless I just had to.

Night and morning we all pitched in with the milking. Bill Stevens, who owned them other cows, worked just as long hours as we did. Nights, after we was through milking and cleaning out the stable, and had brung the milk inside, and strained it into the big vats, I used to go to bed and think about them blamed cows, and how, come morning, nothing would be different. I'd be alone again, out there on the prairie, setting on that mule, watching the cows. Them was the longest days I ever knowed.

Mama'd read a book about cheese-making. Then the fellow from Grand Island, who helped make them big vats to hold the milk, taught her what he knowed. He let a calf suck until it couldn't hold no more milk. Then he killed it, took out its stomach, washed it good, and hung it in the sunshine to sour. The stuff inside the calf's stomach turned out to be rennit, that we had to put in the fresh milk to make it curdle. I never knowed they made cheese like that. Blamed if it didn't make my stomach curdle, just watching him.

We hadn't no more than got started good with our cheese-making when Father and Uncle Boone and Julia drove into the yard in the wagon. Julia stayed with us while the men went into Grand Island to do some trading. That night her and Mama and Sadie talked for a long time about how they had to get some schooling. I said I wasn't going to school and turn out to be like Ming Coombs. Mama'd been throwing it up to me again about how good he could talk. But I told her if him and Happy Jack was turned loose on the prairie, I knowed which one would be making it in to camp.

For a long time Mama had been working with the girls nights, teaching them all she could. Julia had set her mind on being a teacher and by then she was fifteen year old. Julia wasn't near as pretty as Sadie, but she worked hard, and was awful smart. She figgered that if she could get in a term of schooling at Grand Island, she'd be ready to go to the Institute and take her teacher's examinations.

Early the next afternoon Uncle Boone drove into the yard alone. He acted sort of sheepish when he give Mama a letter from Father, saying he wouldn't be home for awhile. He wanted Julia to move down with us for the summer, and close up the house on the homestead, because he'd been offered such a good job that he couldn't afford to turn it down. Uncle Boone had agreed to keep an eye on

our place. By then the grasshoppers had come for the third summer in a row, so we didn't have no crop left to worry about, and the
hay would grow by itself. Uncle Boone could pasture our team of
horses and the longhorns right along with his. I was using our mule
every day to ride herd on them cows. Mama was sort of surprised to
think that Father had sent his horses home with Uncle Boone and
had settled down to a steady job in Grand Island. She begun to figger
that he was real sensible, even if the letter he'd wrote was short and
didn't say much. But after awhile, she got the whole story pried
loose from Uncle Boone. Father wasn't in Grand Island at all.

When Father and Uncle Boone had got within about six mile of
town, they come to a long wagon train, stalled right in the middle of
the road. It was the Cummings' party, headed for the Black Hills.
They had a good outfit, and was using either two or three yoke of oxen
on each wagon. But when they got to Prairie Creek, them lead oxen
had sulked and laid down, and wouldn't get up again. It was plain
to see that them fellows driving was getting no place fast. They had
one of them sit-down strikes on their hands. When the lead oxen
quit all of them others laid down, too. They'd been there most of
the day, and by that time, them oxen was so sot on staying where
they was, that it had begun to look to them fellows like they wasn't
never going to get to the Black Hills.

Father jumped out of his wagon, as soon as him and Uncle Boone
got up to where they was. Cummings started right in telling Father
his troubles. He said they'd tried all sorts of schemes to get them
oxen up and started again, but nothing would work.

Father spoke right up, and says, "I'll get them going."

Cummings says, "Man, if you do, I'll pay you well. I'm so beat
I'm going back to Grand Island to get a little rest. When you get
ready to start, let me know."

Father says, "We're ready now."

So he took charge and he told them fellows that had got the oxen
unyoked to yoke them up again.

Then Father picked out a man to work with each of them oxen, and
he says, "I want every one of you men to wring off two wisps of
prairie grass like this. Twist them around real tight. When you've
got a couple of wads made about half the size of your fist, get over

and stand by the head of your ox. Be ready and when I give the word move fast."

After he seen that all the men was ready, he says, in a real loud voice, "Stuff the wads of grass up the nostrils of your ox, tight as you can. Then get out of the way."

Uncle Boone said them oxen laid there a minute, puffing and blowing. Then their eyes bugged out 'till you could of roped them with a grape vine. They knowed they was being smothered to death. Then the lead team riz up first. All the other teams staggered to their feet, too. And it wasn't no time until the whole blamed bunch had took off, running down the road, blowing wads of prairie grass in all directions.

Them oxen was all through sulking. The drivers, who was good enough runners, caught up with their teams and started walking alongside, guiding them with their goad sticks. Father just stood there in the road laughing because he'd broke the strike.

Cummings seen he'd met up with a good man. He come over, thumped Father on the back and offered him fifty dollars cash and his board and a free ride to the Black Hills if he'd just be along to take charge if them oxen ever laid down again.

Now Father had been sort of dickering around, quiet-like, ever since he'd heard that the Black Hills was throwed open to prospectors. He knowed he couldn't pull up stakes and move us up there, in Indian territory. But no man can set comfortable by the fire when there's gold in the hills only five hundred mile from his door. It cost money for an outfit, and it was quite a piece to walk. The first stage that went into the Hills from Yankton, in March of '76, had charged twenty-five dollars for riding one way. The board and lodging along the way brung that up another ten dollars. Freight run so high, shipping it by the stage, that folks riding in couldn't take regular outfits or enough grub to carry them through no time. And that was figgering from Yankton far to the north of us and considerable closer to the diggings. Taylor Brothers at Yankton had got out a hundred-page guide book that sold for fifty cents and it had two maps of the gold mines, and pictures, and everything a body would ever want to know about how to get there and what to take. Father got hold of one of them books, but when he tried to read to Mama about how "there was a fortune in gold nuggets waiting for every man brave enough to go after it," she just went right on talking about how we was all going to work hard and pay off what we owed on them cows.

Since Father was planning on getting in there sooner or later anyhow, he figgered he couldn't afford to turn down Cummings' offer. Them oxen was moving ahead every minute. He had to decide quick. So he had Uncle Boone turn his wagon around and him and Cummings got in and rode to where them oxen was still making double time, heading for Dakota Territory. Cummings give him a piece of paper to write the note to Mama, and Father reached in the back of the wagon and got his rifle. That's how it was that Father took off for the Black Hills without no outfit, or extra clothes, or saying good-bye, or nothing. Uncle Boone said that when they was driving off, Father leaned out of the covered wagon that him and Cummings had clumb into, and yelled, "Take good care of my folks, and the homestead, Boone, until I get home again." That was the last anybody in our family seen or heard of Father all that summer.

Before Father got back, Mama was doing considerable complaining about how hard it was for her to be on her feet such long hours. Us children was worried about it, because up until then Mama had been a great hand to keep still and just make the best of things. Soon as Father got back from the Hills, he seen that things was too much for her, so him and Stevens talked it over. Winter was coming on. The cows would soon be dry. The only thing for us to do was to move back to the homestead. Them Sioux would soon be snowed in theirselves, and they'd never been knowed to do much damage during the bad weather.

Mama was sure proud to think that the cows was paid for and that we had a little money ahead. Father hadn't done so well locating a claim up in the Black Hills. Them fellows pouring in from Cheyenne, Bismarck, Yankton, and Colorado had staked all the good claims ahead of him. Seemed like no matter how hard we tried, we was never first. But he'd seen the Hills and had worked for a fellow for awhile who had a claim on Spring Creek, and was running six sluice boxes, and taking out between sixty and seventy dollars a day in fine gold flakes. Only the fellow who owned the claim hadn't found no real nuggets, and by the time he paid four men to pick and shovel, and another one for forking, and another one in the tailrace, the fellow owning the claim wasn't taking out no real money at all. So as soon as Father got a grubstake, he'd quit working for him and went up prospecting on Nigger Gulch, but all the claims that showed pay dirt was already staked. Deadwood Creek was the best, right where it joined Whitewood Creek down in a deep canyon on the north edge of the Hills. But when Father got there in June of 1876, more than a thousand miners had snuck in past the guards and was living along them steep banks, most any way they could. The ones that had struck it rich was staying in Wagoner's Hotel that was made of up and down boards and a bunch of tents throwed together. But a night's lodging there cost a pennyweight in gold, and meals and everything else come high. Many a miner was sleeping in a wickiup made of poles and boughs with dirt throwed over top, because he was so busy digging he didn't have no time to cut the logs or think of building a roof over his head. Before the end of March of 1876 every foot of ground in Deadwood and Whitewood gulches was staked. Father said the gulch was alive with folks, some living off the mines, and the others living off the miners.

He'd been up there all summer and covered most of them Black Hills. He said he'd never seen such beautiful country nowhere but the mining wasn't near all it was cracked up to be. Some fellows had struck it rich; they was the ones the newspapers wrote the stories about. But a lot of fellows was working terrible hard on claims where they wasn't even making their salt. But he'd seen flour selling for sixty dollars a hundred. He figgered the thing for us to do was sell the cows and take the money and buy flour for two dollars and fifty cents a hundred in Grand Island. He could haul a wagonload of flour to Deadwood, and even selling it for ten dollars a sack, he'd be lots farther ahead than he would be sapping cows.

But Mama didn't favor selling them cows at all. There wasn't no point in arguing with her about it right then. He wouldn't be able to make the trip anyhow until spring, and by then the cows would be fresh again and they'd bring more money.

Father rode home on a little Indian pony. He'd traded his gun to a squaw man for it. The Cummings party had left in such a hurry that he didn't have no real chance to check up on their plans. They never come out by way of Grand Island. That wagon train broke up soon as it reached the Hills. The oxen and wagons was sold and used by freighters hauling between Cheyenne and the Black Hills. Them fellows paid Father the fifty dollars all right, but food was so dear he'd spent that and all the money he'd made working on Spring Creek while he was prospecting. When winter started coming on, he'd traded his gun to the squaw man for the Indian pony because he couldn't figger out no other way to get home, except, walking.

We hadn't been back at our place very long until Mama took sick in the night. Father got out of bed, stirred up the fire, filled our kettles with water and set them on the stove. Then he sent Sadie and Myra and me over to get Aunt Sadie, and he said for us to stay with Uncle Boone for the rest of the night. By that time Julia had gone to Grand Island to work for her board and room and go to school. Nobody was over at our place but Father and Mama and Aunt Sadie. Next morning Uncle Boone and me went over to do the chores. Father come out and said he didn't want me in the house until Mama got through having the baby.

I never heard how it happened. We had a brother Charley, all right. He breathed a little while and then he quit. I just tiptoed in and seen him alive once, lying there on the bed alongside of Mama. Right then he looked more alive than she did.

But next morning when I went back from Uncle Boone's house, where we'd stayed again that night, Father was planing boards and making a coffin. Mama'd had Aunt Sadie get into the little box of things she'd brung all the way from Pennsylvania. Aunt Sadie was cutting up the skirt to Mama's wedding dress to line the coffin. Next day we was all real quiet when we followed Father out for the burying. He'd picked the place and dug the grave ahead of time, but it didn't seem like much of a funeral because Mama couldn't come. She watched from the window. Us children and Uncle Boone's family was all slicked up for it. It was too late for most wild flowers but the girls had picked what they could find. Father carried the coffin across the field in his arms. After we got there, Aunt Sadie read a piece from the Bible, and we all said the Lord's prayer together. Charley was buried in the southeast corner of our homestead, where he wouldn't seem too far away, and still he'd be out of the way for the plowing.

No, I never knowed what went wrong with Charley, and I don't think Mama did, neither. Because after that she sent for a new doctor book, and from then on she studied them kind of books harder than ever. And when a woman needed her, no matter how far away she lived, or who she was, Mama went and took care of her while she was having her baby. If they didn't have no money, she went just the same. When times got better and a few folks could pay her, she kept her nursing money separate, in a green glass Mason jar, that had raised letters on it, saying patented November 30, 1868. Mama had real good luck with them jars. We'd shipped them from Pennsylvania to Virginia, and from there to Grand Island, before we'd hauled them out to Arcadia in the wagon. But the one she kept the money in had a little nick at the top, so it wouldn't seal. It held other stuff just as good as ever, and when Mama had enough money in it from her nursing, her and Father bought a handsome tombstone, with Charley wrote on the front of it.

For awhile, after Charley died, Mama didn't seem to be thinking much about what we'd do next. But Father was considerable worried. He said we'd never get ahead if we didn't sell our cows and invest the money in something that would show a profit. By then we'd had the cows two summers, and they was paid for. But we wasn't making no money off of them. Why, we couldn't no more than hold our own, even if we didn't figger in our time. All of us had worked terrible hard the first summer we had them cows, and after we'd sold the butter for ten cents a pound, we hadn't made enough to feed ourselves and still pay for new clothes to take the place of the ones we'd wore out while we was milking the cows. Working in that cheese factory hadn't been no answer. Anyhow, Mama was the only one who knowed how to make cheese, and Father said he wouldn't let her tackle it again. We sort of figgered that her doing that heavy work and lifting might of been what had made Charley die. Besides, we couldn't prove up on our homestead if we lived fifty mile away. That loft where we'd stayed wasn't much of a home; why it got hotter than a burnt boot up there in midsummer.

We only owned twelve cows, but poor Stevens owned twenty-five head. When he didn't have no place to sell the milk or nothing to do with it, he was twice as bad off as we was. The reason he put in the cheese factory was that them cows had wore him to a frazzle.

One night, before we went down there to help, he was so beat he leaned up agin a cow's flank and went to sleep, setting there on the stool, milking her. Now Stevens was a real big man, and after a couple of hours of holding him up, the cow got tired and moved over. Stevens was throwed off balance and took a header right in the gutter. He was a terrible sight when he come to the house to get washed off. While he was getting hisself into that mess in the barn, Mrs. Stevens was so wore out trying to keep ahead of all the milk that he'd brung to the house that he found her sound asleep, setting there beside the churn. She hadn't even missed him.

No matter how hard we worked, us homesteaders wasn't making it, and when folks heard that the Black Hills was open to prospectors, they figgered it was a godsend. We'd raised three crops for the grasshoppers by then, and the men decided mining wasn't near as risky as farming. The railroads had quit building branch lines and had laid off their extra hands during the Panic of '73, and they hadn't started up again. Most of the men left their women and children alone on the land whenever they had a chance to make a dollar or two, but after Fort Hartsuff was finished and the soldiers moved in, there wasn't no work around close. Excepting for doing a little trapping winters, us homesteaders didn't have no way of earning an extra dime.

Because he went into the Black Hills with the Cummings train in '76, Father knowed that a lot of them poor devils was going to get fooled on the mining, too. He'd studied it all out. Them fellows, who'd gone in on foot or rode in on horseback or by stage, was bound to be out of grub come spring. He could really cash in if he got a wagonload of flour to Deadwood. We talked it over and seen that there wasn't nothing to do but sell them cows, all excepting one that we'd keep for ourselves. So Father started hunting for a buyer and planning his outfit. He'd be heading for the Black Hills soon as the weather broke and he got a crop in. He knowed I was hankering to go along, but he didn't promise nothing, right then.

Mama hadn't no more than got back on her feet again after having Charley, when Mitch Mason come to the door saying they needed help bad. Mitch and his wife had settled on a homestead a piece from us. They was all right but they'd had tough sledding and she was real young, besides. Folks around used to talk behind their backs about how they done things. Just like one of them fellows, riding through to the Black Hills, told about how he'd stopped at their house to buy some bread. Mrs. Mason didn't have none baked, but she did have several loaves of dough raised and ready for the oven. She brung one to the door, and stood there, holding the dough out to this fellow setting there on his horse, and says, "Do you want it like this, or would you rather wait until it's baked?"

It was just bare daylight when Mitch come to get Mama. He said their little girl had been having the croup all night and was getting so bad she couldn't catch her breath. Mama dressed and they hurried right over, but the baby only lived for a little while after she got there. It had diphtheria.

Mama sent Mitch back to get some sulphur to burn so she could fumigate, and to take a letter to Father, while she stayed with Mrs. Mason to lay the baby out and to help with the cleaning and scouring. After Father read the letter, he went right to work making another litte box just a mite bigger than Charley's. I went over to get Aunt Sadie. She come back with me and cut up the rest of Mama's wedding skirt to line it. After Mitch got back from taking Mama the sulphur, he said him and his wife had talked it over, and they'd like to bury their baby right at the edge of our hayfield, alongside of Charley.

Father says, "Come right ahead, Mitch. We've got lots of room here."

Mitch wasn't no hand with carpenter's tools, so he pitched in and dug the grave while Father finished making the coffin. Soon as Aunt Sadie put the lining in, the two men drove over to get the baby. Uncle Boone rode around to gather up as many of the neighbors as he could get together in a hurry, while Aunt Sadie washed and combed us children before the company got there.

After awhile we seen the wagon coming. Father was driving and Mitch set on the front seat beside him. Mrs. Mason and Mama was setting on the back seat holding the coffin across their knees. The folks had hurried things along as fast as they could on account of the baby having diphtheria and the weather turning warm, and all. We sure give her a nice funeral. Mama and Aunt Sadie stood across on one side and spelled each other with the talking and the praying, while the rest of us all lined up with the Masons. But I got goose pimples right after they was through with the praying and Father was shoveling in the last of the dirt and tamping it down. Yes, sir, I felt mighty queer when Mitch Mason stepped right across the grave and hit Father a big whack between the shoulders, while he was still bent over, and says, "By God, Hawthorne, I hope I can do the same for you some day."

Spring come on fast in '77. Julia was far closer to Mama than most blood kin ever get, and having her come home from school for the summer, and the sun shining, and the green things popping out of the ground, put new life in Mama again. It sure was good to have her bustling around, talking, and laughing, and saying we had the best farm land in the West. Before the snow melted, she had seeds coming up in boxes and tin cans that was setting on the window ledges inside our house. As soon as the sun had warmed the ground, the whole bunch of us was working outside from daylight 'til dark, getting the plants and the garden in. Father and me planted corn and plowed the firebreaks, but Mama was the one with the green thumb. Nights, neighbors was dropping in, so the men could ask Father about what to take to the Black Hills. He was giving advice, free and easy. I was working just as hard as I knowed how because I'd heard him say that he figgered on taking two outfits in, and I knowed blamed well he'd hate to be putting out anything to pay an extra driver.

When he sold the cows, Father got considerable money, along with two wagons and a yoke of oxen. When the man come to drive the cows away, they took them Texas Longhorn steers along, too. But I always figgered Father more or less give them away to get them off the place. A fellow named Parl Rounds, from over around Loup City, seen there was lots easier ways of making a living than by farming, so he set up business as a cattle buyer right there in his light-wheeled buggy, and he done his bookkeeping inside his hatband. Parl was the only fellow around with time enough to drive all over and find out who could buy and who had to sell. He never lost no money that any of us heard of. At first he started out buying cattle, but it wasn't long before he had money to loan on mortgages, then, after Uncle Boone proved up on his homestead, he got his place and laid out the town site of Arcadia. But when we was selling our cows, none of us was more than halfway proved up on our homesteads. We had them cows to sell, but we wasn't near ready yet to afford a mortgage.

Uncle Boone didn't have quite enough logs hauled to finish his house, so him and Father made one more trip to the Cedar Canyons for logs, and they took me along with them. We knowed it would make Father a mite late getting started to the Hills, but Uncle Boone had been taking care of our place and Aunt Sadie had looked after the post office when Julia went down to be with Mama at the cheese factory, so Father said it was only right that we should pitch in and help get their logs. The day we left for the Canyons, Aunt Sadie's mother, who was a real old lady, come out to the wagon, and asked me if I'd bring back a little cedar tree to plant by her grave. She wasn't used to the prairie and she wanted an evergreen to droop over her grave when she was gone. She knowed I'd be glad to, and when I come back I brung quite a bunch of them little cedar trees, and old Mrs. Coulter and me planted them along close to where Charley and the Mason baby was buried. Then she picked out the spot that she liked best and asked Father to save it for her. After we planted them little cedar trees in by them first two graves, everyone around Arcadia just took for granted that the corner of our homestead was their cemetery, too.

Because I'd done so good with my driving on that trip to the Canyons, Father told Mama that he needed me to drive our team of horses to the Black Hills while he drove the ox team. Golly, was I glad when I seen she wasn't going to throw a monkey wrench into our plans. Uncle Boone lived on the next homestead. Jim Mapes promised to keep an eye on us. Mama and Julia together was looking out for things, and Father knowed he didn't have nothing to worry about at home.

After the Black Hills was throwed open, we'd see wagon trains going by our place every day or two, heading that way. Lots of times men layed over, down at the spring, until more folks come so they could travel in a bigger party through the Sioux territory that laid on ahead.

Emigrants and miners wagon trains don't look nothing alike. You can tell an emigrant wagon train from as far as you can see it, and I was blamed glad that I was going to be traveling with a bunch of miners who'd just have their camp outfits, and grub, and mining supplies along, and that we wasn't going to be slowed down by a bunch of women and children. Why, lots of emigrant wagons even had a big cook stove setting right up in the center, with a stovepipe sticking out through the canvas top. On one side they'd tie a plow; on the other side, a bunch of chickens in a coop, or maybe a beehive. They most always had a cow following in back. It seemed like every emigrant family thought of something different to take along, and that was all right for folks going out to homestead, but Father and me was men going into a man's country.

That's why I told Sadie, and Belle, and Clyde and Sam, who was the cousins nearest my age, that I was going into Grand Island with Father and for them to be keeping a real close watch out for me when I come back through Arcadia with a load of provisions. I made it mighty plain that I'd be hauling supplies into Deadwood, the roughest toughest mining camp in the whole West.

When we got in to Grand Island, Father and me slept in the hay at the livery stable with the rest of the men who didn't have no women-folks along. Next morning we went up town to dicker for the flour and other provisions he figgered on buying. Somebody had upped the price of flour on us. Father went all around and then he come back to where we started from at Koenig and Weebe's Steam Flour Mill. They ground and sacked that flour right there in Grand Island and they give him as special a price as they could, but he could haul all the flour we had money enough to buy in one of our wagons. So, he sent me back to feed the teams while he went out to find some freight to haul to the Black Hills in the wagon I was going to drive.

When Father come back he'd agreed for a price to take a German woman and her outfit up to the Black Hills where her husband was mining. I told him women wasn't going in there like that. He said she was ready to pay good for the trip, and it was up to me to do all I could for her, and to treat her just as I would my own mother. Father crawled in and went right to sleep, but I laid there and wondered about what all them folks in Arcadia would think seeing me drive through with her after I said I was going to be traveling with the miners. And I knowed blamed well what Clyde and Sam would be saying.

Next morning, Father and me loaded the old lady and her outfit, and it turned out to be a danged sight worse than I ever figgered it could be. She hadn't left nothing at home. We even had a cow tied on the back of the wagon. I milked her night and morning. What milk we didn't use was poured into a barrel that hung down under the wagon bed. That barrel swung back and forth churning the milk into butter before night and giving us buttermilk to drink besides.

That old German woman was nice, and we set on the wagon seat together all the way from Grand Island to Harney, clean up in the Black Hills. Her and me got along fine together for better than four hundred mile. But, golly, I hated to drive into Arcadia with her and her outfit, and that blamed cow hitched onto our wagon. We stopped there overnight to make up the wagon train, and pick up the bread and other provisions Mama had made for us.

No, I heard it, but I never bothered to remember that old lady's name. I just said "Hey" or "You" or nothing. But you haven't got no idea how embarrassing it was for me when we'd have to stop and fall out of line. On account of the Indians, her and me was put in the middle of the train. The other drivers would sort of grin and wink at me when she wasn't looking their way. She couldn't go far on account of snakes and Indians. Being the only woman travel- ing in a train of one hundred and thirty men, she didn't have no other women to sort of bunch around in a circle with their backs turned and their skirts spread wide. Having that old lady along with me, out there on the prairie, wasn't so easy on neither one of us.

Before we left the spring, all the folks heading in to the Hills had held a meeting to elect a captain. It was all right for people to jog along alone or in little bunches when they was in homestead coun- try, but after they left the spring, they was blamed fools to travel with less than fifty men in a party. Father and me was extra lucky to be going in right when John and Pete McCathern and their two nephews come along with a bunch of wagons. They was heading for Deadwood, taking the first sawmill into the Hills.

The McCatherns was good men, open-faced and outspoken. Their two nephews was driving for them. The youngest one, Link Young, and me got to be real good friends.

Word had come that the Sioux was at it again. Wagons was

camped all over, down around the spring, waiting for a big-enough party to move on ahead. The night we got there, they held a meeting and counted noses. We could muster one hundred and thirty armed men, including me. No, we never counted the old German woman, she was just something extra throwed in. Them fellows, traveling alone, wasn't a bit like homesteaders, who visit back and forth between wagons. Homesteaders, excepting the McKellers, help each other. They need their neighbors when they're putting up a ridgepole, or having a baby, or a burying. But them prospectors was only traveling together because them Sioux had took to the warpath again. Up until then, I watched many a man slipping up the trail, with a pack and gold pan and shovel strapped tight on his back, looking over his shoulder to see no one was following. Them prospectors, heading out with us, was so danged closemouthed that we never knowed most of their names, or nothing about their plans. I've watched some of them fellows reach inside their shirts and pull out a hand-drawn map and study it and then slide it back out of sight again. Nobody told nothing. Nobody asked nothing. We was all traveling alone together. We knowed our train would be breaking up soon as it reached the Hills, because every prospector was looking out for hisself, first.

The McCatherns had the biggest outfit in the train. Pete had done considerable driving and could cut a circle to size better than any man I ever seen. Them men made a good choice when they elected him captain, and agreed to let him lead off and to follow his orders until we reached the Hills. Then Pete stood there by the big camp fire, and he told about the trail that we'd be following out across the sandhills. We'd be striking out for the Niobrara, and then moving on from there to White River, and going into the Hills through Buffalo Gap. We had hills to climb and rivers to ford, and miles of open prairie, and there was Indians out yonder. So Pete talked to us about how we couldn't have no stragglers, and he picked out fellows quick on the draw who'd lived on the prairie, to ride at the ends of the train. Then he told us about how to make camp and post guards.

Yes, sir, I wish you could of seen us making camp our first night out. Pete had sent some men on horseback on ahead, right after noon, to try and locate a likely camping spot with forage and water.

They come back and reported and he sent word down the line that we'd be making camp about four o'clock. That was to give the horses time to graze, and get corralled before dark come on. Buffalo chip fires stink so you never make them no bigger than you have to, so after dark there ain't much light in camp, which is a good thing if you're in Indian country.

When it come close to time, Pete rode on ahead, too. He studied the ground, and then he made a swing back and clumb into the lead wagon agin. When we got to our camping site, Pete begun to draw a circle with his eye. We followed real close together, and he went clean on around. When he was done, we had a circle of covered wagons, close enough so we could unyoke for the night. It ain't like doing arithmetic problems on paper, where you got an eraser and an answer book. We was all watching close, and when we seen that circle we knowed Pete was nobody's fool.

While the rest of us worked in camp, Pete sent some fellows out on horseback to ride herd on the cattle, as soon as they was unhitched. He said this camp was sort of a dress rehearsal, but when we got into Indian country, one of the greatest dangers was that the Indians would stampede our horses and drive them out of there, and that we'd be left afoot. While they was grazing, he had the men in camp take the chains the oxen used to draw the wagons, and we chained the outside back wheel to the outside front wheel of all the wagons in the circle. That was to keep the cattle from breaking out or the Indians from breaking in, or a bad wind from tipping them top-heavy wagons on their sides.

The ox yokes was laid up agin the back wheels, on the inside of the big circle. We dug our rifle pits right back of them neck yokes. They was about three foot deep, and long enough for a man to crouch in while he was loading his rifle. Us fellows driving horses didn't have no ox yokes to use as a breast works, so we dug our rifle pits deeper and laid the horse-collars in front of us.

Pete McCathern come around and says, "Make them pits two foot wide, and not more than eighteen inches from the hind wheel. Get them deep enough so's you've got room to raise up and fire, and then squat fast. Practice crouching on one knee and ducking out of sight while you reload. And be damned sure you don't get no dirt in the muzzle of your gun."

Then it come out that a lot of them fellows was just railroaders throwed out of work by the first big railroad strike this country ever seen. It come in 1877, just when the news of gold in them Black Hills had got noised around good. Fellows who get mad enough to quit their jobs is bound to be ready to head for a greener pasture if they figger there is one over the next hill. But when they started telling Pete where to head in, he says, "You men who won't do what I say get your wagons and make a train of your own. Each man driving with us is going to dig a rifle pit every night. You've got to be ready to cover the flank of the fellow next to you."

They didn't have no choice, but they sure figgered it was blamed silly to be so careful when we was still in homestead country. But Pete went right on calling the turns. Before sundown, he had all the cattle gathered up and drove through a little gap he'd left in the circle of wagons. Then they closed the gap and Pete posted the first shift of guards. Blamed if it didn't turn out that I was glad to have the old German woman along. Why, I was the only man in camp that et a real good supper that I didn't have to cook myself. Of course, I was the only one who had to dig an extra shelter pit back of mine, too.

From then on every day was about the same, only there was more of it. We went up and down over them sandhills. In the little valleys we'd find good forage where the sand had blowed away and the grass growed green. We couldn't see far ahead, and there wasn't nothing much where we was, excepting piles of sand that had been blowed around and sort of settled. Most of the way we followed a clear marked trail. One night, when we made camp, I was setting there barefoot, alongside of a little buffalo chip fire. A couple of lice crawled out of the sand and over my foot. I set there watching them and thinking about the fellow who lost them, and how he'd been setting right there where I was. It was good to know that folks was on ahead.

We left home around the first of June. I remember where we went and what we seen on that trip to the Black Hills. But I ain't sure where we was at any special time, on account of losing track of the days. The ox teams set the pace. Where the roads was good, I could of let them horses I was driving step right along. But a wagon train has got to keep together. Father figgered his ox team was doing good when it made twelve mile a day. Most of the men driving heavy wagons was using two or three yoke. The horses blowed up when we hit them sandhills. None of our outfits was making it through. We was loaded so heavy there wasn't no way out but to double up. After we hit them bad sandhills up toward the Dismal, Pete called a meeting and said we'd have to make two camps and post guards, while we took half the wagons through each day, and then come back the next day for the rest.

One afternoon, when the lead team was stuck in the sand, and the old German woman and me was just setting there, waiting in the wagon, with the sweat pouring over us, a fellow, driving the wagon back of us, come up and says, "This is a hell of a way for a boy to be spending the Fourth of July." Then he pulled out a bottle and says, "Here, take a swig."

I says, "No, sir, I've took the pledge."

He says, "Well, I'll be damned."

Then he went back and I could hear him telling a bunch of fellows standing there about it and they begun to laugh fit to kill. But drinking come so close to us that it wasn't nothing to joke about.

Father was a good man when he was sober. Mama was a proud woman. She done her best to hide what was going on from us children and from the neighbors. But them men from our valley had got to hitting the bottle regular when they was working over at Fort Hartsuff. There at the last, none of them was bringing home money to their families like they should. The work stopped, but the men kept right on going to the fort and hanging around. When Father'd come home from them trips, Mama tried cooking his meals and being pleasant. When that didn't do no good, she tried crying on his shoulder. Then she sort of give up, and for awhile she done some plain nagging. After that, she just kept still.

The night before we left home, the meeting broke up soon as Pete McCathern got done talking to the drivers. I went back to the house alone because Father was staying down to help the boys celebrate. We was pulling out for the Black Hills, come daylight.

It was bright moonlight. When I got close to the house I could see Mama, plain as if it was day. She was prettied up, standing there, waiting. She had on her grey dress with the real full skirt and the big, round, handmade shawl, the same color as her dress. She'd folded it double, so that the little pink scallops hung down all around the edge. Her hair was parted in the middle and drawed back into sort of a bundle at the back of her neck. Her chin was up and she was wet-eyed. I'd seen Mama look like that before when she'd got up from her knees after she'd tucked us children in and heard us say our prayers.

Then I seen that while she'd been waiting for Father and me she'd been studying that load of flour that was all we had left from that big herd of cows. I knowed she was thinking of the summer spent making butter, and of the time we was down at Stevens' making cheese, and, most of all, of Charley.

But she never said nothing then about Father or the load of flour. She just nodded her head when I said I'd done my best to get him to come, but that he said he'd be along after awhile. I ain't never forgot the way Mama looked that night, or how she took hold of my arm, sort of like she was leaning on me. We walked away from the house, until we stood where we could look out across the valley. Off to the right was that big camp, and all them wagons waiting. Come morning I was pulling out, and she knowed I'd left the nest.

Any boy growing up on a farm knows about blood lines, and how you've got to watch your cattle to see that you keep a clean strain or you'll end up with a bunch of grade cows. If bulls are allowed to run wild, you won't have a thoroughbred in the pasture. The things Mama said to me that night about women, and how there was good women and them women, made sense to me. Mama knowed a lot about women, first hand. She'd nursed women who'd been working at the only business they knowed because they needed her when their babies was being born. She seen how hard it was on them not having a man to stand by, and not even knowing who done the fathering. She said I was dead set on seeing the world, and she didn't have no quarrel with me doing that, but she didn't want me leaving no unpaid debts along my trail. It ain't as easy to start fires and then try to put them out, as it is to shut the damper before the fire gets out of the stove and into the woodpile. Some day, she figgered, I'd meet someone; then was when I'd be wanting a clean mind in a clean body.

When we was starting back to the house, she said I'd never make that girl happy, when I found her, if I let drink get the upper hand and come between us. She said drinking men had a harder time controlling theirselves, and that after awhile they give it first place in their lives. And she put her hand on my shoulder and she talked real straight, for the first time, about Father, and what was happening to us and to her because he wasn't bringing his money home, no more, like he should. She told me about the Apostle Paul and what he'd said about the place of women. But she'd looked into it and she figgered the laws of Nebraska was even harder on women than the teachings of Paul. No matter how hard a woman tried she couldn't hope to rise above her husband. It wasn't just our home or our valley, neither. I've knowed of many a country school where the only children walking through the door in shoes was the ones belonging to the saloon keeper. Mama'd been through enough, first hand, to know what she was talking about. She said if I ever got any money to hold onto it, so I could have a real home some day. Yes, sir, that night before we went back to the house, I took the pledge. No one heard me but Mama. She knowed what it meant when I give her my word that night. So did I. I was almost twelve year old. Come daylight, I'd be leaving home, a growed man.

I didn't have no way of telling when August third come, so I've never knowed where I was or what I was doing on my twelfth birthday. We had more sky on that trip than I ever seen in all my life. Them sandhills can be blamed pretty, night and morning, with dryland gulls flying overhead. But when the sun was straight above, it was so hot that the dry-land turtles pulled in their necks and hid under their shells. I used to look at them and wish that I had something heavier than a canvas wagontop covering me, too.

Before I left home, Mama had give me a real good waterjug, with wicker around it, for my birthday present. I had fastened it to the end of a long pole, figgering I could get a drink of cold water whenever I come to a deep pool. I tied a string to the mouth of the jug. Then after I'd punch it down to the bottom of a pool, I'd pull on the string to turn the neck of the jug up and let the air bubbles out. The bottle would fill with cold water that laid down on the bottom. No, I never used that rigging many times. We never come to very many places where the water was deep enough so that the sun hadn't het it through.

The Niobrara was about the nicest river we come to. The water was real deep in places. Father said that was the first time he'd really got his whistler wet since we'd left home. We was so hot that day some of the men waded right in with their clothes on. The water wasn't deep enough to come into the wagon bed, and we had good rock footing at the ford. All them streams in Nebraska was all right to ford if a man used his head and kept out of the quicksand. The buffalo and Indians had left a clear trail to follow. They made our roads by picking the best places. The smart engineers, going through the mountains out West, knowed enough to follow in their tracks.

Not long after we forded the Niobrara, we found we was in Dakota Territory. The night after we was camped on Wounded Knee Creek, a government scout come slipping in with a warning. The Indians was on the warpath. We was in country that had been give to them Sioux under the treaty, and some of them didn't understand that we'd took it back. He said not to let a man, red or white, into our camp for no reason on earth. Many a squaw man had throwed in with the Indians and was scouting for them because they figgered we'd broke our promise about staying out of them Black Hills. This old scout had got word that the Indians was following our train, and they would have attacked us before, but they figgered the boiler we was hauling in for the McCathern sawmill was a big gun, and they was afraid of us. They knowed about cannons because General Nelson A. Miles had turned them on the Sioux in Montana the summer before. Them Sioux Indians was so mad about what was going on in them Black Hills that they was buzzing around like a bunch of bees that had lost their hive. The old scout figgered we'd make it all right, if they didn't find out that our big cannon was nothing but the boiler to a sawmill.

That night Pete McCathern posted double sets of guards, and says, "Men, from now on, shoot anyone coming within gunshot of our wagons. We can't take no chances with strangers."

Then the guards seen some Sioux slipping along through the grass. The fellows riding herd on the cattle drove them into the corral way before sundown. We never knowed whether them Indians was aiming to stampede the cattle then or attack at sunrise. Pete never had no trouble that night getting them fellows inside the circle to dig their rifle-pits deep enough so they could crouch down out of sight.

We never heard no more complaining from the ones who'd figgered that Pete's sawmill was slowing us down, neither.

None of us slept that night. I dug sort of a trough in back of me, so that the old German woman could lay in it, wrapped in her blankets. She was almost as afraid of having the cattle step on her as she was of having the Indians attack. We figgered they'd strike, just as day was breaking, but nothing happened. We broke camp early as we could, and all the men stood guard while the cattle grazed a little, close by. Fresh tracks showed on the road ahead.

We was climbing up, heading for Pine Ridge. The going was steep, and slowed us down. On ahead we could see real black-looking pine trees. Father said they wasn't near as big as the ones we'd see when we got to the Hills. But we knowed that before we stopped to make camp that night we'd be getting into the Pine Ridge country. Next day, about noon, we reached the top of Pine Ridge. Off to the west, across miles of sandhills, I seen a dark streak agin the sky. I remembered the oldtimers who'd set by our fire back home at Arcadia. Them old fellows was the ones who had told me about white men slipping across that last long stretch of sandhills, and into the Black Hills. Nobody ever knowed what they'd found. They never come out again.

On ahead, we seen them Black Hills, standing tall above the sandhills. They pointed right up at the sky. They stood better than a mile above sea level. Them hills run in a big, long strip, fifty mile wide and better than a hundred mile long. We had a long ways to go yet before we crossed over to Buffalo Gap, down on the southeast corner, but we was going in through that Gap, come hell or high water, and we was going clean through to Deadwood, on the northwest edge, where there wasn't nothing but badlands on beyond. We could see them hills. Nobody knowed what we'd be finding there.

Then, in close, and off to the right, I seen my first two Indians. They was on horses, setting out on a hill, where they showed real plain agin the sky. They was just setting there, studying us. They didn't try to hide. We knowed they was following and watching. From then on we done considerable watching ourselves.

Early afternoon, the next day, we come to a big wagon train, stopped right in the middle of the trail, ahead of us. We couldn't figger out why they'd be stopped that time of day until a couple of their men come riding back to tell us. They'd been driving along when they seen something dark lying in the road. White things was all around it. At first they figgered it was a flock of dry-land gulls. When they got up close, they seen it was a mail carrier, fresh killed by the Indians. He hadn't been scalped yet, and he was still warm. The mail sack had been slit open, and mail was scattered all over him and the ground. Them fellows must of come up right when them Indians was finishing their job.

The men ahead had looked around so much they'd beat out any tracks. But a blind man could of figgered out how it happened. The mail carrier was riding past one of them little coyotes. That's what we called a place where a cloudburst had washed the dirt down through and left a deep hollow, in close to the trail. Them Indians, laying in there, must of picked him off real easy with a close shot. His horse was gone, so one of the men give an old horse blanket to wrap him in. The men was digging a grave alongside the road when we got there. Soon as it was deep enough, they put him in and covered it over. A long-faced fellow who was real religious said a short prayer. Soon as we had him buried, we got out of there fast.

No, I never knowed his name. After that, for awhile, I'd hear folks setting around after dark say, "Yep, them Indians picked off one of Dake's mail carriers, near Pine Ridge." Them days, we never thought much about names. We just kept track of folks by what they done or by what was done to them.

The night we made camp on White River the water was the color of milk from the chalk that kept crumbling off and dropping in. Off to our right was Devil's Butte, where sand crystals flashed in the sunshine. But the old prospectors claimed that many a man had turned back and give up making that climb. Rattlesnakes close-guarded every trail to Devil's Butte.

But we had our worst trouble on the whole trip at a place called Squaw Ranch. It was run by a Frenchman who had married a squaw. Father had told me about him and how he was the fellow who'd traded the pony for Father's gun when he didn't have no way of getting back to Arcadia except to walk. Of course, by that time Father didn't have the pony. He'd give it to Uncle Boone for taking care of our place while he was in the Hills the summer before.

No, sir, we didn't have no idea until we got to Squaw Ranch that

Father was a wanted man, and that the vigilantes had posted a reward for anyone bringing him in, dead or alive. Pete McCathern just chanced to hear about it when he was over talking to the Frenchman. Pete clammed right up after he picked up all the dirt he could without being too nosey about it. He come back and got Father and me out of bed and took us over to his wagon. He had Father get down out of sight, under some blankets. And he piled boxes and stuff around, so he was hid. Then Pete and me set there talking back and forth to Father, trying to figger out what to do next.

Now the story the Frenchman told was that Father had traded the gun to an Indian for his pony. Father knowed blamed well he hadn't. He'd traded the gun to the Frenchman for the pony. But he was a squaw man, and he'd traded his wife's brother's pony to Father for the gun. After he'd done it, the only way the squaw man could square hisself with his Indian-in-laws, was to say he'd just been acting as a sort of agent, but that Father had made the trade with the Indians. Them days, a man could get away with murder a lot easier than he could with selling guns to them Sioux. So, the vigilantes had posted a reward; they had a rope and was ready to use it. The squaw man was the only one around there who could identify Father and clear him. But it begun to look like he was figgering on identifying Father to collect the reward.

Pete said there wasn't nothing for Father to do but get out of camp before daylight. Father thought so too, until he remembered about them Sioux and the mail carrier. Father didn't have no horse to ride, but Pete said he'd loan him his horse until we got far enough away so's it would be safe for Father to join the train again. After that, I drove the ox team and the old German woman drove the horses.

While we was setting there, studying things out, I heard Pete say, "God, Hawthorne. Stay out of sight. Here they come."

He motioned for me to go away so the fellows riding into camp wouldn't see us together. When Pete went out front and leaned agin the wagon wheel, he looked the camp over, just like he didn't have a thing on his mind but picking his teeth.

The squaw man was there all right, and so was a bunch of Indians as well as some of our own train. We was traveling with a rough bunch. I figgered some of them fellows would have turned in their own mothers if they was offered a big enough reward. First they went over to Father's wagon and looked all around. But all they seen was a load of flour and a little bundle of food and bedding he kept up in front beside him. Father didn't have no place to hide in his wagon. Then they come over to our wagon and some of them went right inside and poked around in the old German woman's stuff, and made her mad as a hornet. They come out and started questioning me.

One of our own men asked me where Father was. I looked him right in the eye, and says, "Shall I tell him you're the one looking for him?"

He sort of drawed in his horns and swallowed on that one. Then he says, "No." Father kept in practise. He was knowed to be quick on the draw. The squaw man started asking me questions, but I didn't know nothing about nothing.

When some of the men in our wagon train begun putting in their two-bits worth, Pete walked over with his hand on his hip, sort of fingering the grips on his revolver, and he says, "I'm the captain of this train. We don't have the man you are looking for in camp. No one here has traded a gun to the Indians for a pony. Goodnight." Then he turned to our own men and says, "You fellows had better turn in for the night."

Soon as the camp was quiet, I snuck back to Pete's wagon with a bundle of food for Father. We never knowed the straight of it, except that them fellows was figgering on turning Father in for a reward.

After that, Father was on his own, out in them sandhills. He had to keep out of sight from us, and he had to be on the lookout for them Sioux. The second night he snuck back into camp and slept under Pete's wagon. He told us he's seen some elk that he'd thought was Indians, until they turned and run. Before daylight he was out of there and back in them sandhills again.

The night we camped on Cheyenne River, a runner come in, dead beat. He was calling for help for the stage ranch at Buffalo Gap. The Sioux had moved in from both sides, the folks living there was under seige. Father seen the runner coming into camp. He knowed from the way he was riding that there was trouble on ahead, so he come into camp to see what was up. By then we was all so scared nobody paid no attention to him. I got my gun, figgering on helping save the stage ranch, but Pete says, "Mont, you stay in camp. You've got a woman to look out for."

It was late afternoon before the men got back. They said the Indians had pulled out when they seen them coming. It was so late we stayed in camp the rest of the day. After dark, Pete called a meeting of all the men that wasn't on guard. He told them Father's side of the gun deal, and said he'd settle it personal with anyone turning him in for the reward. We figgered he was out of danger anyhow.

Pete said, "If we make a long day of it, we'll be in Buffalo Gap by next sundown. From there we have better than a hundred mile to go through them hills. Likely we'll run into some of the robbers who've been holding up stages and wagons between here and Deadwood."

The men going to Custer figgered they'd go in a party along the trail when it turned off down past the Gordon stockade. The rest of us voted to stay together until we reached Deadwood. A bunch of the fellows never done no voting or talking. They just set there, glassy-eyed with the gold madness. I'd been watching them close as we neared the Hills. A few of them had teamed up with partners. They snuck off in pairs to study a map that they'd hide in their shirts if they seen anyone looking their way. Other fellows wasn't talking to nobody.

All the next day we watched them Black Hills grow bigger, and taller, and blacker. Under foot, and off to each side, the sand dunes was covered with buffalo bones and prickly pears. The Indians believed that the Great Spirit, who lived in a cave in the center of the Black Hills, had give them the buffalo to use for food and shelter. He'd put the mineral springs there to cure their diseases. Yep, them Indians figgered we didn't have no business moving in on their Great Spirit, and building Deadwood, the roughest, toughest mining camp of them all.

After our soldiers learned them Indians that they didn't have a chance agin cannons and long-range rifles, they knowed they couldn't kill us all, no matter how hard they tried. Just like with our train, they followed us for better than a hundred mile, waiting and watching to see if they could catch us off guard. Because they figgered that boiler was a cannon, they was scared to attack, and we made it in without losing a man. But we lost so much sleep, I always figgered they should of been sued for mental cruelty. We was plain lucky to still be wearing our own scalps, and we should of knowed it. But as soon as we got close to Buffalo Gap, a lot of them fellows, who'd been scared stiff for days, begun strutting around, chewing and spitting, and talking about how they never was afraid of Indians anyhow. The old German woman poked me in the ribs and laughed when she heard them bragging to strangers hanging around out in front of the saloon. Mostly they was showing off for the blamedest little bunty of a woman I ever seen. She had one glass eye, and a face that would stop a clock and set it back a couple of hours. But she done all right for herself, because them fellows hadn't seen a white woman, excepting the old German, for better than two months, and she didn't have no competition. The settlement at Buffalo Gap was piled high with buffalo bones that they'd ricked up like cordwood to get room enough to throw up a few log cabins, and a stagecoach stop and corral. The Sidney Trail met up with ours right there where the Indians used to wait on each side to shoot the buffalo as they went in and out through the gap.

Them hills was a blamed sight prettier than I ever figgered they could be. We followed the stage road in for better than forty mile. At first there was quite a pull up from Buffalo Gap. Along where the dirt is real red the wheels sink down terrible when it's wet. I always figgered Nebraska growed the biggest hailstones there was, until we went to the Black Hills. On our second day out of Buffalo Gap, the sky to the west of us begun to blacken up. I never seen nothing come on as fast as that hailstorm. Before we could take cover, we was hit. Some of them hailstones was as big as apples. They pelted the oxen and horses, and tore through the canvas covers on some of our wagons. The men riding on horseback was soaked to the skin before they could find a place to tie in under the trees. One man come crawling into our wagon with his face all cut and bleeding from them sharp hailstones. A little deer stumbled in agin a wagon so close that the fellow inside jumped out with his hunting knife and slit her throat. We had fresh camp meat for supper.

I've seen hailstones kill little pigs and chickens in Nebraska, but after it cleared so we could drive on through them hills, where the trees was dripping down and the wheels made sucking sounds down in the mud, dead game birds and rabbits lay all along the road

ahead. The ground was covered with leaves and small twigs that
had been whipped off the trees, and all the grass on both sides of
the road was beat down flat. Then the sun come out, and we begun
to get our heads up and look around. Way above us was them mountains. They was terrible big, and twisted into more shapes than I ever
figgered there could be. But underfoot we drove on hailstones, clean
to the next pony express station at Fairburn. We made camp there
that night.

We was so beat we never done no looking around until morning.
That was when we really seen Harney Peak. They just don't come
much bigger—it's the highest mountain in the United States east
of the Rocky Mountains. All around and spreading out on both
sides of the top was granite cliffs, and ridges growing thick with them
black pine trees, and rock walls filled with mica that flashed like
mirrors when the sun hit them. But blamed if that old German
woman would look at them mountains. She'd got all dressed up in
her last clean Mother Hubbard, and she was wearing a real pretty
black and white checked apron. She'd put crisscrosses of white em-
broidery in each of them black squares. Her hair was combed back
so slick and tight I don't think she could of closed her eyes without
it jerking her mouth open and she's scrubbed her face until it was as
shiny as them steel spectacles she was wearing. All she wanted to do
was break camp and get over to the foot of Harney Peak where her
man was mining at a diggings called Harney too.

But by afternoon we seen we wasn't as near as she had hoped for.
We spent all that day following along the main trail to Rapid City.
That night we camped out along with what was left of the McCathern
train, before Father and me dropped out with our wagons the next
morning. By then we'd lost full half of our men. A big bunch of
fellows had left together, soon after we got into the Hills, heading
due west for Culver City. From then on we begun to lose them fellows who'd got hold of them maps from nobody knowed where.
Many a man, who'd rode along with us all the way from Arcadia,
slipped off alone with his outfit during the night without saying a
good bye to nobody. Pete had told the guards to let them fellows with
the gold fever go whenever they had a mind to. They kept looking
back to see if they was being followed before they slipped off into

the black woods. We never knowed where they went or what they found.

After we turned off from the main trail, it seemed terrible lonesome driving along with the old woman setting beside me, and nobody but Father and a load of flour on up ahead. We was following a clear marked trail and heading straight for the foot of Harney Peak. Sometimes Father and me would stop our wagons to get out and look at rock ledges, and waterfalls, and petrified moss, and pink quartz, and grey slate, and rocks thick-speckled with silver, and white crystals that stood on a little knoll, and looked like real flowers blooming. Even after you see them Hills, you can't believe nothing in the world can be like that. After living in the South, and then out on the plains, and not knowing about trees, excepting them cedars that growed in the canyon, I figgered I'd never want nothing better than just driving along, looking at them rocks and mountains and thick pine trees.

Not long after we crossed Iron Creek, the road took a sharp pitch up. The oxen on ahead had slowed down until they was barely moving at all. The horses begun to puff and blow. When they stopped the old German woman got out and walked. But that didn't lighten the load enough. We went a few feet farther, then we knowed we was through. It was a real hot day and there wasn't no hope of us getting the wagons up that steep hill.

Father told me to stay with the wagons while he walked over the hill to Harney to get a team to come and pull us the rest of the way. The old woman and me stayed in the wagon.

When Father got to Harney he seen that it was just a place where a bunch of prospectors had throwed up log cabins to live while they mined for placer gold on Battle Creek. But all they could get out was just what was in the gravel along the rim.

They knowed the most of the gold was down in the bedrock in the bottom of that stream, but they didn't have no way to get at it. Them miners had a big camp at Harney—it was just two mile below where Keystone stands now—but they was all on foot. There wasn't an ox or a horse in Harney. So, when a bunch of miners stopped working to rest their backs and see what he knowed about things outside, Father says, "I've got a woman down here who wants to come and live in Harney, but I can't get her and her outfit up the hill."

Father said he never in all his life seen a bunch of men act like them fellows. Most of them hadn't been around where a woman was in months. They never waited to ask no questions.

He figgered them boys must of drawed their own conclusions, the way they begun passing the word around and dropping their picks and shovels and gold pans. Better than a hundred of them took out of there on the run, carrying ropes. When they got down to where the old German woman and me was setting under the shelter of the wagon top, some of them like to died laughing. Her and me couldn't figger out what ailed them. Then one of them yells, "Boys, this camp's been needing a mother."

Next thing we knowed them fellows had unhitched our horses and tied their ropes onto the wagon. I got out to take care of the horses. With better than a hundred men pulling on the ropes and shoving, the old woman rode up that steep half-a-mile hill so fast she never had no chance to get out and walk.

Her old man had been whipsawing out some boards on down below. By the time he got word that she was in camp, all the boys knowed her and was calling her Ma. She was real pleased to think they was glad to have a woman come to live in Harney. The boys, who was farm growed, was making as big a fuss over that cow as they was over the old lady.

When Father and me got the team up the hill, we found that they'd unloaded the wagon and carried everything inside the cabin for her. She was making a terrible fuss over that little, bandy-legged old man of hers, and they was spitting out German at each other by the mouthful. On account of having them oxen and that load of flour on down at the foot of the hill, we didn't stay the night. But the old woman wouldn't let us go until she'd fed us good. I never figgered, when I first met up with that old German woman in Grand Island, that I'd feel like I did, when I looked back, just as we was going over the crest of the hill, and I seen her standing in front of her cabin, waving good bye to me.

Down at the foot of the hill, the road branched. Father and me took the turn to the left, because it led straight through to Rapid City. That way we'd be making two legs of a triangle, while Pete McCathern and them other boys was covering the long one that led straight north to Rapid City. That's why Father never tried to sell no flour at Harney. He figgered the thing for us to do was to move right along and catch up with the rest of the boys at Rapid City. Then we'd be traveling together again from there, on through to Deadwood, off in a far corner of the Hills.

That night, we camped on a creek, not far from the bottom of the steep hill that led up to Harney. In all my life I've never had nothing as good to drink as the cold water that come from the little spring that run right into that creek. We broke camp at daylight, and reached Captain Jack's Dry Diggings by noon, that same day.

By the time we got there the big rush had moved farther north. We only seen about five hundred miners. The ones Father and me talked to was just trying to get enough dust ahead to pay their way home, or they was working to make enough to get drunk and forget their troubles until they had to start working the diggings again. A lot of them fellows was Civil War veterans who'd come West to railroad. When the jobs blowed up, they tried homesteading. When the grasshoppers et their crops, they'd took to mining. A bunch of them fellows settled right down to living at Captain Jack's Dry Diggings. They'd built their log houses, and they'd just eat and drink what they could buy out of each day's panning. Later on some of them tried building a flume to bring water in from another creek, but it was too far away and they had too many mountains between. After the store and dancehall burned, and the rest of the folks moved on, a bunch of them fellows stayed right in that little valley; by then they was calling the place Rockerville. The last ones left had to take care of the buryings and carry the bodies up the hill to the cemetery on a little flat place opposite the diggings. I never could figger out why them fellows didn't have gumption enough to pull out too.

Father and me didn't have no choice but to take our flour and drive on early the next morning because ten dollars a sack was the best Captain Jack who run the store offered us. Father figgered the price was down on account of them freighters bringing provisions straight through from Fort Pierre to Rapid City. If we sold a few sacks of flour here and there, it wouldn't pay us to go on to Deadwood. It was bad enough for me to be driving an empty wagon up there. If Father got rid of his load too, we'd never get ahead freighting because we wouldn't have no freight.

We covered fifteen mile before we come to Rapid City. It was laid out on a flat, inside the gap in the hills that led out to Fort Pierre. After Sam Scott, Jim Carney, John Allen, and John Brennen seen they wasn't going to make it mining, they went to work with a pocket compass laying out streets and throwing up buildings. Them four fellows moved so fast that folks coming in through the gap started calling their town Rapid City.

When we got there Rapid City was a year and a half old. Stages, drawed by six horse teams, was running regular from the American House. Most of the them was heading due east to Fort Pierre on the Missouri River. The others drove considerable farther than that, straight south, but they made railroad connections with the Union Pacific at Sidney, Nebraska.

A big posse of mounted men stopped us right at the edge of town. When they seen we was strangers, coming in from the south, they let us go through, and said we'd find Pete camped at the foot of the big hill that had a bunch of scraggly trees growing on the top. The leader of the posse told us there'd been a hanging, and the vigilantes had made a mistake and hung a fourteen-year-old boy because they figgered he was riding a stolen horse. When the Governor of the Dakota Territory got proof that the boy was riding a horse his father had bought and paid for, he'd sent word out that he was offering a reward for the killers. Up until then the vigilantes had been making the laws theirselves, and they didn't see what business the governor had taking a hand in affairs out in the Black Hills.

I asked Father why they stopped us and talked like that. He said he figgered it was to keep us from taking a hand in what was going on in Rapid City.

Soon as we pitched camp, fed and watered our teams, and turned them into the corral, Father and me walked up to the top of Hangman's Hill with Pete. The way he'd got the story, the vigilantes picked up this boy when he was riding along with two fellows that had horses they'd stole from the stagecoach company. They brung them into Rapid City for a trial. The two older fellows confessed, but they stuck to their story that the boy was innocent. The trial went on into the night. Next day some folks claimed that the fellows holding it was doing more drinking than listening.

Come morning, the boy and them two fellows with him was dead, and the fellows that done the hanging wasn't telling nothing about it. Them bodies swung there in full view of the town, until some of the folks got tired of watching them turn when the wind blowed, so they went up the hill and cut the ropes, and dropped their bodies down a steep bank on the side away from town. Then they rolled rocks down on top of them until they was all covered over. I never seen a sign of them three dead men when I looked down over the bank. All that I seen was three cut ropes fastened to the biggest tree that growed on top of the hill. But when the wind changed and started blowing toward us, the smell coming up from below was something terrible.

Going back down Hangman's Hill, Father and Pete got to talking about that reward. Pete had seen it wrote out in black and white. Governor Pennington, who lived in Yankton, had offered a thousand dollars reward for evidence proving who done it, because he was trying to run the state hisself and figgered on stopping them vigilantes from hanging innocent people. The men in our train wanted to stay over and run down them killers.

All the next week we camped right there, looking and listening. The townsfolks acted like we'd picked a risky business. Mickey McGuire, who run the International Hotel, told Pete he figgered on keeping his own nose clean and out of other folks business. William Gramberg, the grocer, said if he had any clues he'd be keeping them to hisself. Father done his sleuthing down at Pat Murphy's saloon. It cost him considerable money and he never heard a thing worth knowing. I got to talking to one real nice old man, who was setting out on a box in the sunshine with his back up agin the front of the livery barn. I told him how bad I felt about that boy dying so young, and how I wanted to find them fellows because that dead boy was just two year older than me. But all the old man said was that it might be smart for me to try to live a little longer myself.

We never found out who hung them fellows but we found out who they was. The two older men was Red Curry and Doc Allen. They admitted they was horse thieves, so nobody thought no more about them. But the boy was something again. Some folks called him Hall, but his real name was Kid Mansfield, and his father owned a hotel in Austin, Minnesota. They'd come out to the Hills together, but when they found it so crowded there, his old man figgered he'd head for Yellowstone and send the boy back home with the next

Pete and Fennis Freight Team that come through Sturgis. They was a good outfit and had been running mule teams into the Hills regular. Mansfield was in a hurry. After waiting around several days, while they didn't show he met up with them two fellows who was riding to Sidney horseback. He asked if his boy could ride along. When they said yes, he bought a horse and saddle and give him enough money to pay for his food on the way. The fellow who sold him that horse lived at Sturgis, only thirty mile north of Rapid City. He swore that the Kid wasn't no horse thief. But that didn't do much good, after he was dead.

At the end of the week, we give up and moved on, heading for Deadwood. Old man Wright stayed right there and kept hunting around until they sent him to the asylum, to get rid of him.

We camped an extra day at Centennial Prairie, so's the horses could rest. That was the first full day I ever set alongside the trail and watched the stagecoach and the long bull trains go by. It takes a blamed good man to handle them long teams with one of them braided bull whips, loaded with shot to give it weight. One outfit, carrying machinery in for that big mine they was opening up at Leed, was driving ten yoke of oxen. Another fellow come by driving six span of mules with only one line. But the fellow I always figgered was boss of the lot was the one who come through there driving six yoke of Texas longhorn steers. It ain't no wonder that some of them drivers was knowed far and wide for the way they could handle their teams on the road. When they got to a town, some of the other fellows around took care of the stabling and the handling of the freight. But when it come time for a big bull team to pull out of town, folks would stand around waiting and watching. Then you'd see the lead driver come strutting out of a saloon, with his bull whip in his hand, and acting like there wasn't nobody in all the world but him. All the folks listened for the crack of his whip, and then watched his dust, as he headed on down the trail.

I never seen a worse road than the one going into Deadwood. Some fellows was working on a toll road, that went in from Sturgis, but they never got it built until a year after we was there. We all pitched in and helped each other. Father loaded part of the flour in my wagon. But the folks I really felt sorry for was the McCatherns. You ain't got no idea how much weight and bulk there is to a sawmill, going over them rough narrow roads, and falling into deep chuck-holes, and having to pull off to the side to let the bull trains go by, and then getting stuck and having to unload a part of your outfit and haul ahead and then come back for the rest.

Nights we was so tired we'd fall asleep on guard duty. One night I dozed off listening to Father tell about how Preacher Smith had been murdered by the Indians, not far from where I was setting right then. The closer we got to the gulch, the rougher the road got and the more it was traveled. It was every man for hisself on the road to Deadwood. Nobody asked no favors, nobody give none. But as long as I live I won't be forgetting the look on Pete McCathern's face when we stood looking down from the place where we had to lower the wagons two hundred foot to get them on Main Street. Nobody'd ever tried harder than them boys to get a start. They figgered they'd have her made, soon as they got the wagons lowered down over the cliff, and their sawmill set up and turning out lumber in Deadwood.

But all Pete says, after he'd sort of doubled up, like he'd been hit in the belly, was, "Well, so long fellows. We'll be shoving off for the north. I hope they'll be needing a sawmill at Spearfish."

Yes, sir, you could of knocked me over with a feather when I looked down in that canyon and seen there was a sawmill set up and running at each end of Main Street in Deadwood.

A fellow from our train who was laid up with a sprained ankle said he'd guard our wagons while we clumb down the hill to look the place over. You can't shove 25,000 people down into a narrow canyon without them crowding each other and busting out at the seams. Deadwood was ugly and it was rough. We seen many a building with a dressed-up front and tumble-down back. But only the folks with money was going inside them dance halls, and saloons, and gambling houses. Main Street was a mile and a half long, and had seventy-six saloons. The town and the diggings was all in together and sluiceboxes lined both sides of Deadwood and Whitewood Creeks. The fellows taking gold out was doing all right for theirselves, but most of the prospectors we seen walking along the street and camping along the hills looked blamed seedy. I don't know what they was doing about law, but there sure wasn't much order in Deadwood in '77.

Father and me didn't have nothing much on our minds that first day except selling that load of flour. By afternoon more dressed-up folks showed on the street. A bunch of them fancy women come along with big bustles. They was painted and sort of smiling and looking around at folks, big as you please. A couple of plain-dressed women, going along carrying their shopping baskets, was making a point of letting folks see that they wasn't the other kind. I knowed which ones was the gamblers because they was all dressed up and real clean.

While we was walking along, an old fellow stopped us and says, "Say, ain't I seen you in Grand Island?"

Father and him got to talking and his name was Woods. He said he was knowed as old Dad Woods, and that he figgered since he'd come to the Black Hills and blamed near broke his back with a pick that the name fit him better than it done back home. After they swapped news back and forth, Father told him that we was down looking around for a place to stay and trying to figger out how to get our outfit down over the edge of the canyon, so's we could sell our flour.

Dad Woods said he'd hollowed out a little place for hisself in the bank, and hung a canvas in front. It wasn't deep enough to be no real dugout, and he cooked over a campfire out in front. But we was welcome to hole up with him while we was there. He hadn't been getting much mail from outside, it cost fifty cents to send a letter to Deadwood.

That give us our lodging. Then Dad Woods went back with us and offered a lot of free advice from where he set on a stump. On account of his back being almost broke from picking, he never done no work if he could get out of it. So Father and them other fellows from our train, who was figgering on locating at Deadwood, went to work. We got ropes and we lowered them wagons one at a time down that two hundred foot cliff, and I seen why it was that so many fellows, when they looked down into that deep canyon sold their teams and wagons for anything they could get, and clumb down, with nothing but packs on their backs, to go to prospecting. I ain't sure yet whether the ones who went to mining or the ones that took to freighting made the best choice. But from the time Father went in there in '76 and seen fellows fighting to pay sixty dollars a sack for flour, and the time we got in there in '77, with a whole big load of flour to sell, them freighters had sure played hob with the market.

By that time the horses was so poor we left them in a corral at the top of the hill, and paid a fellow for looking out for them. Oxen get along fine on green feed, but when horses is working, they need grain. After we unyoked them oxen and led them around by the trail, and got the outfit hitched up again and headed down the street, we was too beat and dirty to see nobody. So we kept right on going until Dad Woods told us we was below his place. We tied the oxen in agin the cliff so's they'd be as out of the way as they could get. Then Father and me clumb the cliff, to Dad Woods little dugout, and we crawled in without eating no supper and slept the clock around.

Next morning when we went down to the creek to wash, Father got out his comb and give his beard and our heads a careful going over before we went up town to sell our flour. Dad Woods had told us how to find the biggest grocery store in Deadwood. We drove along, trying to keep from running over folks or locking wheels with the other wagons that was hauling along Main Street, until we come to the grocer's and tied our oxen to his hitching post.

We seen thousands of people in Deadwood, but the one that surprised me most was meeting up with old Mam Blacky, face to face, right there in the grocery store. She was setting alongside the gold scales that was in the middle of the counter that run clean along the far wall opposite the door. She'd been putting on weight and had got to be the biggest cat I ever seen. Why she was looking around like she owned the place, and the fellow behind the counter was just working for her. When I run over and picked her up and begun petting her, she acted real friendly, but he didn't.

I told him she was my cat, and that one of them fellows coming into the Hills had stole her. I figgered on taking her home. I'd got her back from Ming Coombs place, so there wasn't no reason why I shouldn't be taking her back again.

But he said she was his cat. A fellow had brung her in there and sold her to him for one hundred dollars. Mam Blacky was the first cat that ever lived in Deadwood. A cat that's a good mouser more than pays her way, and it was plain to see that Mam Blacky hadn't put on all that weight from groceries. Then he reached out, put her back on the counter, and said she was his cat and he wasn't giving her up to nobody.

Father sort of cooled me off while the grocer left us for a minute to make a sale. When he come back he talked real nice to me about how, when he'd come in there the year before, he'd bought a pony for twenty dollars, but that he'd had to pay eighty dollars a ton for hay to feed her. He needed Mam Blacky in his business. She caught her own food and helped him take care of his. I seen she'd never had it so good, except when she was living with Ming Coombs and drinking all the cream off his milk, so I shut right up and listened.

Father says, "I've come to give you first chance on a load of flour."

He says, "Man, I don't want no more flour."

Father says, "You sold a sack of flour here for sixty dollars last year. I was in the crowd, and heard the miners bidding for it."

The grocer says, "That was last year."

Father seen he'd hit a buyer's market. So he says, "All the money we've got in the world is tied up in that load of flour, setting in front of your door. We've got it in here, and lowered it down into this damned hole and can't get it out again. What would you do with it if you was in my place?"

That grocer turned out to be a real nice fellow. If anybody besides me had to have Mam Blacky, I'm glad it was him. He hauled one leg up on the corner of the counter, and he started right in telling Father his troubles. He'd spent a lot of money putting up his store, but he done all right until them fellows who brung in the miners had started in freighting. Every day them freighters was coming in over six main trails, and that wasn't counting the outfits coming in like we had over the sandhills from Grand Island. They'd all heard about flour bringing sixty dollars. After the first few loads of flour come in during the spring of '77, the bottom dropped out of the market. He put all the money he could get together into flour when it hit twenty dollars, because he figgered it would go up agin. But it kept on going down. Then the freighters begun selling flour right off their wagons up at the top of the cliff for whatever the miners would give them. That grocer was long on flour, and he figgered he was just about as stuck as we was. Hundreds of men was walking the streets hungry, but it takes money to buy flour.

By that time Father wasn't doing no talking at all. We was heading back out the door when the grocer called after us, "If I had that load of flour I'd drive five mile down the creek and try to sell it in Lead. If you can't get rid of it there, come back here. I'll take it off your hands for what you paid for it in Grand Island."

Things was really booming in Lead. Mose and Fred Manuel had figgered out a way to get gold out of quartz, and they'd built their own crushing mill. It was called an arrastra, and a bunch of real important mining engineers was there, seeing about putting in the Homestake Mine. When we got there they was putting on some kind of an exhibition. Father and me tied the team where we could keep an eye on our load of flour, and stepped over to listen. A fellow named Heffelman was doing the talking. I think he had something to do with the bank. I kept slipping up closer to hear him tell about how mining was becoming scientific, and that this meant that big business was coming to the Hills. This was the new order, prosperity would come to every man as soon as the stamp mills got built and working. That one small mill had proved that capital and machinery could get gold out of quartz. Blamed if he didn't sound just like that Seven Day Baptist I'd heard in Arcadia, only he had said all the world needed was the second coming of Christ.

Then he took a deep breath and pointed his finger right at me, and says, "Young man, come up here to the platform."

I turned tail to get out of there, but a big, usher-sort-of-a-fellow got me by the shoulders and a couple of other fellows give me a boost, and there I was right up on a kind of a high stand, looking down at all them people.

Then that fellow pointed to a box setting there on a little table alongside of him, and he says, "Sonny, lift that box off the table."

I tried my blamedest, but at first it wouldn't even budge. I kept trying until I got it up about six inches off the table. I jerked my fingers back quick when I dropped it or they'd of been mashed flat.

Then this Mr. Heffelman patted me on the head, and showed all his teeth to the crowd out front, and says, "My boy, you will always be able to say that you came to the Black Hills and you held as much gold in your hands as you could lift."

Then he patted me again and says, "Thank you." Them fellows lifted me down and that's the nearest I ever come to getting any of that gold out of the Black Hills.

Father and me tried the grocery stores in Lead. They was long on flour and short with us. Father didn't have much to say as we walked along beside the oxen, heading back to Deadwood. When we come to a place where there was a little grass, he let the oxen graze, and we stood watching the miners, working at the sluice boxes down along the creek.

At No. 2, below Discovery, we seen a guard, setting with a rifle across his knees, keeping folks away. The miners, owning that claim, had took close to one hundred and fifty thousand dollars out, the first four months it was worked.

Father says, "Mont, I been thinking."

I says, "So have I."

He says, "I ain't going home broke."

I seen how he felt. It was blamed hard to think of all them weeks on the way and the hard work we done hauling that flour better than five hundred mile, just to use it for ballast.

Then he says, "Mont, I want you to start back alone with the team and the wagon. I'll sell the flour here for what I can get and invest the money so's it will turn a quick profit. But you better leave soon. I want you to follow the Sidney Trail. Take the long way home."

EIGHT

THE LONG WAY HOME

Jim Kinney, who'd drove his wagon in with us, hailed Father, when we was heading back with the flour, and says, "So long, Hawthorne. I'm leaving for home in the morning."

Father says, "Jim, can Mont drive back with you?"

"Sure," says he. "A bunch of other fellows are pulling out then. We'll be glad to have him go along."

So Father and me left old Dad Woods setting on a stump, watching to see that nobody got into them sacks of flour, while we split our outfit. I took just what bedding and provisions I'd be needing on the trail. After we clumb the hill to the corral, Father looked my revolver over and checked to see that I had plenty of cattridges. That night I slept alone in the wagon. We wasn't taking no chances having me left behind.

The last thing, before I left Deadwood, I walked over to the store to tell Mam Blacky I was pulling out. It was a lot harder to say goodbye to her than to Father. I figgered I'd be seeing him again.

Come morning, I was the first man ready. Right at daybreak, eleven wagons of us drove out of the corral that was at the top of the cliff above Deadwood. We was heading down the Sidney Trail.

Jim Kinney was a short-tempered, friendly, little Irish fellow. Because Father'd spoke to him about me, he said that I was to follow him all the way. He was driving a team of horses, too.

Some of them fellows had been doing a lot of talking about Indians and road agents. One big-mouthed, blow-hard of a blatherskite pointed to a place in the road, and says, "That's where them road agents slaughtered Slaughter last month." Then he throwed his head back and laughed fit to kill.

Jim Kinney spoke right up and says, "You know damned well them road agents was after Harry Lake who was carrying that fifteen thousand dollars for Stebbin, Wood and Company's Bank at Deadwood. If John Slaughter had attended to his driving, and let them rob his stage, he'd be alive today."

Kinney figgered the road agents would leave us alone. Any robbers looking our bunch over would see we wouldn't pay off for their trouble. The fellows who'd turned road agents in the Hills was after big money. Five of them held up the Fort Pierre stage at the water hole on Cheyenne River. They said they wasn't going to rob nobody with less than three hundred dollars. The driver and passengers clumb out. The road agents felt them all over, counted their money, and searched through their stuff. When they seen that none of them had three hundred dollars, they let them go right on. A fancy woman, riding on that stage, didn't play fair with them fellows. When she was leaving Deadwood, she'd weighed in her dust and got folding money. She twisted it in a tight roll around her head, combed her hair up over it pompadour, and pinned her hat on with long hatpins to hold it solid. Them robbers never found it at all. They searched her, but they was looking in the wrong places.

Me and Kinney figgered we was safe enough anyhow. The Sidney stage hadn't been robbed for over a month, and then not a soul had got killed. We was a lot more worried about Indians than we was robbers. We didn't have no money, but we was all wearing our scalps yet.

At first, going back out, we camped along at about the same places. The night we stayed at Rapid City, we inquired to see if anybody had collected that thousand-dollars reward. They hadn't. From there on to Buffalo Gap, we followed the main road, instead of going around by way of Captain Jack's Dry Diggings and Harney. About half way out of the Hills, we come to French Creek. A bunch of wagons was camped there already, so we pulled off to one side. I'd built my little fire and was setting there on my haunches beside it, cooking supper, when I heard someone yelling for me. I looked up and here come a bunch of fellows with the dangedest looking woman I ever seen. She was real tall and built like a busted bale of hay. She wore men's clothes, and had been chewing tobacco and letting it get away from her.

I felt like crawling into a hole and pulling it in after me, when I heard her say, "Where's the boy who's driving out alone?"

Kinney spoke up and says, "Mont, I want to make you acquainted with Calamity Jane."

I'd heard considerable about Calamity Jane, but she wasn't nothing like I figgered she'd be. She'd had so much to drink she teetered, and pretty near fell on her face in my fire. I felt like a blamed fool—having her put her arm around me—with all them fellows standing around listening to her tell about how I was going to be a great freighter some day. She didn't know me or my plans. The trouble with Calamity Jane was she talked too dang much, and if I hadn't been so surprised about her carrying on like that over me, I'd of told her so.

From Buffalo Gap on, we followed a different road all the way. The Sidney Trail skirted the hills to the west for some distance after we went out through the gap. Then it struck off south and ended at old Fort Sidney. Because it was the rail point nearest the Black Hills, Sidney had got to be quite a place during the gold rush. Better than fifteen hundred people was going in and out of town every day, and considerable more than that had moved in to stay. Lots of folks stopped over in Sidney to blow off steam. One dance ended with three corpses propped agin the wall. So many fellows went to Sidney to raise hell and shoot up the town, that the Union Pacific warned all through passengers to stay on the train so's they wouldn't get picked off by stray bullets.

Father'd made me promise not to give no one a ride while I was driving down the Sidney Trail. He said the horses was beat to begin with, and that some of them fellows was dangerous and might make away with me and my outfit.

I never seen hungrier men than come stumbling out of them Black Hills. They was eating skunks, snakes, wild rose haws, and them apple-like things that come in the fall on prickly pears. They'd rub hard to clean off the stickers. If they get stuck in a man's tongue, it's serious. I seen one greeny that got them prickly pear spikes in his feet when his shoes wore out. They hurt his feet so bad he put his hands out and set down fast. One of the bull teams come along. The fellows seen him rolling around at the edge of the road, so they picked him up, throwed him on top of a load, and hauled him to a stage ranch. After that, each time they come through, they'd give him a little food. He'd been there, laying on his face, in a shed, for close to a month. Them bull-team drivers was all betting with each other on how long it would take them prickly pears to fester and work out of his hands and feet and backside.

The trail led along a sort of a razorback edge of a hill. We was leaving the Badlands and getting close to Red Cloud's Indian Agency when a soldier rode up and says, "What the hell are you doing here?"

Jim Kinney says, "This is the Sidney Trail, ain't it?"

The soldier says, "I don't have all day to talk to you. Make camp, and stay right here until you get the order to move on again."

Then he turned his horse around and went galloping off down the road.

We seen smoke coming up from the bottom of Cottonwood Creek, so Kinney and me clumb down over our wagon wheels to look into the little valley on the flat. Over two hundred Indian lodges was there. Some was tore down, some was being put up, and some looked like they'd been setting there considerable time. Them Indians was running around, like a bunch of chickens with their heads cut off.

Then Kinney says, "God, Mont, look!"

And right on the opposite bank of the valley, leveled at them and at us—if they miscalculated and aimed high—was a company of soldiers from Fort Robinson, with their heavy cannons pointed, ready to fire.

We'd been give our orders. There wasn't nothing to do but get off the road and make camp. But we was all hoping them Indians didn't stir up no more trouble, and if the soldiers did have to shoot, they'd remember to aim low.

During the Indian wars, some of the Sioux give in earlier than the others and moved into the government agencies to get the rations and blankets they'd been promised. That's when Sitting Bull and Crazy Horse, and a lot of the others took to the hills. After the Custer Massacre, General Miles was put in charge, and told to take their guns and horses. So he sent General Terry out to bring them in.

But Sitting Bull and Gall took off for Canada and surrendered up there. Crazy Horse and his band still stayed in the mountains. The army couldn't take their guns away from the warlike Indians because they was gone. After their ponies was took, the reservation Indians had to play ball with the agency.

When them army men couldn't get close to them other Sioux they sent Crazy Horse's old uncle, Spotted Tail, and two hundred and fifty of his head men up into the mountains to talk the fighting Sioux into coming down to Fort Robinson. Old Spotted Tail had been promised that he'd get to be chief of all the Sioux and a first lieutenant in the United States Army if he'd get them Indians to come in and surrender. He was gone two months. When he come back he brung Chiefs Touch the Clouds, Roman Nose, the two Bears, High and Low, along with close to a thousand other Sioux.

For awhile Crazy Horse kept them guessing. But before long his band come in and camped close to the agency too. Then when Crazy Horse didn't like the way things was going there, him and some of his people tore down their lodges and started for the hills again. But the soldiers come after them and said they couldn't go off like that no more. Crazy Horse and a few of his head men rode off to the fort to talk things over. The army marched the others right back to Cottonwood Creek Canyon, and was pointing guns at them when we got there. I talked to men that was inside Fort Robinson that day, and they said Crazy Horse rode in with his head up, talking and acting just as friendly as any man would coming to a peace meeting. A big bunch of agency Indians and whites was riding along with him. Crazy Horse was dressed in a blue shirt and buckskin leggings. He wore one eagle feather in his hair to show he was a chief. When he got off his horse, he throwed his red blanket over his shoulder and walked through the door of the room where they told him the meeting was going to be held.

Crazy Horse never knowed he was in the guardhouse until he seen the bars on the windows and the chains hanging agin the walls. He was trapped. That's when he turned to get out of there. Little Big Man grabbed him by the arms. Crazy Horse drawed his knife, turned sideways, and slashed Little Big Man's upper arm clean to the bone, cutting his arm muscle right in half. Then the officer of the day give the order, and they run him through again and again with a bayonet. Both agency Indians and whites was in that crowd closing in on him, and they never backed away until he was dying. Then his father and old Touch the Clouds broke through the circle. His mother heard and come too. Them three set beside him, until they closed his eyes.

That's how it was that on September 7, 1877, word come to the Oglalas, camped below us in that little canyon, that their chief, Crazy Horse, was dead. For three days we set in our camp, on the hillside above them, listening to them Indians wailing for him and for theirselves.

At the end of the third day, the government sent an old Indian scout to tell us we could start down the trail again at sunrise. He set by our fire and talked long into the night. He knowed the West, and he knowed the price folks had to pay, who had guts enough to come out and do the settling. But just before he left, he says, leaning his head agin his hand and looking into the fire, "I've killed many an Injun in my day. They scalped my folks when they burned us out. I hate the sons of bitches. But I can't see bringing nobody in with promises, and then killing him like a rat in a trap."

The Indians had been moved from the Platte on up to the agency there by promises of more guns and ammunition and food. But after the Custer Massacre their guns had been took away from them, and just before we got there, they'd had their rations cut off, too. Congress allowed it was time for them to move on again. So the Indian agents told them that they had plenty of rations all ready issued and waiting for them at the new agency.

Next day, when we headed down the trail, we seen thousands of Indians, milling around and talking things over among theirselves, trying to make up their minds whether to move again or starve right where they was. Them Indians was mad enough to fight, but they didn't have nothing to fight with. The buffalo, their ponies, and their guns was gone. They didn't know nothing about farming or working at nothing else. All them agency Indians done was to hang around waiting for the next handout. They was the same Indians who'd kicked up such a fuss when they'd been moved north from the agency on the Platte, just five years before; now they was madder than hornets again about having to leave there and go two hundred and fifty mile to the Missouri, to get their next rations.

At noon, we let the horses graze while we fixed our lunch in close to the Spotted Tail Agency. A half-breed rode up on the prettiest palamino I ever seen in my life. Us fellows all gathered around to look at him. I'd of give my eyeteeth to own him and I knowed the other boys felt the same way. Then the half-breed says, "I'll trade him straight across for a rifle, and keep my mouth shut in the bargain."

We knowed it was dynamite. But I could see how the boys felt. A man could go a lifetime without seeing a horse like that, much less getting to fork him for his own. It wasn't no wonder Wyoming Johnny spoke up and says, "I'll swap my 45-70 Springfield and a box of shells, straight across."

Jim Kinney says, "You'll swing if they catch you. This fellow has Indian blood."

Wyoming Johnny says, "I'm looking at his white side."

Then several of the boys got to talking to Wyoming Johnny sort of low so I wouldn't hear, and they all begun looking my way. But I didn't know what was up until I heard one of the fellows say, "Let the kid hand him the gun. He's too young to hang."

But after the mess Father got hisself into, and knowing about that boy getting his neck stretched who was only two years older than me, I could feel the rope getting tight around my neck, too. I told them I wouldn't do it. But Wyoming Johnny says, "How you going to like going down the Sidney Trail by yourself?"

I didn't have no choice. So I handed the half-breed the gun, and Wyoming Johnny led the pony away. We was hoping that was the last we'd hear of that trade. But after we'd made camp that night a bunch of squaw men and agency Indians rode in, big as you please to get the palamino. They said it was agin the law for us to trade a gun to an Indian. When we tried to get the rifle back, they said we ought to be thankful they wasn't turning us in to the government. Then they rode out of camp, leading the horse. Wyoming Johnny was out his rifle. We heard afterwards they'd been working that same scheme regular. They got a lot of guns that way, until one outfit heard about it ahead of time. They drawed their revolvers, called their bluff, and ordered them out of camp. Next morning, though, the horse was gone and so was the saddle. Them breeds working that trick was right back in business again.

Soon as we got past the agencies, we begun meeting folks who'd been held back by the soldiers. Them bull trains was a sight to see

along that Sidney Trail. Besides having twenty-five wagons, a regular freight train always had a chuck wagon along, and all sorts of
extras. They carried spare tires, spokes, yokes, and tongues. I seen
one outfit stop by the side of the road and set up a hand forge while
a blacksmith welded a brace under a wagon. Most of them drove
twelve oxen to the wagon, and each wagon had a water keg fastened
on one side.

Them bull trains would break camp early in the morning, and
move on for six or eight hours in the cool of the day. Then the wagon
master would give the signal, and they'd make a regular circle at
noon, just like they would at night. Only they done it different than
Pete taught us, when we had to follow the leader clean around the
circle. When a bull team circled to make camp, the first team turned
to the right, and the second team turned to the left. They kept going
back and forth like that, just leaving a little place open for a gate-
way, but drawing the wagons in close with the left front wheel of
each wagon touching the back right wheel of the one on ahead.
When they broke camp they drove right off, first from the right, then
from the left. A bull-team driver was always ready for anything with
a Bowie knife in his boot, a couple of revolvers in his holsters, his
rifle slung over his shoulder, and his bullwhip in his hand.

The steel-lined Deadwood stage passed us by just like we was standing still. The outriders was armed and two more guards was locked
inside with all that gold. Fresh horses stood harnessed and waiting
at every stage stop. None of us fellows, going home with empty
pockets, had much to say that day.

Almost every other stage I seen, going by us on the road, had someone leaning out the window, terrible sick, and all green around the
gills. The leather springs swung them sideways, and the rough road
bounced them up and down at the same time. I never had money
enough to find out just how sick I'd get in one of them things myself.

Once a week the mail left Sidney for Deadwood. During Indian
times the mail carrier got to riding at night, so they couldn't see him
coming. A horse can see the road in the dark when a man can't. Summers it's always better to ride at night on account of the heat. The
mail carrier used to have from 2,000 to 3,000 letters in them saddle-
bags. I wished I was him until I found out he was just a hired hand

and didn't get to keep the fifty cents folks had to pay to get a letter carried in over the Sidney Trail.

For two whole days before we got to it, we seen Chimney Rock, standing up straight and tall. It ain't no wonder the pioneers, crossing the Oregon Trail, used it for a landmark. Close by was the place where the Sidney Trail, going north and south, crossed the old Mormon Trail, heading west. There wasn't no sense in us going on down to Sidney. We could follow back over a clear marked trail, laid out by Brigham Young, and wore down by the Mormons that followed him. We only had about a hundred and fifty mile to go from there, until we reached the town of North Platte. Then another hundred and fifty mile on top of that would bring us to Grand Island. From there on, it was some sixty mile to home.

Golly, we was glad to see the North Platte River. After we got to it, we never made no more dry camps where we done without water and cleaned our dishes, rubbing them in the sand. Nights I'd go down and set with my feet in the water and try to forget how hot it had been.

After we turned off on the old Mormon Trail, we never done no complaining. By then, Jim Kinney had sort of elected hisself our Captain, and he said he'd lick the first bastard that done any bellyaching about that road. Jim figgered we wasn't walking and so we didn't have no cause to complain. Why, we hadn't been through nothing compared to them three thousand Mormons, who left their winter quarters at Omaha, and made it on foot clean out to Salt Lake. They didn't have no outfits. All the goods they had in the world was what they drug along in little handcarts or carried in packs on their backs. Yep, you got to hand it to them Mormons. They was long on guts and religion, or they'd of turned back before they ever started.

Even that part of the old emigrant trail that run in close to the North Platte River wasn't no picnic. We hit hills and swamps and sand. It begun to look like I'd never make it home with our horses. I couldn't find no place to get grain for them. The old-timers used their heads when they drove oxen or cows on the long pulls. Horses don't have no bottom when they're living on green feed, or dry hay.

Most of the farm houses between Chimney Rock and North Platte wasn't there no more. The Indians had burned them places and scalped the settlers so recent that new folks hadn't had time to clear the title, get located, and file. It give the cattle drovers a good range to put on some weight before they shipped their beef into the stockyards at Chicago.

When the Texans first started driving their cattle north, over the Abilene Trail, they found plenty of pasture in Kansas. For awhile they was strong enough to fight the homesteaders and have things their own way. Nebraska had passed the herd law, making every man responsible for the damage done by his own cattle. But a law like that can't do you much good when you're living way out next door to nowhere. Them days, many a homesteader learned that the cattlemen had the upper hand, and that having a drive of Texas longhorns pass over your land was as bad as having the grasshoppers move in on you.

The cattlemen give up driving through Kansas to Abilene, after the armed bands started meeting them and taking their longhorns for theirselves, if they wasn't strong enough to shoot it out and make it on through. Some folks figgered they was honest homesteaders, with real reasons for hating the cattlemen. But many a night, when I set by the spring in Arcadia, I'd listened to old fellows tell stories of how the rustlers played they was homesteaders long enough to move in on them herds and shoot it out with the drovers. Then they split the herds, and turned rancher theirselves.

The coming of the homesteaders and the barbed-wire fences broke the cattle drives over the Abilene Trail. A homesteader didn't have no way to protect his fields until 1874 when barbed-wire fencing went onto the market. After that, a homesteader with a rifle and neighbors who'd stand by had a chance to hold his own.

From 1865 to 1885 new cattle trails kept leading out of Texas. Each one laid farther to the west than the last. The Ellsworth and Newton Trail, that took off from Forth Worth, Texas, to Ellis, Kansas, and from there on across the Platte, into Nebraska, wasn't no good by 1876. That's the trail that run up past our homestead on the Middle Loup, and come in around Yankton and led out to the unbroken prairie of the Dakota Territory. After us homesteaders filed on the pasture land and run barbed wire around each quarter section, the cattlemen couldn't even get through.

The cattle we seen, south of the Red Cloud Agency, had been drove in over the upper end of the Dodge City Trail that was used regular by the cattlemen from 1876 to 1884. Them longhorns, grazing on the prairie grass between the Badlands of the Dakotas and the U.P. Railroad, was the same kind of mean, cussed, wild critters that used to come charging at us up on the Middle Loup. A man ain't safe with longhorns unless he's on horseback.

I'd of give a lot to have had a good horse myself, right then. For several days I'd seen it coming. Our team of horses had got so poor, I could count every rib as they went stumbling along. I'd been walking for miles doing my best to get them through to North Platte. We was twenty mile out of town when one horse lost his feet and went down. I got him up, but the other one was through, too. Jim said they'd wait for me while I walked over to a ranchhouse we seen on a little knoll about two mile away. I looked around before I left and the field was clear, but right about when I hit the middle of it, I heard them. When I seen the longhorns coming my way with their heads down, I knowed it was too late to run, so I got down on my knees and wormed my way along in the tall grass. They run past there, where I'd been. Then they circled, getting ready to charge again. But by that time the fellow who lived in the house and was riding herd on them started looking for me, too. He let out a yell, and I stood up and answered. He galloped over to where I was and kicked his left foot out of the stirrup. I stuck my foot into the empty stirrup and swung up behind him. Soon as I was in back of him on the horse, he used his spurs. We got out of there at a gallop.

That fellow turned out to be real friendly, and honest to boot. He made a business of fattening longhorns there on his range before they was shipped to the stockyards in Chicago. After we got back to where the boys was waiting, him and Jim helped me turn the horses into his fenced pasture. We left the wagon in close to his shed. Then I took his name and he promised he'd look out for them until Father or me come to drive them home.

Jim took me to North Platte in his wagon. The town had started out to be tough when it was a division point for the railroad. But when the Sidney Trail opened, the gamblers and folks from the sporting houses had moved to Sidney. That give the church members a chance to have their innings. They elected Anthony Reis mayor because he'd promised to clean up the town. A new law was made that no woman could enter or visit a saloon. The reformers really played hob when they passed that one. It backfired. The men could go to the saloons and drink, gamble, and raise hell in general. Their women-folks couldn't get inside to check up on them or to take them home. The men liked it fine.

I said good-bye to the boys, and went down and hung around the depot. When a freight train come through I asked the engineer if I could ride home. When he heard what had happened he put me right up in the cab with him. I said I was the Hawthorne boy from Arcadia, and he said his folks lived in Grand Island. By then I was so wore out, I fell right to sleep.

Next morning, when he woke me up, he says, "Say, didn't you tell me your folks live in Arcadia?"

"Yes," says I. "We've got a homestead there."

He says, "Ain't your mother the Mrs. Hawthorne who's running the cattle corrals and living in the Tar Box house, right down by the railroad tracks in Grand Island?"

He started in telling me about how she looked and that she had three girls; two of them close to courting age, and the other one a lot smaller. It sounded so much like my folks, I figgered I'd better stop in and find out what Mama was up to. When the train pulled in to Grand Island, I jumped off and run up there. Sure enough, it was Mama. She was standing out in front of that little square box of a house, dressed in a long Mother Hubbard and wearing a big, white, starched apron. A tall fellow in a ten-gallon hat was standing with his horse's bridle over his arm, while he counted out a bunch of money into her hand.

Soon as she looked up, she grabbed me hard. Then she turned and introduced me to him, and says, "Thank you, Mr. Olive. This will pay for the corral for the rest of this week. When you need to ship cattle again, I'd be obliged to have you let me know in advance."

Mama sure was glad to see me. I didn't even have to tell her about the flour. She always figgered that with Father no news was bad news. Her and the girls had worked hard all summer on the homestead, but with the cows gone, they wasn't even holding their own. When the leaves begun to turn, she started looking ahead. Cousin Belle and Julia had both passed their examinations and had teaching jobs waiting for them at $16.00 a month. Sadie and Myra needed to get their schooling. Aunt Sadie took over as postmistress. A fellow named Ruff Braiden, who was looking around for a homestead in close to Arcadia, was glad to live in our house and take care of things until he got located. Uncle Boone took our family right along in the wagon at the same time he made the trip in to a country school where Cousin Belle was to start her first teaching and board around.

Going in to town, Mama worried some about where they was going to stay. One time when I was in Grand Island with Father I counted, and there was thirty-seven houses—but it had growed some since. She had the wagon cover along just in case things come to the worst and they had to camp out.

Mama's big windfall come when she heard that a fellow, down at the railroad, couldn't get a reliable man to run the corral and live in the Tar Box house that went with it. The men, who didn't have a business or a farm to keep their noses to the grindstone, had all pulled out for the Black Hills. Mama said she had to talk fast at first, but she knowed there wasn't a reason in the world why a woman couldn't handle that corral just as good as a man. They was so tired of having the records mixed up and some of the money held out that she got the job. That give them a house to live in, so they moved right in and took over.

The corral gate was handy to the door, and the runway went right past the house. She could see what was going on and collect the money. The cattle was run in through the main gate. On each side was smaller corrals and separate gates, so the different lots didn't get mixed. Clean on down at the end of the main runway was the chute where they run the longhorns into the cars to haul them to the stockyards. The cattlemen bought most of their feed at Michelson's barn and livery stable. They filled the water troughs from a well in the corral, and took care of their own gates and the loading. Mama always had more customers than she had corrals. Herds of cattle had to wait outside of town until there was room for them to be drove in. All Mama done was collect the money and keep the books; she had more free time than she ever did at the homestead. If Mama was called away on a nursing case, one of the girls collected the money while she was gone.

Julia was teaching at a country school and boarded around during the week. She come home Friday nights. The girls spent most of

Saturday washing and drying their hair and fixing up their clothes. By then their hair had growed down to their shoetops; they had to get up early of a morning to get it braided. When they was home together they always done each other's. Sadie's was lighter-colored and curlier than Julia's. Them two girls was always joking and having good times together, but Julia had to be real quiet and dignified when folks was around, on account of being a teacher and setting a good example. She wore grey alpaca dresses, with white collars and cuffs, and big white aprons, just like all the teachers done. Sadie was younger and still in school. She was always teasing people, and laughing, and showing deep dimples in close to the corners of her mouth. I never seen nobody look as pretty as Sadie when she was starting off to school of a morning, wearing her red knit hood.

A bunch of single fellows was working for the railroad and living in Grand Island. They come around pretty regular, but Mama figgered our girls was way too young to be give the run of the town. She treated all them young fellows real friendly, if they wanted to come in and set in the house. But she wasn't going to have her girls out sparking in the dark, before they was even growed up. Jim Mapes was working in town at the blacksmith shop. He dropped in most anytime, just like he done when he was living on the homestead.

Saturday nights, Mama was always so busy, keeping an eye on the girls, that she never paid no attention to Myra and me. Teeny Tielson and a bunch of other children would come over, and we'd sneak out to see the show. The first movies ever I seen was acted out right there at the corral. The outside fence was made of heavy up-and-down boards. It was six foot high, with two-by-sixes nailed horizontal at the top and the bottom and in the middle. Us children could slide out past our woodshed, walking on that middle two-by-four, and holding onto the top of the fence. After we got out, about a hundred foot from our place, we could look clean across the corral and into the window of Kelley's house. Every Saturday night their boys would all come home and bring their friends. The old man and the old lady wasn't no hands to set on the sidelines. I never been to a show since that was half as good as watching them Kelleys get drunk, and have a knock-down drag-out fight on a Saturday night.

Sundays we all dressed up and went to Sunday school and church.

Several different brands of religion was holding meetings in Grand Island. We always went to the Methodist.

I seen that Mama was fixing to get me back in school, so I went out and got a job taking care of the town herd. The boy who'd been doing it was down with diphtheria. Folks was glad to have a big boy like me that had rode herd before step in and take over. 'Twasn't long until they held a meeting and raised my wages from fifty cents a week to seventy-five. It wasn't hard work. All I done was get up about daylight and milk our cow, then I'd ride a horse around town, gathering up all the cows that folks had tied in the sheds back of their houses. I'd take them out a piece looking for good pasture. I'd set and watch them graze all day, and take them back in so's their owners could milk them before dark. Mama'd brung our cow along from the homestead. Beside making that money, I was saving us what we'd of had to pay out for our part of the cost of herding. No, it wasn't much, but that was what they paid. A hired girl, working full time, only got paid a dollar and a half to two dollars a week and board. Them folks, paying me, figgered I had a fair job. It wasn't like I done the milking. Nobody made much, but nobody charged much. The barber asked a nickel or a dime for a haircut or a shave, depending on how long it was since the fellow had the last one. The railroad men had to put out money to a barber when they was away from home.

Mama cut our hair herself.

One morning, before we was up, I heard terrible screaming in Danish. I knowed Mrs. Licktey, who lived across the road from us and couldn't speak no English, was in trouble. By the time I got my breeches on, Mama was in her wrapper and out the door.

Mrs. Licktey met her in the middle of the road. The little girl she was holding in her arms was all black in the face and strangling to death. Mama seen what was wrong. She grabbed the child, run her front finger down its throat to break the membrane, then she rolled it over and begun spanking its bottom to get it to breathing. Mrs. Licktey kept screaming as she run back to the house. Then we seen that she was coming back through the door with a baby in her arms. That one had stopped breathing. Its flesh was all spotted and discolored and black. Folks don't know nothing about membranous diphtheria, who didn't live through them days when there wasn't no antitoxins. At first a baby just acted like it was having croup, then all of a sudden it took a turn for the worse. Just like with Mrs. Licktey's baby. It was gone when we got there.

Mama told me to run for help, so I told the McAllisters and they got word around. Women cooked food and sent it in. The carpenter down at the railroad track give his time and made a tight little coffin. Mama wouldn't let nobody come inside the house to help on account of the contagion. She dressed the baby, put it in the coffin and nailed the lid on herself. Then she carried it out in the yard and set it on a box. The folks come and took it away for the burying. Mama and Mrs. Licktey stayed right inside the house taking care of the other child that was still terrible sick.

It was real hard on Mrs. Licktey losing her baby like that, with her not speaking English, and her husband still off somewhere in the Black Hills. Mama could keep an eye on us from across the road, but she never come home until there wasn't no danger of us catching the diphtheria. Anyhow, she had a big nursing job on her hands to help that other child get its strength back. If you see anybody took sudden with the membranous diphtheria, stick your finger down his throat and then give him something to make him throw up quick. After that give him a teaspoonful of whiskey in a little water every half hour both day and night. Sure you got to wake him up. How you going to build up his strength unless you keep right at it? Whiskey was used to get folks back on their feet, but blackberry brandy with ginger was used for the stomach-ache. No, I wouldn't call that drinking, not if Mama or a doctor give it.

Before long, the weather got terrible cold. The snow was too deep to drive the cattle to pasture. We sort of wondered if Father might get home for Christmas, but he never showed. Then something happened that sort of took the Christmas right out of all of us. The eastbound train come in regular at eight-thirty of a morning. We didn't have no watches, so Mama watched for it and then sent the girls off to school. It stopped over long enough for the folks on board to eat their breakfast at the Railroad House. Right after it pulled out a man come running to get Mama. He said there'd been a bad accident and for her to come quick. She grabbed her little brown bag and we both took out of there on the run, figgering it probably was Father, coming home.

When we got there we found that a young fellow about twenty-year old had rode in on the brake beams, clean from Sidney. He was almost froze when he got to Grand Island, so he crawled off to see if he could get thawed out and find a little something to eat. He was around back, seeing if the cook had some leftovers, when he heard the train starting to pull out. He made a run for it, and got under all right, but his legs was so stiff and cold he couldn't move fast enough to pull them up out of the way. The wheels run over both of his legs, right up agin his body.

One of the men that seen it happen run up town for the doctor. This fellow, who knowed Mama done nursing, come for her. When Doctor Gaines got there, he says, "I'm glad you're here, Mrs. Hawthorne. Where can we take this boy to examine him?"

A man spoke up and says, "The carpenter shop has a table."

The switchman had already tore his own shirt off his back and tied strips real tight around the boy's thighs, but it didn't near stop the bleeding.

That boy never let out a whimper when they lifted him over onto a plank and then sort of scooped his legs along. They carried him into the carpenter shed and laid him on the table. He just kept looking right straight into the doctor's face while the doctor was shaking his head over his legs. Doctor Gaines couldn't do nothing for him. The bones was all ground to pieces clean up into his hip joints, and the flesh was cut away, too. The doctor got out fresh bandages, and him and Mama worked trying their best to keep him from bleeding to death so fast.

The telegraph operator come and took his name to send a message to his folks. The boy said he didn't want it sent because there wasn't no use in worrying them. He'd been trying to beat his way home for Christmas. The men at the depot sent the message anyway. Late that day an answer come from his folks, way off in Iowa. They'd like to help, but they didn't have no money.

That morning, right after Doctor Gaines had finished with the bandaging, he'd asked Mama to step outside the carpenter shop for a minute. Then he told her that he had to leave to take care of other sick folks that was needing him. There was nothing to be done for the boy but to see him through to the end. Mama said she'd stay and do that.

When the doctor come back in for a minute to say good-bye the boy looked up from where he was laying on his back and said, "If I've got to die, couldn't I set up and have a pine block to whittle?"

They lifted him up on the carpenter's bench, moving his legs along, easy as they could, until he set braced with his back agin the wall. We'd gathered the fresh shavings and piled them in all around his legs to make it as soft as we could, and to help soak up the blood. There wasn't no way on earth for them to stop that bleeding, or to save his life. He knowed it, too.

His eyes was big, and deep blue-black. From the time the carpenter put that chunk of soft pine and a sharp jacknife into his hands, he never seemed to see nothing or nobody except that chunk of wood he was whittling into little shreds. The only times he'd take his eyes off it was when Mama would wring out the cloth in cold water that she was holding agin his head. Then maybe he'd stop and rest a minute and take her hands and hold on tight. The reason I got to stay right there was that she needed me to bring cold water and run other errands for her.

All that day, and on into the night, he set there whittling and talking to Mama. He told her about his whole life. His folks was poor. He was the oldest of a big family. He had to get out on his own soon as he could. He'd looked everywhere for work. But times was tough all over. He'd been clean to California. In the spring of 1877 over thirty thousand men was out of work in San Francisco alone. So he pulled out of there and went up to Colorado, but he couldn't get no work there. Then he'd tried mining in the Black Hills. When he got back to Sidney, broke, he clumb on the brake beams. Then it happened.

Word got around that the boy was dying. Railroad men, in overalls, would come to the door and look in, wishing they could do something to help. All that long afternoon that boy never said a word to make nobody feel worse than they did already. Once he looked up at the carpenter and says, "Am I keeping you from getting your work done?"

He never made a face, he never let a sound of pain get past his lips. By late afternoon, them shavings was a mass of blood, and his hands was so white he could hardly hold the knife, but he kept right on with his whittling. Then a real stylish dressed woman come flapping in at the door. She'd heard about the accident and had come down to see what had happened. The first thing she says was, "Doesn't it hurt?"

That was when we seen that awful look go over his face, and he says, "Lady, I'm human, just the same as you. Wouldn't it hurt you to have your legs cut off?"

Mama motioned for her to get out. Some of the others went outside, too. The carpenter, who was an awful good man and stayed right there to do all he could, closed the door. After a while, when the boy got too weak to whittle no more, Mama and the carpenter eased him back agin the pillows she'd had me bring from our place. The boy held onto her hand when he was telling her about how much he wanted to see his folks again. He asked Mama to write to his mother and tell her he'd done his best to get work so he could send some money home to her. Every place he'd been, there was too many men ahead of him.

After he was gone, Mama closed his eyes. Then she laid him out straight and held his arms folded until they was set. The carpenter said to leave him right where he was until they took his measure and made his coffin. Some of the railroad men was waiting outside to help him. By then Mama was so wore out, the men told me to take her home and see that she got some rest. The folks around the depot and the eating house wanted to help with the burying. Mama was glad she could write to his folks about him having a nice coffin and funeral.

Of course folks had to have a measure took to have a casket made. How else would they get a fit at the shoulders? Them days, all coffins was made to measure. The widest part come right at the shoulders, and they tapered toward both ends. The shoulders was the hardest part to make on account of having to saw into the sideboard several times to make it bend around. Them little cuts had to be made real careful; if they was too deep the board would break. Homemade coffins was a lot more work than the bought ones with straight sides like we see nowadays, but I always figgered they looked nicer, made coffin-shape. If folks was poor and short of cloth, they had to be put inside without no lining. Usually their families had a shawl or something they could use. Having a coffin made by folks who knowed you and cared always seemed more personal to me. Like with the carpenter. He knowed what that boy was made of, because he'd seen how brave he died. When they was laying him inside the coffin, the carpenter reached over to the top of the bench, picked up that whittled piece of pine wood, and laid it in alongside of him. Yes, I was there and seen it happen, because Mama'd sent me back down with her shawl to wrap him in.

Soon as Christmas was over, Mama said I had to get some schooling, so I went to work for a fellow named McDonaldson, over at Shoppe's Mills about fourteen mile from town. He was an old '49er, who'd gone out to California and mined in around Sutter's Fort. When that goldrush blowed up, he come back and homesteaded. On account of me being such a good milker, I got my board and room free and enough time off to go to school every week day for two months. The teacher was real pretty. I won a card with a picture of a girl feeding a white swan on the front of it. That prize was give because I could stand up and say the bones in my body, in their right order, naming every single one of them, faster than anybody else in the whole room.

While I was there milking cows, word come that George McKeller had shot Ed Chapman in the grocery store at Loup City. Ed went in to buy grub and mind his own business when George come in drunk and started jawing around, calling him names. I never did get the straight of what they was arguing about, excepting that it had something to do with a pig. They begun to scuffle and George got Ed's right thumb in his mouth and bit down hard. While he had Ed out of commission, George drawed and fired from the hip, shooting a hole right through his own jacket and right through Ed. Then George run out of the store, jumped on his horse, and galloped off. Soon as Ed Chapman was dead, folks chipped in on a reward. Then everybody started looking for George. George was hiding close to home where he could get his meals regular. When Old Man McKeller seen that reward posted, he turned George in hisself. The McKellers figgered George would get off with a fine like he done when he tried to shoot Father. They felt terrible bad when a regular trial was held, over at Ord, and George was sent up for life to the State Penitentiary at Lincoln.

Ever since I'd got back from the Black Hills, I'd been raising an awful fuss about not getting to go home. School was out by the first of March. Father had got back, broke, with a hardluck story. Spring planting time had come. So Father hopped a freight train and went down to get the team. The horses was in fine shape. That fellow I'd left them with at North Platte knowed his business. While Father was driving the horses back to Grand Island, me and Mama packed, and turned the corral over to a fellow who was waiting with his family to move in when we moved out. Mama said we'd have a roof over our heads, so even if we had lost the cows, we was still better off than we was the first time we went to live on our homestead.

Father didn't take us out by way of Dannebrog. He struck off from town on the road that went across the plains to Prairie Creek and then over the sandhills to the South Loup. From there we followed up the Middle Loup on the west side, where the pulling was easier, until we come to the ford that took us back across the Middle Loup, in close to our homestead. Father must of miscalculated at the ford. We never knowed whether we hit quicksand or a deep hole. The horses stumbled and water come right into the wagon box. We was so busy hanging on and saving ourselves, that we didn't notice at first that part of our stuff was gone. Father was sure a good man with horses to bring us through alive that time. But when we got to the other bank, Mama's handwove Revolutionary coverlid was gone. When Father seen how she felt about it, he unhitched one of the horses, clumb on its back, and took off downstream, poking in the deep holes with a long cottonwood pole. We never figgered he'd find it and snag it out, but we hadn't no more than wrung ourselves out, than he come back, carrying the red, white, and blue coverlid. Mama hadn't shed no tears when she lost it, but she cried real hard when he give it back to her. He patted her shoulder and says, "That hole come in the corner, Martha, when I was working it loose from the bushes. But the colors don't fade a bit under water."

Braiden, the fellow living in our house, hadn't got located yet. Him and Father talked it over, and Braiden decided to move into the empty house that Buckskin Bill's wife had moved out of, after she got tired of waiting around for him to come back to her. Buckskin Bill only come in there in the first place to help George McKeller vote them school bonds, and he never had done no work on the place except for throwing up that cabin. The reason nobody figgered Buckskin Bill would show around there again was that the woman he'd run off with had a husband and two brothers living close by, and they was all danged good shots. So Braiden moved in, fixed up the house, put in a crop, and figgered on filing soon as he could. We got along fine, neighboring back and forth during the summer while we was raising our crops.

Come harvest, who should come riding across the cornfield, pointing a revolver at Braiden, and ordering him off the place, but Buckskin Bill. When Braiden stopped to argue, Buckskin Bill shot him in the right eye. No, it didn't kill him because his cheek bone sort of slanted the bullet sideways. But it plowed quite a furrow along the side of his face, and his right eye set catty-wampus and wasn't no good afterwards.

Father was working close by and run over fast when he heard the shooting. Buckskin Bill tried to get the drop on him first. But Father drawed and shot him right through the hand, knocking his revolver on the ground. Buckskin Bill never waited to get it. He wheeled his horse around and headed up the road towards Ord. We found out afterwards that Father had shot off one of his fingers, but they never noticed it laying there at the time.

Soon as they got down to our house, Mama went to work doctoring Braiden, and Father and me rode all over telling the neighbors about the shooting. A posse was organized; they voted to run down Buckskin Bill and hang him for wife-stealing. They lit out after him but he had a good horse and considerable of a start. When they got to town, they split up and swung out around, cutting off all the roads. Buckskin Bill was cornered. The posse was all ready to head him off, soon as he made a break.

But what did Buckskin Bill do but go right up to the jail, knock on the door, and give hisself up. After a doctor come and sewed up his hand, the jailer locked him in a cell with an outside window, looking out on the street. When the posse got tired of waiting and rode into town to get something cool to drink, there set Buckskin Bill, with his face right up agin the bars. He was acting awful smart, and laughing and yelling at Father and the rest of the posse. Things like, "I'm so full of bullets now, every time somebody shoots a new one in, two more pop out the other side."

The men got so disgusted with him carrying on like that, they give up trying to lynch him and left for home.

Winter was coming on. Julia and Cousin Belle went back to their teaching. Sadie moved to Grand Island, where they taught the upper grades. She worked for her room and board at Cooks; Mama knowed them. They was Methodists. Myra was smart as a whip, and got along fine in the one room school there in Arcadia. After I left McDonaldson's I never went to school another day in my life. Father and me had a lot of work to do getting in wood, and fixing up the buildings.

Soon as we got back to Arcadia, we begun hearing stories about clashes between cattlemen and homesteaders. A homesteader needs water; so does a cattleman. Having the homesteaders stringing their fences along the creeks and plowing under the prairie grass was hard on fellows like Ben Gallagher, William Paxton, Jack Morrow, John Burke, the Gilmore Brothers, and Rankin who run Texas heifers up by the Dismal River. They had a lot of money tied up in them rangy, stringy longhorns, and they couldn't get it back out unless they was in prime condition at shipping time. Them cattle had to be fattened close in, on prairie grass; then they could run them through the corrals at the railroad, and route the cars straight through to Chicago. That way, there wouldn't be no heavy shrinkage.

When the cattlemen moved north, they needed room to spread out on the open range. Twice a year they held roundups and branded their cattle. A calf knows its own mother and will follow her. They didn't have no trouble separating and counting their calves. The cattlemen was always accusing the homesteaders of stealing their calves before they got them branded. When a homesteader is accused of cattle rustling, the best thing for him to do is to pack up and git. If he knowed he was innocent and stayed on, the verdict was generally: "shot by parties unknown." But many a homesteader, figgering he didn't have a chance nowhere else, stayed on to toughy it out. The law said that when a homesteader once filed he couldn't change his location.

The Olives had made a drive through from Texas with fifteen thousand head of longhorns in 1877. They was running them right across the river to the west of our homestead at Arcadia, using the Middle Loup and the South Loup for their side fences. Tough old Texas cowboys rode both ends of their line that reached clean up to the Dismal River, on the north.

Mama had introduced me to I. P. Olive the day I come back from the Black Hills and he seemed real pleasant. But Bob Olive had the

black temper and was knowed as a killer back in Texas. Both them
Olive men was said to be bad ones to cross and they'd give warning
to homesteaders and cattle rustlers to get out and stay out of their
new range in Nebraska. I begun to wonder about Mitchell and
Ketcham, who'd been living over on the South Loup to the west of
us. Ketcham was our blacksmith and done good work, reasonable.

We was lucky to get to Nebraska early, and locate in a little valley
with a spring on our place, and a river close by. Most of the other
folks, who come after us, didn't have it so good. They had to file way
out on the open prairie. One day, when I was down at the river fishing, I asked an old fellow, who'd been coming there regular to fill his
water barrels, why he didn't dig a well. He says, "Son, I did try sink-
ing one. I worked down far as I could through the clay. Then I got
a windlass and went down close to two hundred foot, and never
struck a drop. I figger if I've got to haul my water two mile, I'd rather
do it on the level than I would straight up."

During the real cold weather, that same old fellow lost his starter
and come over to our house for a fresh one. His cabin was so open
that everything had froze inside. After that, he'd put his bread dough
in a pan and wrap it in cloths. Nights, he slept with it under the
covers with him so it would raise.

Father'd been watching the sky, and one morning at daybreak
when it looked real clear off to the west he got me up extra early to
have a long day. We forked the horses, and headed straight off west
from the ford on the Middle Loup. It was quite a piece over to where
Mitchell and Ketcham was homesteading on the South Loup. We
wanted to get there, have our horses shod, and get back home again
before dark. On the way over we seen big herds of Olive's longhorns
grazing, but nobody bothered us, and we got to where we was going
inside of three hours.

Ketcham was a bachelor. His homestead adjoined Mitchell's.
They'd knowed each other for years. He et his meals with them in
their cabin. Mrs. Mitchell had been married to another man first.
She had a daughter by the name of Tamar Snow, who'd growed into
quite a chunk of a girl, since I seen her last. I went over to visit with
her. But her mother was all red-eyed, and so was she. They was
gathering up their stuff getting ready to pack it into the wagon, fixing to move.

Olive's herders had come by early that morning, and pointed to a calf's hide, hanging on the fence to dry. They said it was rustled from their herd and they wasn't going to have no rustlers on their range. If they wasn't packed and out of there within forty-eight hours, things would go hard with them. Mrs. Mitchell claimed that the calf had belonged to their own cow. When she come fresh, she had a bull calf. They'd fed it until it was big enough to veal, then they'd butchered. She figgered the Olives had made up that calf story just for an excuse to get them off their range. Her and Tamar went right on packing and crying, so I went back to where Father was talking to the two men. When I passed the fence, I stopped to look at the calf hide. It didn't have no brand on it.

Ketcham shoed our horses because he figgered he had plenty of time, and he needed the money bad. They didn't have much room in the wagon, or much to pack in what room they did have. Mitchell went right to work helping the women. Before we left, Father and me shook hands all around and said we was sorry to see them go. They didn't have no place to move to, nor no idea which way to turn next.

Going home, Father said it was a damned shame for them to be out their work, and their chance to ever prove up on a homestead again. Some of the rest of this story I heard Mrs. Mitchell and Tamar tell in the courtroom in Hastings, when Father was called as a witness. But I'm going to tell it just like it happened without it being all scrambled up, like it was when them lawyers got through with it.

After we left, they finished loading their stuff in the wagon. They knowed something more was up when they seen Black Sam, who worked for Olive's, riding up. He says, "Ketcham, I want you to shoe my horse."

Ketcham says, "Can't, my tools are loaded. We're moving."

Now the story the Olive's lawyer brung out in court was that Bob Olive had been made a deputy and had rode over to arrest Ketcham and Mitchell for cattle rustling, and he only begun shooting when they resisted arrest. But Tamar and Mrs. Mitchell claimed that four horsemen rode up and begun shooting soon as they got within rifle range. Fellows around, who'd worked for Bob Olive, figgered he'd flew into one of them black rages of his, soon as the boys come home and told about seeing that calf hide hanging on the fence.

Both sides agreed that the Olives shot first. The women begun screaming. They clumb down off the load and run for the house. Before he could take shelter, Olive got Ketcham through his shooting arm, winging him so bad he was out of it. By that time, Tamar had got her wits back enough to pitch in and help her father load. Until Ketcham got shot, all that Mitchell had to use was one of them old single-shot Sharps. It was accurate but slow to use in a running fight. Ketcham showed Tamar how to load his Spencer carbine; it was a repeater. She shoved seven cattridges in at a time. But with that gun, a man had to hold low, to shoot high.

Old Mitchell was close to seventy-year-old, and he'd worked hard all his life. Having this come on him so fast, sort of upset him. Tamar said he was shooting all around them fellows, doing lots of missing and no hitting until he placed a good one, and got Olive right in the kidneys. They seen Bob Olive double up low, and wrap his arms around his horse's neck. For awhile they figgered he'd hit the ground. That sort of brung them other cowboys to their senses, too. They turned his horse around. One rode close to him on each side, holding him on as they got him out of there.

Then Ketcham and Mitchell and the two women jumped in their wagon and drove off in such a hurry, they forgot to tie the cow on behind. They struck straight off for Loup City, driving as fast as they could, figgering on giving theirselves up to Judge Waugh. But he wouldn't take them in because he didn't want to have no trouble with the Olives, and the shooting hadn't happened in his county. He told them to go out to an island in the Middle Loup, and stay hid until they heard from him. So they found a place where they could ford. When they got out on the island, they seen that the cottonwoods growed so sparse there wasn't near enough shelter to hide the horses and wagon. It was early December and terrible cold, but on account of smoke showing they was afraid to build a fire. They laid under the wagon for three days, huddled together, trying to keep from freezing. By then they figgered Judge Waugh had give them the run-around, so they started out to find another county seat where they could give theirselves up. They knowed what it meant for a homesteader to have shot one of the Olives. That's why they was too scared to set still and wait, even if they hadn't been drove out of there by the cold.

After Bob Olive was shot, he begun bleeding like a stuck pig. The men with him got him as far as a dugout, where he made his will, and laid down to die. He lingered on for two days before he breathed his last. Meanwhile, one of the fellows with him had rode off for help. When the other men come, I. P. Olive offered seven hundred dollars reward for the capture and punishment of the murderers of his brother. Part of the boys had to help cart the remains back to the home ranch. The rest of them took off, looking for Mitchell and Ketcham.

They made their first stop at their homestead on the South Loup, to burn the buildings. Mitchell and Ketcham had built sod houses, so all that happened was that the roofs burned and fell in. Their tracks was easy to follow because they wasn't trying to hide. All they wanted was to give theirselves up, and be locked in a safe place until time to stand trial. When Olive's men reached the Middle Loup, they found a homestead where the woman said Ketcham had come in to get bandages for his arm. By then, the cowboys was hot on their trail.

Late that night, Wheat, who was one of Olive's riders, stumbled in at our door. He was about half froze and covered with icicles. His horse had fell and they went under water together down at the ford. Mama worked with him most of the night trying to keep him from being frost-bit permanent. We set up listening to him. He was the first to tell us what had happened. He said that when they got to Loup City, they seen some other wagon tracks crossing the ones they was following. They knowed that Mitchell's wagon was on ahead but they sent him to check on whether they'd split up, and one of them fellows they wanted had caught a ride north. Wheat talked terrible bitter agin them two homesteaders. I liked Wheat. And I liked them Olives. Why, Bob Olive used to stop at our spring for a drink of water, and then he'd come up to the house and set there eating Mama's homemade bread and chokecherry jam, just like he was one of us boys. Still, you couldn't ask to meet finer men than Mitchell and Ketcham. There was two sides to that story. Before they got it finished, several folks was dead.

Mrs. Mitchell and Tamar said they contacted Judge Waugh when he was leaving Loup City. Sheriff Barney Gilan and Phil Dufraud, a deputy, was told to ride down with them to Kearney, the county seat of Buffalo County, where they was going to give theirselves up. They was scared. But they felt a lot easier, having the law along to protect them, when Olive's men come galloping down the road after them. But all the sheriff and that deputy done was to turn their backs and shut their eyes, so they could say they never seen it happen. That gang drug Mitchell and Ketcham off the load, and rode off with them, looking for a tall tree. Excepting for the fuss the women put up, the only argument come when Sheriff Gilan thought he might not get that seven hundred dollars reward. But Olive give it to him right off. Him and his deputy took out of there with the money, leaving Mrs. Mitchell and Tamar to drive the horses to town.

The hanging took place in Devil's Gap Canyon, not far from Plum Creek. They swung Ketcham first. While part of the boys was using the only good elm tree in sight for him, the others shot Mitchell. Then they hung him, too. After their bodies was cut down, they tried burning them, but the wood was too wet to get up a good fire. So, they buried them right there in the canyon.

That probably would of ended it. A report was wrote out about it being an accidental death at the hands of parties unknown, but Mrs. Mitchell wasn't satisfied and she went to see Ketcham's brother. He was an old Indian scout and come there nosying around demanding a trial. By the time they got the bodies up, and hauled to Kearney, they was in bad shape. But folks got so interested that when the train stopped over in Grand Island the coffins was opened up in the baggage car so folks in town could take a look at the remains of Mitchell and Ketcham. One fellow took some pictures of them, showing that they was gashed with knives, shot with rifles, hung, and then burned. They've still got copies of them pictures tucked back out of sight in the historical rooms in Lincoln, Nebraska.

The trial was held down south of us at Hastings. It had just got to be the county seat of Adams County, after they'd changed it from Juniata, by going up in wagons and moving the county records down in the dead of night. Everybody figgered Hastings was a good place to hold a trial because it would be one of them new deals with everybody starting out from scratch. Judge Goslin, who was running the trial, said no man could enter the courtroom unless he was searched first and his guns left outside. The Judge kept his revolver laid out handy, right on the table in front of him.

Feeling was running high agin the cattlemen, and when word got around that Father had been called as a witness for the Olives, folks wouldn't hardly speak to him. But all he had to do was to get up on the witness stand and swear that Wheat was setting by our fire, trying to get thawed out, on December 10, 1878, when Mitchell and Ketcham was killed, so he couldn't have had a hand in it. The Olives run in a bunch of fast-talking lawyers. Everybody thought, from the way they played up that story about Bob Olive being a deputy, out arresting cattle thieves, that they'd all get off scot-free. But I. P. Olive drawed a stiff jail sentence, and he never got out of there with a pardon until he'd served a whole year of it. I think he was sentenced more for paying out that money to Sheriff Gilan than he was for what was done to Mitchell and Ketcham. No, Gilan moved on farther west; there wasn't no point for a man with seven hundred dollars in cash spending his time just being a sheriff.

After the lawyers got his money and Olive got his pardon, him and his son went out to Colorado. He was playing billiards there one night when a stranger come in and picked a quarrel with him over nothing. The stranger drawed and shot him six times with his own gun. After that he reached over, picked up Olive's own gun, and emptied that into him, too. Olive's son heard about it, and run in to settle the score. The stranger had reloaded by then, so he shot and killed the boy, too. He just stayed right there beside them two dead Olives, until the miners took him in to stand trial. When the miners' court in Leadville heard about what had happened to Ketcham and Mitchell, and how this old Indian scout, doing the killing, was Ketcham's brother who'd tracked the Olives out there to take the law in his own hands, they set him free, dismissed the case, and said them fellows had died in a justifiable accident.

Lou Fredinsburg, who'd been a real good neighbor of ours from the time we first moved to Nebraska, was away from home at the time of the killing of Mitchell and Ketcham. None of us had made a real crop that year on account of the drought, so as soon as harvest was over, Lou went to trapping. Him and four other fellows had spent the winter in the north central part of the state up around the lakes and on Long Pine Creek, where the canyon is deep and wide. They done so well the other boys didn't want to start for home. But Lou had promised his wife that he'd be home by the first of March for spring planting, and she'd worry if he didn't show.

So he sold his furs to a trading post up there, and waited for a real clear day before he struck off for home alone. He got along fine the first day, but that night the snow begun to fall. Then come a freeze. He was lost for five days and his feet froze on him. Lou knowed he didn't dare let his feet thaw until he got to help, so he kept on stumbling along, night and day. When he did have to lie down to rest, he'd roll his blanket around the rest of him, but he always left his feet out so they wouldn't thaw.

Lou didn't have no idea where he was going, except that he was following along downstream. Finally he come to some fellows out hunting. They took him to Fort Hartsuff, where there was an army doctor, and he went right to work on Lou, cutting off both his feet before gangrene set in. Lee Heron knowed we was friends, so he rode over from the fort and got Mama to go with him to break the news to Mrs. Fredinsburg and the children. Then when Lou was well enough to come home, Father went over in the wagon and brung him back. After his legs healed up, Lou tried to farm his homestead, but it was blamed hard for him to get along, stumping around without no feet. So the Fredinsburgs left Arcadia and moved on farther west, hoping to find some work for Lou that wouldn't take so much walking.

Mrs. Fredinsburg and Mama kept writing to each other. Them women that homesteaded out there in Nebraska, and helped each other when their children was being born, got to be real good friends. The Fredinsburgs ended up at Battle Ground, Washington, and that ain't very far from here. The Browns settled down below us here in the Willamette Valley. A lot of them families that homesteaded in Nebraska never quit moving until they hit the West Coast. Cousin Belle married and moved to Oregon. Only Clyde and our Hill cousins, who come out sometime after we did and filed on claims up along the bluffs north of Arcadia, stuck by the old homesteads. Yep, about the only one that didn't have somebody in his family heading farther west was George McKeller, and he was an old bachelor and didn't have no family. But he might of been trying to move out West the day the guards shot him, when he was climbing over the wall of the state penitentiary. By that time, George had wore everybody out so bad around there that the other prisoners give the guards a big hand when they heard that George was dead.

All the time I was away on that trip to the Black Hills, I'd counted on getting back home again. But when I got there nothing was the same. Neighbors was moving on. New folks was coming to take their place. Aaron had married Amanda and was living in his own home. Nights, when he did stop over at our place, I could tell that all he was thinking about was her. Julia and Sadie was most growed up and away at school. Myra was too young to be much company. There was times when I almost missed them blamed cows. But the thing I missed most was something I seen leave one night when Father come in late, after spending the evening with them fellows that was running the still on up above our place.

He'd been drinking too much other times, but that night he was the meanest he'd ever been. Soon as he come in, Mama sent Myra over to Aunt Sadie's for the night. Her and me stayed to see if we could reason with him and get him into bed, so's he could sleep it off. When he went over to get some water to put in the washpan, and didn't use the dipper, Mama says, "Sam, be careful." He picked up the wooden water bucket and poured water all over the front of hisself and the floor. Having her say that was what set him off. Next thing we knowed, he'd throwed our only oak bucket on the floor. After he got through kicking it and jumping on it and batting it around, there wasn't nothing left but a bunch of kindlings, a bail, and two iron hoops. By then he was so wore out, we didn't have no trouble getting him to bed. He never even sobered up enough that night to know what he done.

Next morning, Father slept late. When he woke up, Mama was cooking his noon meal, using the staves of our only bucket to make the fire. He started to ask her what had happened to the bucket. Then I watched his face set, as he figgered it out for hisself. He knowed how little she had to do with. Why, that was the only bucket she'd had to carry water in all the time we'd lived in Nebraska. Father looked sort of like he wanted to say something, if he could only think of something that ought to be said. Then Myra come back, chattering away like things was just as fine as they could be.

When Mama finished cooking, she called us to set up at the table. After she put our plates in front of us, she come around to her own place. We bowed our heads while Mama asked the blessing, just like she always done. But I noticed Father was having considerable trouble with his swallowing. We wasn't half through, when he shoved away from the table and went outside. Then we heard a horse gallop off. Mama went right on eating and never said nothing about it, so I didn't neither. That night the horse was out in the barn, covered with lather, and a new oak bucket set on our table. It had been fresh filled with cold water from our spring. Mama never mentioned our old bucket or the new one to me, and I don't think she did to Father. But nights, when she didn't think nobody was watching her, something showed in Mama's face that made me wish we could of kept our old bucket.

Julia and Sadie come home for the summer, bringing word from Dr. Gaines that the typhoid-diphtheria had got out of hand in Grand Island, and asking Mama to please come and help him. She figgered folks there needed her and we needed the money she'd be making. Julia and Sadie took over running the house, raising the garden, and doing the baking and the canning. Mama got out Father's old carpet-bag, and packed what clothes she needed. Then she picked up her little brown nursing bag, and caught a ride to town with one of the neighbors. It was better than two months before we seen her again.

Nothing much happened that summer, excepting hard work. Jim Mapes had growed into as fine looking and strapping a fellow as you'd ever hope to see. He'd come back to the valley, and was doing odd jobs here and there. By then it was plain to see that Sadie was the one he'd took the shine to, but she was too young to be spoke for.

Moving them Sioux again opened up a lot more country on beyond. Folks was coming and going. Nights, we rented out the floor downstairs for sleeping. The girls baked every day in the lean-to kitchen at the back of our log house. They served meals, and then sold homemade bread besides. Father and me and the girls slept upstairs in the loft. Mama had made two real nice rooms up there by hanging sackcloth curtains on wire. Our old sod house had been took over by the district school; Ming Coombs was the teacher.

On the Fourth of July, everybody in our valley went down to Loup City to the celebration. Uncle Boone was racing the Indian pony that Father had traded his gun for. He didn't win, but he come blamed close. We'd had a big day and started back, crossing the bridge right at Loup City and fording back over the Middle Loup close to home. A terrible storm come without no warning. Our wagon was ahead.

By the time we crossed at the ford, the water was up close to the wagon box, and the rain had soaked us to the skin. The wind blowed hard . . . lightning was striking close.

We'd just got home and into the house when Cousin Belle come running to tell us their wagon had been struck by lightning. Aunt Sadie was shook up the worst. The new baby she'd been holding in her arms was black in the face, and dead. We went right over to do what we could. Next day, at the funeral, old Mrs. Coulter was taking on about how she'd had that cedar tree brung down to droop over her grave, and here her grandchild was buried alongside it first. That was a queer thing about old Mrs. Coulter. She didn't live very long after that, but she lived long enough to help bury Aunt Sadie and five of them eight grandchildren of hers, right in close to that little cedar tree. Folks went fast with typhoid, them days.

When Mama come home from nursing in Grand Island, she was wearing a new hat and looking real spruced up. She'd brung presents to us all. The nicest one was for Father. But what surprised him most was that Mama had a white ribbon bow, pinned on the collar of her coat. Yes, sir, Mama had joined the W.C.T.U.

A bunch of women had held a convention in Chicago and every one of them had promised to wear a little white ribbon bow, and to get other women to work for temperance too. Frances Willard had quit her teaching at Northwestern University and was going all over the country organizing Temperance Unions. Them women figgered there wasn't much chance of changing men when they got sot in their ways. But if they could stop child labor, teach children temperance, and win the vote for theirselves, something might get done after all. The only chance the women had of getting the vote was to get their men to vote to give it to them. That was going to take plenty of tact and sticktoitiveness.

Mama started right in working on Father. The Union Pacific Railroad was fixing to move its shops to Grand Island from Omaha on account of the trouble they'd been having with flood water coming from the Missouri. Soon as she'd heard about it, she'd got the rent of a boarding house that was being built close to where the shops was going to be, and she'd spoke for a job for Father. If he went right back to Grand Island, he could go to work steady at regular pay. Her and me could finish with the harvest and bring the food we'd raised down with us to feed our boarders. If she set a real good table, them railroad men would pay as high as three dollars a week for board.

It didn't take Mama long to see how things was going between Sadie and Jim Mapes, and she didn't like it. For one thing, she fig- gered Sadie was too young. Then, good as Jim was, he did take a drink once in a while. Besides, he hadn't lit long enough to take root and wasn't in no shape to start providing for a wife. She talked to Sadie and asked if she couldn't wait. Sadie said she'd try.

Mama hurried around getting Father outfitted and helping the girls get their clothes ready for school. Sadie was real agreeable about going back to working for her board at Cooks, and never once men- tioned hating to leave Jim. Mama kept still too, but she felt pleased about putting sixty mile between them until Sadie had time to grow up and change her mind. Just as they was leaving in the wagon, who should come around the corner of the house, with his clothes wrapped neat in a bundle, but Jim. He'd been figgering on riding in with them all the time to get a job, helping build the Union Pacific Shops at Grand Island.

That's how it was that only Mama and Myra and me was home the day the cloudburst come and cleaned us out. Early that morning, Jerome Hill, one of them cousins that had moved in about four mile above us, rode down to help me harvest corn. He stopped where Mama was cutting cabbages for sauerkraut, to say he'd never seen a nicer garden or a nicer day. That afternoon a black cloud come in from the northwest. It give us a good soaking and went over. Then the sun come out bright again. 'Twasn't long after that when another cloud, bigger than the first, rolled along close to the horizon. While it was heading our way, that first one swung around and come back, too. They met overhead, bumped, and let go.

In no time after the thunder and lightning begun, the water started to pour down on us. The creekbed overflowed. All of two foot of water run out on each side. Winters the creek had cut down eight foot deep. Summers it almost dried up. That morning, Jerome and me had crossed to the far cornfield, by climbing down the bank and jumping from rock to rock, without even getting our feet wet. Jerome had left his horse on the far side when he first come. Soon as the storm struck, Jerome galloped off for home; his wife was alone there with a new baby. He told me afterwards that his horse had waded in water up to his belly, on level ground above our place. Four mile above, at his homestead, it hadn't rained a drop.

I didn't have no way to get back across excepting to swim. Our creek had turned into a regular lake with water running right through into our house. We figgered the house might float off any minute, so we moved out to the barn. When the water come all over the floor there, Mama put Myra in the manger, then her and me waded around until we got the two pigs up on top of the feed bin. They grunted and squealed all night. The old cow bawled. The chickens kept cackling away from over on the fence where they had roosted. The three of us spent the night up in the mangers. We never got no sleep.

Come daylight, we seen that the water was going down, so we went out to look around. Right in front of our house enough dirt had been scooped out to more than fill a big-sized room. A lot of it had come into our house along with the water. Up above us, where the cloud-burst had hit first, about half an acre of dirt had washed out to a depth of six foot. Our hog trough had floated clean across the Middle Loup River. Some big cedar logs, that had been piled at the far side of the house, had floated out across the cornfield, mowing off the stalks on the way. Grasshoppers ain't nothing compared with being hit dead center by a cloudburst.

Mama sent word to Father. He took time out to drive up for us and to help us pack what was left. Seemed like something always come along to make our moving lighter. When Father got there he showed he had something on his mind, then he give Mama a letter from Sadie. Her and Jim loved each other so much they couldn't wait no longer. They'd got married just like Mama would of wanted them to at the Methodist parsonage. They was sorry we couldn't have all been there, but Father had stood up with them, and Jim had a good job helping build the shops in Grand Island. Sadie had signed her letter, "Your happy children, Jim and Sadie."

Mama wasn't no woman to cry over spilt milk. She thought a lot of Jim, and she knowed he'd be good to Sadie. By the time she got the neighbors told, you'd of thought she'd figgered that wedding out by herself. When Mrs. Coulter told her they seemed sort of young, Mama says, real quick, "Many a girl has ben married at fifteen without getting as good a boy as Jim Mapes."

When we got to Grand Island we went right to the boarding house the folks had rented, and left our stuff. It was a real nice house. We knowed we'd like it fine. Then we slicked up and went over to see Sadie and Jim. They was living in a little place down the street. When we got there we had to knock several times before Sadie come to the door. She looked terrible and stood leaning agin the casing like there wasn't no life in her. Jim had the typhoid fever. She'd been nursing him night and day. Then she'd got it herself, but she was still trying to keep on her feet, so she could take care of him.

Mama took charge and had us all flying around. We got them moved up to our place where there was more room. Jim's mother come to help. Julia left her school and pitched in too when Sadie took a turn for the worse. At first they was afraid for Jim, but about the time he begun to rally, Sadie got so bad she was burning up with fever. Toward the last Sadie was out of her head. She'd set up and look around the room where everything was strange and say, "I want to go home. . . . I want to go home." They was wringing out sheets in cold water trying to break the fever and get her cooled off, but nothing done no good. Sadie'd been married just two months and a half and was sixteen years old by the time she died, November 15, 1880. Nobody had to break the news to Jim. He'd had their beds put in the same room so they could be together.

Jim says, "Will you take her home?"

Mama says, "It's the least we can do."

He asked Father to go down to the furniture store and get their best bought coffin and charge it up to him. He'd seen some there when him and Sadie was down looking at the kind of furniture they wanted to buy some day. Then Mama and Julia dressed her in her best school dress; it was the one she'd stood up to get married in. After she was laid out, the neighbors, tiptoeing in, said they'd never seen such a pretty corpse. The preacher come and held the service right there in the house, so Jim could hear.

Father and Mama was the only ones taking Sadie home in the wagon. Julia had to stay and help Jim's mother care for him. He wasn't near out of the woods yet. Anyhow, there wasn't room for us children to go. When they was leaving, the minister went out to the wagon and said a prayer. Father helped Mama up on the wagon seat before he went around, clumb up on the other side, and picked up the reins. Their backs was real straight as they drove off down the road. The flowers on the coffin had all flattened out under the hot sun. They'd have to be driving night and day for over sixty mile, borrowing horses along the way. The last thing Sadie had said was, "I want to go home."

Seemed like it was a terrible long way to go.

NINE

RAILROADS NEEDS COAL

Soon as he could be moved safe, Jim's folks took him down to their farm so that Julia could go on with her teaching. After Father got back from Sadie's burying, he went right to work helping to build the roundhouse. Mama put Myra in school, straightened things around, and in no time she was setting two big tables full of board- ers, regular. That's when I got my first job, working for the railroad.

Father hired our team and me out for three dollars a day to work on the grade they was running straight south to Hastings. The fathers always got paid when they hired their boys out that way. But by the time he paid for my board and for feeding the horses, there wasn't much left. I moved right along with the crew, sleeping on a corn- husk mattress in a tent, and trying to keep up with the other men. It was real hard work, too. Many a hot day my shirt front was stiff with blood. No matter how bad your nose bleeds, you can't stop to do nothing about it when you're driving scraper. The fellow filling stayed in one spot, but I had to keep moving right along over to where we dumped, so I wouldn't hold up the line.

When we got through with that stretch, our outfit went down to work on the Columbus and Elkhorn Railroad close to Madison. There was something sort of funny about the way all them little railroads kept branching off from the main line. Course, the plains couldn't ever of been settled without the railroads. But this had something to do with land grants, and how the Union Pacific couldn't build more lines and get more grants, but it could help subsidiary companies, and then buy them out after awhile. The railroads took big risks and they done smart figgering during them years when close to one tenth of the land in the United States was turned over to them as land grants.

The first locomotives had burned cottonwood. Fellows cut it from along the banks of the Missouri and delivered it at Omaha for around eight dollars a cord. The railroad couldn't get no more cordwood until it hit the Platte River, two hundred and twenty-five mile away. Everything close in had been cut and burned. No matter how hard they tried the woodcutters wasn't making nothing, neither. Fremont had wrote in his reports that there was coal on beyond. The railroads sent prospectors out with the engineers to find it. Unless it come in big veins, they was licked. The covered wagon pioneers had burned buffalo chips to get across. There wasn't nothing on top of the ground. The railroads had to find coal. They opened up coal fields in Iowa and at Council Bluffs, on the east side of the Missouri. It wasn't the best coal in the world, but a half ton of it was better than a cord and a half of wood. Then the railroad made a test run from Cheyenne to Omaha averaging thirty-four and three-fourths mile an hour, on a stretch five hundred and seventeen mile long. Railroads needs coal, and they was getting the best there was from new mines that the Union Pacific had opened up at Carbon, Wyoming.

Father and me was quitting the railroad and going back to the homestead for spring planting, so I said good-bye to the fellows on the grading crew. But when I got back to Grand Island with the team, a contractor had offered Father good money if we'd take the horses, and help do a rush job on the Julesburg-Denver Short Line.

We was sick of raising crops for grasshoppers. That cloudburst had been followed by a hard winter—our fields was bound to be in bad shape. This job meant sure money, so we took it. Mama stayed right where she was, running the boarding-house in Grand Island.

The contractor loaded our crew on flat cars, with just our bed rolls and a change of clothes apiece. We like to froze to death setting out there in the open, but we wasn't the only ones hit in that snow storm that come deep and fast in the spring of '81. Why, the range cattle had crowded in on the tracks until the engineer had to put a couple of men out on the cowcatcher to roll the dead ones out of the way so the train could get through. We only stopped at Ogallala and

Julesburg long enough for the boys to make a beeline for the saloons to thaw out their innards. We was all blamed glad to get to Sidney, where we made camp and got organized to strike off, cross country, on foot. Our first job was grading the Narrows on the South Platte, where the railroad would run between the cliff and river. The engineers sent us on ahead while another crew laid track across the level country btween there and Julesburg.

After we finished grading the Narrows and worked out another deep cut, we struck off across country again. Our outfit was so big and we was hauling so much equipment that nobody got to ride but the drivers. By then we'd covered better than a hundred mile of Colorado on foot, but we found out we hadn't even started yet. We headed due west through sagebrush, over hills, past lakes, and across prairie, until we come to Fort Collins where we done more grading.

Then orders come for us to hurry southwest to Denver, but when we got to Greeley we was told to make camp. The job ahead had blowed up because President Garfield had been shot and might not pull through. For sixteen days, fifteen hundred men waited there. We wasn't getting paid; we was just waiting. A fellow give us a talk about how the Union Pacific was lining up their grants right through the mining country and aimed to build five railroads across the Continental Divide in Colorado.

But while we waited nothing happened all day except when the train come through about ten-thirty every morning and the conductor on the run from Denver to Cheyenne throwed a rolled-up newspaper to a runner, who'd sprint five blocks with it up to Grimes Hotel. He'd pitch the paper up to Grimes, who was standing on the little fenced-in balcony that was built out over the porch of his hotel. Then Grimes would unroll it and raise his voice real loud so we could all hear him read. The men, who'd bet money on President Garfield pulling through, had to pay off on September 18, 1881, when word come that he was dead.

Right after that, Father said we'd been off work for so long that we'd et up most of our money. He told the contractor we'd be willing to go most anywhere, rather than to head back home to Mama, broke. Next night, word come for us to get everything loaded. It was pitch dark when they give the order for us to get aboard. I was riding on a flatcar, leaning agin my bed roll. It was leaning agin the scraper.

All of a sudden I realized we was heading south, towards Denver. The rest of the boys didn't know no more than me. Come daylight we seen high mountains ahead and knowed we was close to the Rockies. At noon we unloaded in Boulder, Colorado.

Soon as we'd had dinner we started up town with our teams and scrapers, until we come to a place where a new railroad grade had been throwed across the street. That dirt was so full of round beach rocks that it took us better than two hours to get their road tore up and our own grade made, crossing over top of theirs. The roadbed we'd tore out belonged to the Burlington System. They'd got there first and done their grading to hold the right of way. Since they didn't have no rails, our contractors figgered it didn't count. But the City Marshall come and told us to stop, so we pulled off a piece and waited.

Then our boss come along, handed us shovels, and told us to go to work again. Of course we wasn't being paid to think, but we was in Boulder for two weeks, and nothing we done while we was there made sense. The Burlington had a bunch of men working right across from us. I was on the U.P. side, shoveling hard as I could. A big red-faced Irishman would throw a shovelful of dirt right back, as soon as I'd throw it over on his side. Finally he says, "Boy, take your time." After that we both slowed down and got along fine shoveling dirt back and forth to each other.

When we went in there the U.P. had rails all ready to put down as soon as we finished the grade, and them other fellows didn't have no steel. But after they come down and threwed all our rails and ties into the river, we didn't have none, neither. Some of the railroad men had kidnapped the judge and hid him back in the hills, so we couldn't be arrested. By the time the law moved in on us from outside, both crews was fighting with fists and shovels.

They arrested the bosses and took them off to jail, so we sold our horses, and bought tickets straight through to Cheyenne, Wyoming, on the train. A letter was waiting there from Mama. She was making out fine, keeping boarders, and Jim was back working in the shops in Grand Island. But men was waiting in line for jobs down at the railroad there, and money was terrible tight. Father and me was setting on the front porch of the hotel in Cheyenne, trying to figger out what to do next, when a big, soft-bellied, snaggletoothed fellow come up and made hisself acquainted. He was one of them promoters, out getting miners for the coal department of the Union Pacific Railroad. He told us about what a good town Carbon, Wyoming, was, and said we could make our living there easy, working in the mines. I told Father I wasn't going back to Nebraska, with a job like that waiting for me to the west. He seen it the same way I did. We decided I was to go to Carbon and get located while he went back to get rid of the homestead, and to help Mama and the girls move. That Promoter was such a smooth talker that Father was hankering to get to mining, but he didn't like to break the news to Mama that we was starting all over again.

Carbon was the first coal-mining town the Union Pacific ever had. Maybe they run it like that because they hadn't got around to figger out nothing better. When they first struck them rich veins, down in southeastern Wyoming, they give the Wardells, who was coal people from Missouri, a fifteen-year lease. When the miners went on strike and they couldn't deliver, the railroad took over, put D. C. Clark in as superintendent, and told him to bring in more men and produce coal or else. The Wardells was ousted by a court order. Jack Wardell run the company store. It was a stone building. After him and that fellow with him piled grocery boxes in front of the windows, and holed up in there with their rifles and ammunition, they had a regular blockhouse. They'd held out for a long time, living on the groceries and taking potshots at the fellows that come to deliver the summons; but by the time I got there, they was starved out and had give up. Then Beckwith and Quinn got hold of the building and put in a store there.

Nobody done no planning at Carbon. The town just growed out of the desert. Except for the regular buildings at the mine, and a few stores strung along down by the depot, every man had to provide for hisself, and there wasn't nothing much to provide with. There wasn't a tree in sight, nothing growed at Carbon but sagebrush, and greasewood, and prickly pears. Building sod didn't grow in that thin, dry soil. All the water had to be hauled in tank cars from Medicine Bow River, twenty-five mile to the east. It was stored in a board cistern; folks had to pay Ford, the waterman, twenty-five cents for a whiskey barrelful. The company give you your job; but you provided your own tools and squibbs and powder. You sharpened your tools yourself. Except for the job, you was on your own. Nobody ever thought of company houses in Carbon.

Over on the hilly side to the left of the tracks heading west, where the boulders wasn't too big, folks had made dugouts back into the bank. Over on the other side, back of the stores, they'd piled up rocks to make stone houses. Nothing was wasted at Carbon. Men fought over the packing cases around the stores and mines. Every speck of wood in town was used. Walls was patched together out of anything folks could get hold of. Blasting powder for the mines come packed in big tin cans. Some of the miners worked extra hard, just to get them cans emptied sooner. They'd take them home and flatten them out to make roofs for their houses. Overlapping the round heads that was cut out of the ends made them go farther.

The day I got off the train at Carbon, I walked all around, looking. I got to thinking about how Father was bringing the folks to Carbon on a one-way ticket. I hadn't seen Mama for a long time. It would be awful good to be with her again, but I didn't hanker to see her face when she got her first look at Carbon. That night, when I was trying to sleep in an old shed of a boarding-house, I got to thinking about the homestead back in Arcadia, and about that big spring of cold water. Don't it beat all how a man never knows when he's well off?

Next morning early, I went over to the mine to check in. Over six hundred miners was working at Carbon. New recruits was coming in every day. Things out West was booming. It took coal to keep them trains rolling from coast to coast. The railroad had done away with the covered wagon trains; and the old sailing ships, coming around the Horn, was being give a run for their money. Carbon was on the main line. All trains going east and west stopped there for coal. Settlers was filling up the treeless plains; folks in Nebraska and all along the way needed coal bad. There was work for everyone. No boy in Carbon, after he was weaned, was idle long.

The way they run the mines them days, they could use everyone in town. Now me, I was fifteen years old by then. I had callouses on my hands. They looked me over and set me to undercutting coal with a handpick. I worked with an old miner whose partner had been killed in a cave-in. He didn't take kindly to having a kid put in there with him. But I done my best; by the second day he was talking to me just like I was anybody.

I knowed enough to show up with my own tools, sharpened good, and I'd had considerable experience handling a pick when I was working for the railroad. But coal mining was a blamed sight different than I'd figgered it would be when I was thinking about it above ground. For one thing, it's terrible dark down there. Unless you've been in a coal mine, you can't believe that things can get that black. All of us miners had little pit lamps, with a hook that hooked into the leather band that we wore around our heads. Them little pit lamps looked like baby coffee pots. The lid fitted tight, with an air hole in the top to give it a draft. We'd lift up the lid and fill our lamps with about a half teacup of oil. Then we shoved the wick down the spout and left enough sticking out to make a real good blaze, soon as it was lit. A pit lamp shines wherever you are looking, but all around it's black. These new-fangled mining engineers can't figger out why, with all them open flames and the gas and coal dust, we wasn't all blowed to pieces, using them blamed lamps. I've waded through coal dust up to my ankles, with the flame shooting back over my head from my pit lamp, and never thought nothing about it because I didn't know no better. Guess that's the sort of thing that started that old saying, "The Lord looks out for fools and children."

At Number 2 mine, where I was working, the tunnel went back a long ways. Charley, who was working with me, claimed that tunnel was four mile long. I figger we walked that far to get to our room. The coal in the vein we was working run about seven foot thick. We had to pick it real careful, being sure to leave about six inches of coal overhead so she wouldn't cave in on us. When we come to the end of that vein we hit regular fire clay where she run out; then they moved us on to another place. But usually a man and his pardner worked a long time in the same room. Some places the vein run twelve to fourteen foot thick. Other places it made a dip, maybe of a hundred feet or thereaways, where there was just dirt. Then we'd hit another vein up higher again.

To start another room we'd pick in about three foot and cut an overhead. Then we'd move over and start another entry way in, running the two in side by side and about ten foot wide, leaving ten foot between them. Then we'd go back like that about seventy-five foot before we'd cut a hole through connecting the two. That was so air could come around.

Somebody was always trying to figger out some way to get air to the miners. At Number 2, they sunk a shaft from the surface to the tunnel, about half way back. They hadn't struck coal at all until they'd run the slope back so far from the entry that we wasn't getting no fresh air down in the mine. Up around the collar of the shaft, they built a house, thirty foot square, with big doors on each side and a tight roof. When the wind blowed, they'd open the door on the windward side, and them other closed doors and the roof would force the air down the shaft and into the mine. One hot day, when there wasn't no wind, one of the miners went up to tell the superintendent that we wasn't getting no air down in the mine. He says, "Hell, Joe, we ain't got none up here, neither."

Down in the pit, at the bottom of the shaft, they'd have two rooms running back side by side, with a passageway between, so the air would follow around to the side. Them new rooms wasn't getting no air. Air don't circulate in a pocket. So they put in doors that they could close and force air back into the side rooms. Then in close to each of them doors, they hollowed out a little place about the size and shape of a fireplace. They'd put a little boy in each of them places to pull a string that opened and shut the doors. The smaller the boys was, the easier they fit into a small hole; they had to be out of the way when the mule driver come through with the loaded coal cars.

Most of the little boys I seen, setting back in them little burrows, was about six or seven year old, and real skinny and washed-out looking. They worked the same hours as the rest of the miners, and we was starting so early of a morning that we had to light our way to the mines with our pit lamps, and it was always dark above ground before we quit at night.

Them little fellows set there, all day, bent over just watching and pulling that string when the mule cars come through, and closing the door when they was out of the way. After Mama got there and went to nursing, she said that work was real hard on them children. There was considerable consumption among the little fellows at Carbon.

Of course they wasn't doing heavy work, or dangerous, like the older ones done. That's why them little fellows didn't get much pay. The boys from ten to thirteen years old was getting paid around seventy-five cents a day for spragging. If a boy wasn't wide awake, he might lose some fingers, but spragging was a lot more exciting than setting in a dark hole all day, pulling a string.

You remember me telling you about how the veins don't run even underground. That means there are bound to be a lot of hills in the tunnels. Each miner had to fill his own car and run it to the entry of his room. Then the cars was lowered out of the rooms to the main tunnel, where the mule driver come along, gathered them up, and took them back clean through the mine to the main entry where they was hauled up to the surface with a h'ist. After they went to work in the mines, them mules never seen the light of day. Feed was let down to the lower levels where they stayed and hauled the coal cars.

None of them coal cars had brakes on them, and in a lot of the rooms there was steep pitches leading down to the main tunnel. The wheels on the cars was about fourteen inches across. Them boys, doing the spragging, would set on their knees by the track, with a pile of sprags beside them ricked up like stovewood. Why, a sprag is a little pole about fourteen inches long, and about as big around as your wrist, with a sharp point on one end, like a pencil. When the loaded coal cars start going by, you pick up two of them sticks and as the car starts to pick up speed, shove your sprags right in between the spokes just as they come around opposite you. That swings the sprag right up agin the bed of the car. Then the wheel locks, and the car slides down hill a lot slower. Sprags make good brakes, if you use them right.

Another boy set down at the foot of the incline, taking them out. The sprags that wasn't busted was piled up until he got a car full. Then they was hauled up to the top of the grade and used over again. On some of the worst pitches, they tried lowering the cars down with ropes. But that was dangerous on account of the ropes getting frazzled out and breaking. Spragging was a good way for them boys to learn to move fast.

Charley, who was working with me, said I'd better stay out of the poker games unless I knowed my business. He was one of the best poker players in Carbon, but it had cost him better than three hundred dollars to learn. Anyhow, a stranger like me was smart to set back until he could talk their language. Like if you got in an argument with a fellow and he says, "Be careful or you'll get your nose blowed," you'd have to back down or get the drop on him quick. Because he'd be figgering to blow your head off.

By the end of my first Saturday night in Carbon, I seen what Charley meant. The cowboys and Finns had been feuding for considerable time before I got there. Three of them cowboys—Rooster, Brewster, and Ramrod—come in regular of a Saturday night, and mostly played jokes. They weighed all of two hundred and thirty pounds apiece, and when they come galloping into town, bound and determined to raise all the Cain they could before they left, the breakage was something terrible, but that was about all it amounted to. That big bunch that come in, on my first Saturday night, was something again. They started in picking on some Finns that had got paid off and was waiting to take the train. They busted the bottoms out of some whiskey bottles by banging them agin the bar. Then they held on to the bottle necks and shoved the broken, jagged edges into them poor devils' faces, cutting them something terrible and almost blinding one old fellow. Then they got on their horses, emptied their guns in the general direction of anybody that hadn't ducked out of sight when they seen them coming, and galloped off. Some of us done what we could for the Finns. They was fellows who'd come to this country and worked in the mines so they could get a little money ahead and go to farming. Maybe them cowboys figgered that was a big joke. I thought it was about as funny as a butchering. But I seen what Charley meant when he give me that warning. I figgered that from then on, I'd keep my nose clean and watch my step of a Saturday night.

When I told Charley about the folks coming, he said I'd have to pick the part of the hill where we lived sort of careful. The women there had divided off into regular social sets. The Irish didn't have nothing to do with the Scotch. And the Finns kept away from the Danes. He figgered the bunch we'd fit in with best was the coal miners, who'd come over from Lancashire. I'd met some of them Lankies around the mine. They was big, raw-boned fellows who hunted elk, and antelope, and sage hens, of a Sunday. I figgered they'd be good folks to know. The Bob Jacksons lived in a dugout across from the depot. I boarded with them until the folks come. Nights we'd set and talk. They was one of the first families that moved to Carbon.

Mrs. Jackson and Bob had growed up together in England. He left and come to Pennsylvania, but he couldn't forget her. When he got enough money ahead, he went back to England and they was married. They was short of money for the long trip back, so when they stood up to get married, they used a borrowed ring. After they got to Pennsylvania, he'd figgered on buying her one, but he got down with the fever ague, just like my folks done. Then he had a chance to come out to Carbon with a bunch of other Lankies, and they was hired because they knowed mining. After they got to Carbon, he kept worrying about her not having no ring. By then he had a little money ahead, so he left her and their two little girls while he went off prospecting, clean into the Black Hills. He'd had as hard a trip as any of them. The Indians made off with his outfit, and almost got him. All he come home with was enough gold to make her a wedding ring, but she sure was proud of it.

Mrs. Jackson was a manager. She could make a little water go farther than anyone I ever seen. She burned paper in a whiskey barrel to kill the taste and then scrubbed it good with soap and water. She had a dishcloth and then a wooden lid for the top. After Mr. Ford filled that water barrel, she give him his twenty-five cents, and nobody was allowed to touch the barrel but her. The drinking water was kept in a bucket on the table, with a dipper hanging on the side. But no matter how close she figgered, wash days and bath nights run into money. Coal miners and their clothes get terrible dirty. Anybody who says soap and water is cheap never lived in Carbon.

Saturday night, Mrs. Jackson would call the two little girls in and look them over careful. The one with the cleanest head got washed first. Course, that hardly seemed fair, because that give her a better chance for the next week, too. But Mrs. Jackson figgered the cleanest one should get washed first as a prize for being the cleanest. After she had washed their heads, she used the same water to give them their baths. Then after they was in bed, she used that same water to scrub the floor and wash the outhouse.

Seeing how comfortable the Jacksons made out cheered me up enough so that by the time Mama and the rest of the family got to

Carbon, I was ready to show them the place I'd picked out for our dugout. I'd hunted around until I'd got quite a pile of stuff to start it with, too.

But the morning the folks got off the train, I couldn't think of much to say. Mama just stood there in front of the depot, quiet-like for a long time; looking all around. Then she turned to Father, and says, "Sam, is this it?"

At first he didn't have nothing to say because he hadn't seen Carbon until then neither. Then he cleared his throat and says, "Yes, Martha, this is it. But I understand there's a lot of activity going on under ground."

Julia hadn't come with them. She'd got married. I just took for granted that she'd got tied to Wash Brown. He was Porter's boy, and had growed up neighbor to us in Arcadia. The Browns was all workers, and kept the biggest woodpile ahead and drove the best horses of anybody in our valley. Soon as he was old enough, Wash had filed on a homestead in close to ours. He'd planted it to corn and was feeding hogs and shipping them to Chicago. Wash was thrifty. He'd built his house and had been setting up regular with Julia, but he was terrible bashful when it come to speaking up. In all the years he lived neighbor to us, I only heard him swear once. Then all he said was, "Jesus God." Wash just wasn't no hand with words.

But you could of knocked me over with a feather when Mama said Julia had married Jim Mapes. They was living in Grand Island, where Jim was working in the shops. There never was a finer-looking, big, blue-eyed fellow than Jim, or a harder worker. He tried awful hard to get ahead, but a lot of the time his luck run bad. It had been a year since Sadie had died, but Mama said he still seemed terrible lost without her. Julia thought a lot of Jim, and she figgered he needed her the most.

Father had begun to think his luck wasn't too good neither. When he got back to Nebraska, he'd looked all around for someone to buy our homestead. We'd put in a lot of work proving up on it and getting our papers. But folks was sort of shying away from that part of Nebraska, on account of us being eat out so many times by the grasshoppers. Anybody with money was buying railroad land; they'd opened up a lot of land to the west, in close to the tracks. The real dirt farmers didn't have no money to pay down, anyhow. With all the free land on beyond, they just kept on going until they found a place where they could file. The best Father could do was rent our homestead out, slap a five hundred dollar mortgage on it, and hope that land prices would go up.

After I took the folks over to the place I'd rented until we got settled, Mama sort of got her second wind. She started acting real cheerful and asked me a lot of questions about how I'd been, and she told me how nice it was for us to be together again. But I noticed she waited for several weeks before she wrote to her folks in Pennsylvania about our new home.

I laid off from the mine long enough to help Father get the dugout finished and the roof on. The nicest houses in Carbon was made of flat stone slabs piled one on top the other with adobe plaster between. But the first settlers there had gathered up all the rocks in close. Hauling in stone for a house runs into money. The only folks building stone houses when we got there was the ones who was blamed sure they was going to stay. Ford, the waterman, and the mine officials had real good stone houses.

Mama started fixing our place up soon as the freight got there. She'd kept some real pretty quilt tops that had scorched too bad to make up when our house burned in Virginia. She hung them on the walls and folded them so the holes didn't show. We put up our rag carpet canopy that we'd used on the ceiling of our sod house for a ceiling again. Why, when Mama got through fixing it up, you'd never know, when you come inside our dugout, that the walls was dirt and it run back into the hillside.

Mrs. Jackson had brung her marriage chest with her from England. She had a bunch of them white-linen aprons, made real long, and wide enough to go clean around her. She split some of them for curtains and used some of them for table covers, and kept the others to wear on days when she wanted to dress up extra special.

We all took to them Lancashire neighbors right off. Their children had nice manners and they kept their houses clean. But there wasn't none of them that could hold a candle to them Finnish women when it come to working and scrubbing from daylight till dark. About the only fun they had all week was on Saturday night when they turned out for sauna. I figger having them steam bath houses where they poured water over hot rocks and then set around visiting and getting up a real sweat, was a lot better than the way we done, taking turns climbing into a washtub that was set out in the middle of the floor in front of the stove, with Mama testing the water with her elbow before she poured more in from the teakettle. Mama was always sorry she couldn't talk to them Finnish neighbors of ours, but they couldn't speak English. She knowed they was quality, when she first seen them hanging out their wash, snow white.

Mama was a proud woman, and I never seen a harder worker nowhere. It wasn't no time until our dugout was one of the nicest in Carbon. She'd always had flowers in her dooryard and didn't aim to go without them there. She went out in the desert, keeping watch for rattlesnakes and Indians, and dug up cactus and prickly pears, and Indian paintbrush. She planted them all along both sides in front of our dugout, and whitewashed rocks and set them on both sides the path. Then her and Myra leveled off a little place to one side, and lined rocks around for the walls, and left empty places for the doors and windows. After that, Myra could ask other little girls to come and play with her, in her playhouse. They'd serve afternoon tea and practice their manners, with Mama keeping an eye on them, to see they done it right.

We hadn't no more than got settled when two young fellows stopped in one night. Mama had been baking bread. You can smell good bread a long ways off and them boys seemed real hungry for it. After they et their way through most a loaf, they asked Mama if she'd bake for them. When she said she would, they brung up two sacks of flour. The agreement was that she'd bake up one sack for them and keep the other one as pay for doing the baking. Next day word got around over at the mine. That night men begun to come to our door carrying sacks of flour. Soon, Mama was putting in most of her time baking bread. We had so much flour ahead, she begun selling loaves, too. We had a long narrow table, better than six foot long across one side of our dugout, and she was filling it regular every day with fresh baked bread. Nights her arms would be so tired from all that kneading that I got in the habit of scrubbing up extra good and helping her knead the dough before she put it to raise for the morning baking.

Making all that bread wouldn't of been so bad, if word hadn't got around that Mama was a nurse. She begun taking care of women when they was having their babies. Then, because there wasn't no doctor in camp, they started calling her for accidents, too. One night the miners come for Mama and she had to walk four mile through deep snow to Number 5 mine. A fellow lay way back on one of the lower levels where a coal car had run over his leg, breaking it up close to the hip, and cutting him bad. When they got there, she seen that the break wasn't right in the joint. It was terrible hard, working down there with just the lights from the miners' pit lamps. But she kept her fingers on his leg, feeling them bones slipping back in place, while a couple of miners held him down by the shoulders and two others pulled down on his leg, to set the broken bones. After they got a splint on it, they strapped him to a board and got him to the tipple, where the light was better. Then she seen he'd lost too much blood and was too weak to be carried up over the hill and across four mile of snow to Carbon. The miners brung what she needed and they set up a place right there in the corner of a shed for Mama to stay and take care of him. Nights, Myra would stand by the window watching more than a hundred miners come marching over the hill, coming back after dark from working their long day at Number 5. She'd watch the lights from their pit lamps streaming back over their heads. Their faces was so black with coal dust that nothing showed but black shadows and bright lights, moving across, above the snow. And Myra would cry and wonder why Mama wasn't coming home from Number 5 mine, too. Then come the night when we seen the shadow of her long full skirt as she walked along beside the men who was carrying somebody strapped to a plank. That's when we knowed that the miner who was hurt had got well enough to be moved back to Carbon and Mama was coming home again. After that, when Mama went to the store, the miners all tipped their caps, and we was proud of the way they spoke to her.

Money never went far enough, them days. We was getting from $1.75 to $2.00 a day. Things always seem extra high, when you're dealing at a company store. In the spring Mama sent $5.00 back to Nebraska and asked our kinfolk there to send us as many cabbages and onions as we could get for that much money. We'd pay the freight at our end of the haul. When they come the freight was $22.00. Mama sold enough of them under what the regular price was there at Carbon to get her $27.00 back, and she still had almost half of them left over for us.

The company paid the men different rates because they said some places was easier to work than others. Some of them was getting a dollar a ton digging over at Number 6 mine. Most of them fellows was putting in from twelve to fourteen hours a day because they was on their own. Most of the Finns had worked so hard in the old country that they was willing to work for less and put in as high as eighteen hours a day. Then the company got to talking about how much they was making, and the Lankies, who was old hands at mining, got mad, and said they was running down the pay for all the rest of us.

The worst of it was it took 2,240 pounds to make a ton. Then the company took one car in eight for screenage, and didn't give you nothing for that car. Before long, they changed that to one in four. When the miners found out they was selling the fine coal they called screenage to the settlers in Nebraska, and getting ten dollars a ton for it, they called a meeting.

One fellow got his dander up and went in to see L. R. Meyers, the superintendent. Meyers was all right, but he was under Clark who spent most of his time in Omaha and he had to make a record for him, just like Clark had to make a record to the head fellows that was above him. Most of the miners was afraid to talk back to Meyers, but Johnson was so mad he couldn't keep still. He figgered he hadn't been paid what was coming to him. Meyers was real pleasant, and went over all the figures with him, and says, "Yes, you do have thirty cents more coming to you, after we deduct for the screenage and the leakage."

Johnson says, "You don't need to pay me the thirty cents. Just keep the damned stuff and call it stealage."

By the time we paid for our powder, and squibbs, and getting our tools sharpened, there was mighty little left. The miners got pretty ugly about the way things was going. But they figgered if they struck for higher wages the company would bring more men in from outside. Mostly they was real careful to wait and practice their talking back when they was by theirselves, down at the saloons of a Saturday night.

During the next summer, a bunch of folks come down with the

spotted fever, only we called it mountain fever them days. Mama and me got it terrible bad. All the other real serious cases was hauled up to Laramie on the train, and died there in the hospital. When we started burning up with the fever, Mama had Father and Myra go out and gather a big kettleful of sagebrush leaves. She boiled them a long time, and then added some chopped-up lemons that Father got down at the store. I never tasted nothing as bitter as that tea. From then on, that's all we drunk until we'd downed that whole kettleful. It's the only medicine there is that cures the mountain fever. Why sure it is. I know because I'm here, and them other folks that didn't take it, ain't.

After that epidemic, there was quite a bit of talk about us not having a doctor at Carbon. Word got around that the company had hired one, and at first the miners figgered it was a good idea. But when they tried to hold out a dollar a month for the single men and a dollar and a half for the ones with families, so's he'd be getting a regular salary, I seen Johnson heading for Meyers' office again. He was sore as a boil, and says, "Why in the hell are they calling that sawbones the company doctor if we're the ones that's paying him!"

When the Sioux was moved west, nobody seemed to think nothing about them Cheyenne and Arapaho Indians that was supposed to be hunting there too. But in 1876 they claimed they was being lied to about their reservation, and they made camp right on the Platte River, in eastern Wyoming, and said they wouldn't move until they told the President of the United States that they had a right to a reservation right where they was. But he was busy at the time, and sent an agent from the Bureau of Indian Affairs. When he got out there, they was starving. He promised old Chief Washakie that he'd only move them up with the Shoshones for the winter. Chief Washakie, who'd been friendly to the whites, said the tribes was enemies, but they moved them together anyhow. The Shoshones didn't want the Arapahos on their reservation, and made things just as tough for them as they could. Finally in 1937, the Shoshones sued the government and they got four million dollars for the value of the land and natural resources that the Arapahos had used up during the sixty-one years it took them fellows in Washington to decide that the Arapahos didn't have no business up there where that agent moved them. Yes, sir, after he'd been dead for years, they decided that them Arapahos belonged right there in Wyoming, where old Chief Washakie said they did all the time.

Back when that old chief was moving his lodges in with the Shoshones, a lot of young bucks that didn't want to hand in their horses and guns took to the hills. Other bands was roving out there already. In 1879, the Utes went on the warpath. Joe Rankin from Rawlins, just fifty mile west of us, and Major Thornburg with a party of soldiers took off after them. Word come in to the telegraph office at midnight on September 30 that they had been waylaid in a canyon to the south of us. The men went out to help and found that thirty-five of the soldiers had been killed, and fifty-nine others was wounded. We knowed a lot of them Indians was still out beyond, waiting to pick off anybody they could.

One day, the stable boss at the mines went to look for some mules that had strayed off. When he didn't come back, some of the boys went to look for him. They found him shot full of arrows, and carried him back to the mine where he died that night. Everyone had gone there to hide, figgering the Indians might attack. The mine was handy. We didn't have to build no blockhouse, even if we was living in Indian country. Ever once in awhile a cowboy would come riding in with the corpse of some stranger he'd picked up who'd got scalped on his way out to Carbon looking for work. Our cemetery was filling up. Them Indians kept us on our toes. When the whistle blowed the signal, everybody above ground come running. Then the women and children stayed in the mine all night, and the men stayed up at the entrance with their guns ready. One night the Bob Jacksons heard noises up on their sod roof. They figgered the Indians was up there hiding in the grass, spying down on the rest of the town. At first they was afraid to move. Then Bob got them organized and they made a run for the mine. The whistle blowed, everybody in town come a-running. We stayed there in the mine, huddled together all night. Come daylight, the men organized a strong party and went out to reconnoiter. They went up the road past the cemetery and circled back looking for Indian sign on the hill back of Jackson's house, but all they found was the old sow and her pigs that belonged to the restaurant man. They'd broke loose and clumb the hill to the little hollow where Jackson's roof started to slant up and had bedded down there for the night.

Carbon never had no real Indian attack while we was there. By then the Indians knowed we was too strong for them, but them young bucks was just beyond town, waiting and hating us for what had been done to the friendly ones we'd took away. Many's the night we'd hear the signal and run for the mine, figgering them Indians had lost their heads and was aiming to have one last good fight. There ain't no better way to get to know your neighbors than to stay all night with them in a coal mine, waiting for the Indians to attack. It got so when the cowboys come in off the range, to get liquored up and beat up the Finns, we was ready for them. By then we'd got used to our Finns and knowed they was good neighbors.

Saturday night I'd lie in bed and listen to the Lankies, dancing till daylight to the tune of Lunny's fiddle. Them fellows had growed up on coal mining in England. They never looked ahead to nothing beyond Sunday morning and horse racing and shooting live pigeons on the wing. All they wanted out of life was steady work and to live and die in Carbon. We really knowed each other, and no matter where we went we was still in plain sight. Young folks, trying to do their courting on Sunday (that's the only free time a miner ever has), got to walking up to the railroad cut and setting there on a boulder, holding hands. But that wasn't near as much fun as it could of been, on account of the little boys following them and throwing clods down on their heads from up above.

On the Fourth of July, the whole town always turned out for a big picnic and a full day of sport. That was the best day of the year. The Methodists was holding meetings on Sundays then, and us members was sort of held back until the Fourth come. That's when we'd watch Mike and John Quealy, whose dad was our pit boss, trying to look like regular jockeys in them big, forty-pound, western, stock-saddles, and putting all they had into winning from each other. The Lankies was strong for horse racing, but it got so they was holding back and betting most of their money on the pigeon shooting. There just ain't no more sporty target than a live pigeon, and we was all having a fine time till we found out that them fellows releasing the pigeons was playing favorites by spitting tobacco juice into the pigeon's eye when they wanted a fellow to miss. Most shooters has a weakness. Some can hit a right angle better than a left. The fellows, letting the pigeons go, knowed every shooter's weakness, and would spit the tobacco juice in the opposite eye to the way they wanted the pigeon to fly. That was to make him veer off to one side so a fellow would miss his shot. When we found out what was going on, we had a fist fight that left most of us seeing as crooked as them pigeons. That night everybody went back to town for the calico and overall dance. Prizes was give to the girls that waltzed with a glass of water on their heads if they hadn't spilled a drop.

Yep, that was a big day, and I was sure glad that Julia and Jim had got there to enjoy the fun. All Mama done that day was to set and hold their new baby, but from the fuss she was making over it, I figgered she was having the most fun of any of us. When the Union Pacific finished building the shops at Grand Island and laid off the men, Jim and his brother Joe had come West looking for work. They was lucky, and got on at the mine. Jim rented a little place in close to us, and Julia pitched right in, helping with the baking so Mama could take nursing jobs farther away from home.

We was learning a lot right there in Carbon. A Swede, named Coffee Johnson, had a regular museum in his store. Coffee was a great traveler. He was close with his money and charged high prices on account of having to save up enough to go on another trip. Nights I'd go into his store and stand and look at the bottle of water from the Dead Sea, and sand from the Sahara Desert, and the bullets from Gettysburg, the lion skin from Africa, and the eight-legged lamb that growed right there in Wyoming. That's when I knowed it was time for me to be getting out where I could see new things for myself.

We'd only lived in Carbon two years but during that time I seen things quiet down considerable. The women got to feeling their oats so much that the married men didn't dare cut up when their wives was around. The Territorial Constitution had give them the vote, and they never let nobody forget that they was the first women in the United States to have it. Over in South Pass a woman had got herself elected justice of the peace—our men figgered that sort of thing could spread. Why it got so the only fun the married men had was helping to run the bad folks out of town. The women had egged their men on until they'd elected a sort of a town welfare committee to notify anyone caught doing wrong that it was time for them to move on.

Two fellows come in and set up their business with two girls they'd brung with them. They rented a house, fixed it up good, and figgered on staying permanent. The committee went over and told them to start packing. Them two fellows just laughed and dug right in to toughy her out. Next thing I knowed about it, the committee had them fellows down at the telegraph pole by the depot. Word got around while they was peeling the shirts off them fellows' backs. All the men knocked off work and come running, figgering on seeing a hanging. But the committee just made the prisoners face the pole. Then they wrapped their arms around it and tied their hands together, while all us men got in two lines. Each of us got to give them fellows two good whacks across their bare backs before we handed the switch we was using to the fellow waiting back of us. When the committee untied them fellows and told them to take their women and git, they didn't have to be told again. Of course, some of the miners, whipping them the hardest, had been hanging around their place regular. But the way things was going they couldn't show which side they was really on in public.

Yep, by 1882, when Big-Nose George was captured in eastern Montana and brung back to stand trial for being one of that gang of robbers that had pulled the spikes on the Dale Creek Bridge, figgering on dumping the express into that seven hundred foot canyon, folks had settled down considerable. That gang never did get nothing off that train, because Honesen, who run a store in Carbon, was out that way hunting, and flagged down the train. But what folks in Carbon was mad about was that them fellows who'd been holding up trains pretty regular had shot and killed our two deputies, Tom Widdowfield and W. Vincent, when they was sent out to bring them in. But Sheriff Rankin had got a confession out of Big-Nose George, and had locked him up in the jail at Rawlins. Everybody figgered the law was handling things fine. The public hanging was to be held downtown in Rawlins on April 3, 1882. The mine was shutting down so everybody could go. All they talked about, until then, was the killing of them two deputies and the running down and capture of Dutch Charley and Big-Nose George.

Both them deputies was fine fellows, but Tom Widdowfield was sort of special, because he'd lived in Carbon. We liked his wife and his two little boys, and we knowed how bad they felt, when they never seen him alive again, after he left trailing them train robbers. When the deputies got to Rattlesnake Creek, at the foot of Elk Mountain, they come to a fire that still had live coals in under the ashes. That's when they was shot and killed from ambush. Vincent's remains was shipped back to his folks. Tom Widdowfield's friends chipped in to pay for that big tombstone in the cemetery at Carbon that tells how he was shot while doing his duty.

Soon after they was killed, Dutch Charley was captured over close to Laramie, but Big-Nose George had got away. Sheriff Rankin took custody of Dutch Charley, handcuffed him, and put him on the train heading for Rawlins, the county seat of Carbon County. The telegraph operator had heard they was coming, so the men piled boulders and railroad ties across the track to stop the train. Another bunch had ties ready and piled them in back of the train so the engineer couldn't move it either way. Then the men clumb aboard, and told Sheriff Rankin they was taking charge of Dutch Charley.

They stood him up on a big barrel while they tied the hangman's knot, then they rolled the barrel away, and hung him to the cross-arm of the telegraph pole at the Carbon depot. They left him for several days. Through passengers on the U.P. train always let out yells and pointed when they seen Dutch Charley swinging there. The smell got bad. But the show-offs around town would walk over and grab his shoes and swing him around until the rope up above got all twisted and knotted. One time when it started whirling back, the rope broke. After that happened, they carted him off and buried him in the desert. Nope, they didn't want him buried in our cemetery along with Tom Widdowfield and the rest of the home folks.

But, by the time they captured Big-Nose George, two whole years had passed since the lynching of Dutch Charley. Folks had calmed down and cooled off; they was ready to let Sheriff Rankin take over and hang Big-Nose George according to law. But the blamed fool wouldn't cooperate. Just a week before the hanging, he slugged the sheriff when he was taking him his dinner. Mrs. Rankin had sense enough to slam the outside door of the jail shut before she shot the sheriff's revolver into the air to signal for help. Men come and run him down in the back hall. They drug him out and made him climb a ladder with the noose around his neck. They was using the telegraph pole at the depot in Rawlins. When they took the ladder away, the rope broke and he lit on his feet, running. So they shot him when he was running right up the main street of Rawlins.

Young Doc Osborne come and pronounced him dead. He got to looking him over and thinking about how something ought to be done to preserve a man as well-knowed as Big-Nose George, so he got some plaster, and made a death mask. Soon as it was set, he went right to work and skinned him. Then he sent Big-Nose George's hide to a tannery, and told them to finish part of it natural, but to dye the rest a deep chocolate brown.

Then Doc Osborne had a pair of shoes made out of the hide. They're two-tone, with tops made of darker leather, and the lower parts light-cream colored. They look like regular oxfords, and are stitched real neat and lined with the darker shade. Next time you're in Rawlins, Wyoming, you go into the Rawlins National Bank, there on the main street, down close to the depot. After you pass the counter where folks sign their checks, you'll see a little case, off to the right. Inside, you'll see a picture of Big-Nose George, and the death mask Doc Osborne made. It's got a terrible sneer around the mouth. But the thing you want to look at real good is them two-toned oxfords, made from Big-Nose George's hide. You won't see nicer looking leather no place.

Living in Carbon, in them early days, was like living on an island. The trains stopped for coal, then they went on again. Us folks, mining that coal, didn't have no way to turn, excepting towards each other. We come there to live on a desert. If we hadn't put down roots and worked together, we wouldn't of had no more chance than a bunch of tumbleweeds, blowed·along ahead of the wind. Why, the first fellows trying to build a church in Carbon had to go and get other men to help them. Even with a bunch of them working together, the wind blowed so hard they had to put the framework up three times before they got the roof on.

Railroads needs coal, and they've got to have miners to get it out for them. Carbon was first, but it wasn't long until other coal towns was opened up by the railroads. Some of the folks that wasn't miners at heart moved on. A lot of them Finns had growed up on farms. Soon as they got a little money ahead, they went to homesteading in Dakota. A bunch of them come clean out here to the Hood River Valley, in Oregon. Most of them are dead now. But when we used to meet at the store, we'd stop and visit. They was proud of their children and of the fine fruit their boys was raising. Then we'd switch back and talk about the folks we'd knowed at Carbon.

When the Union Pacific moved the main tracks and all of its equipment to Hanna, six mile north of Carbon, a lot of the old-timers wouldn't move until they was starved into it. But the railroad engineers knowed that the Carbon Basin had played out, and they done their best to help their old miners get moved and to give them the best jobs. Hanna was the nearest town, so most of them went over there and went right to work on Number 1 mine. Just a year after they moved over there from Carbon, a hundred and sixty-nine miners was killed in an explosion in Number 1 mine. Bob Jackson come through that one and he wasn't killed in the second explosion in Number 1 when fifty-nine more miners was killed. By then a lot of his friends was gone, but he lived right on at Hanna until 1923.

When he died there wasn't no hearse in town, but his folks borrowed a wagon and they drove over six mile of dirt road, taking him back to where he wanted to be. They buried him there in that big cemetery that stands out, all by itself, on the desert. Once a year, folks still come from all over, and they spend Decoration Day cleaning up the graves and fixing the fence. Then they have a picnic, and they set and talk about the Carbon they remember. Ever once in a while the antelope get curious because they see something new and white flashing over inside the cemetery fence. But when they go over to look, it's only another old-timer come back to Carbon. One of the newest tombstones belongs to Bob Jackson's nephew, who was killed in the World War. Another belongs to an old miner who was brung clean back from California, because his folks said he hadn't never felt at home nowhere else since he'd had to move away from Carbon when it got to be a ghost town, way back in 1902.

But shucks, Father and Jim and me wasn't real miners. I'd growed up out-of-doors. Days, when I'd go down into the pits, I'd think about fresh air and cold water, and going fishing again. Father come home and told me about finding a little spring of water down in the mine. The next day was Sunday, so he got the pit boss to let him take Mama and Myra down to see it. They walked better than two mile underground, stumbling along following the coal-car tracks.

When they got there the spring was dried up and gone, and Myra cried. That night, when Father was off downtown with the men again, I told Mama I was through working underground dreaming of the time we'd be drinking cold water again. That was in 1883. I was seventeen years old and ready to strike out on my own. I knowed where I was going and I knowed what I was going to do.

I says: "I'm moving on ahead. The Columbia River is the biggest river in the west, and it grows the biggest fish. I'm striking out for there to learn the cannery business. Maybe railroads needs coal, but I've got to work where there's water."

TEN

THE EMIGRANT TRAIN—WEST

When I got down to Jim and Julia's place to tell them I was moving on ahead, they was setting by the table, side by side. The coal oil lamp was right in front of them so they could both see good. The table was covered with books and maps and pictures. I never seen nothing like them roses, or the orange blossoms, or the green trees. The picture I liked best was one that showed the ocean. But Julia was looking most at one of a herd of cows, standing in a field of clover. She figgered her and Jim ought to be moving on, because Carbon was such a hard place to wean a baby. Anyhow, mining there was tapering off. Number 3 and Number 4 had shut down. Number 5 was almost worked out.

Working men only get paid when they're working, but big companies sort of like to have extra hands around so they'll be there when they need them. The last ones to go to work on a job are always the first laid off. Jim seen it coming and there wasn't no point in him moving over to Rock Springs just because a lot of the folks we knowed had. He'd been over and looked around, but he said housing was lots worse than at Carbon. The wind blowed there terrible. Spring and fall, Bitter Creek flooded folks out of their dugouts.

Rock Springs is the place that got wrote up in 1924 as being the largest town in the United States without no inside toilets. Eight thousand folks was living there in '24, but when Jim and Julia talked about moving over in '83, it wasn't near that crowded.

Jim said he couldn't see no point in staying in the mines when he had money enough ahead to get him and Julia and the baby to San Francisco.

Julia wanted to be real sure they knowed what they was doing before they talked it around. That's why she wrote a big bunch of letters to different places, asking about California. The biggest booklet come from the Union Pacific-Central Pacific, because they'd been running through trains since 1869, and knowed more about what questions folks would likely be asking when they was getting ready to move West. But the Texas-Southern Pacific that had built lines to the coast in 1882, and the Santa Fe and Northern Pacific, that was just getting finished, was going clean out of their way to cut rates and help folks get located, too. Jim figgered they was doing it because there was so much land out West going to waste. Julia was suspicious of railroads on account of seeing Father read them same kind of books, until she wrote letters to all the different people about Jim's chances of getting work.

But this was different. The best answers of all had come from the Commissioner of Immigration in California, and the Commissioner of the Public Land Office in Washington, D.C. Why, California had over 100,000 orange trees. Most of the orchards was making a profit of better than a thousand dollars an acre. Some had run as high as $3,000.00 an acre; $800.00 was considered low. They wrote that California wasn't just raising oranges. They was planting hundreds of acres of cotton and most everything else. That's why they was so shorthanded and needed experienced farmers so bad; they'd sent men clean to Italy to get fellows that knowed how, to come out there and raise grapes and make them into wine.

The bunch doing the most to help folks get started was The California Immigration Union that "maintained a general agent at Copenhagen, Hamburg, and Bremen." There was also a "traveling agent in Germany and a general agent for the eastern states." William T. Colman, who'd headed up that big vigilante committee, was president of the Union. But Leland Stanford, who helped drive that gold spike connecting the East and West, and Mark Hopkins, and Peter Spreckles was right in there with him, pitching too. They must of figgered they had a good thing, or they wouldn't of sent all them books out free, just to help poor folks make a fresh start out West.

You just haven't got no idea how much paper Julia got back from sending out that bunch of letters. Everybody had something else to tell. The California Legislature was going to run Japan right out of business when it come to manufacturing silk. All they needed was more farmers to help them. They announced: "The State of California, with the view of establishing the business of silk making as one of its fixed pursuits, offers a premium of $250.00 for every 5,000 mulberry trees (planted), to be paid when they are two years old, and a premium of $300.00 for every 100,000 cocoons."

It wasn't no wonder that Julia was so excited she wouldn't let me get in a word edgewise. When she finally run down, and I told her I was heading for Astoria, and the Columbia River, she give me a big squeeze and says, "Mont, that's wonderful. We'll go to San Francisco together, on the same train."

I never seen her like she was that night. While Jim and me set and talked, she was laughing and humming as she started right in getting their stuff packed. She had to stop a couple of times to nurse Orey, when he woke up and cried. Mama had told her the baby was getting way past weaning time, but it was hard for Julia to know what else to do, when he was crying and reaching out his hands to her and there wasn't a cow in Carbon.

When Mama found that Julia and Jim and the baby was leaving right away too, she took it kind of hard at first. But when Julia told her about how good things was going to be for us all out West, she seen it was the only thing we could do. That was a funny thing about them two. I don't think Mama ever stopped to think that Julia wasn't her own blood daughter, and Sadie was. Mama was one of them women who don't have to do the borning to be a mother. But sometimes it sort of got Julia, having folks say she was a step-daughter. She showed it considerable the day Sadie died. That was when I found her crying out back of the woodpile, saying over and over again, "Why couldn't it have been me."

Of course, when folks get in as big a hurry as we was to move on ahead, they don't have time to be missing each other until the packing's done and they've left home for good. Julia and Mama went right to work figgering out what we'd take, while Jim and me went down to the mine. We turned in our time, drawed our money, and picked up and sold our tools. It wasn't like we needed to give notice. They had more men waiting than they had places for them to work.

After I'd quit, Meyers, the superintendent, come up to the dugout and told Mama he'd been watching me for a long time. Because I was a steady worker, didn't drink, and could be depended on, he'd figgered on putting me in the pump house at Number 6. It meant a job in the daylight. Any other time I'd of jumped at the chance. But he'd come while I was down buying my ticket, and I couldn't see turning back then.

Jim and me got three tickets to San Francisco from the railroad agent in Carbon. We'd been told to be sure and buy them from a fellow we knowed. Scalpers was palming off counterfeit railroad tickets around all the big depots, and they'd figgered out a lot of different ways to make it work. One of the best was to have a woman standing outside the depot crying. If she was a good looker, men was bound to stop and comfort her. When she'd find where one of them fellows was going, that would turn out to be where she was going too. Only she'd just found out she couldn't because her mother had just took sick and was dying. She'd come down to turn her ticket in, and they wouldn't give her money back; she'd open her bag, fumble around a minute and show her ticket. It looked like a good one, all printed and stamped. The fellow would bite and take it off her hands. When he got on the train the conductor would tell him it was a phoney. The conductors had to be terrible careful about them counterfeit tickets. If they took the wrong kind, they was charged up agin them, so they made folks get off or sold them other tickets. That's why we bought ours in Carbon. I give the ticket-taker enough extra to get me to Astoria by boat. He said to check the sailing date when I got to San Francisco.

We could of got a better rate, if more of us had been going. The way it was, we had to pay straight coach fare from Carbon to Ogden, where we'd change cars from the Union Pacific to the Central Pacific. If thirty-six folks went together, they got a special rate. We was saving a little money by going from Ogden on by emigrant car. They give a free baggage allowance of a hundred and fifty pounds apiece. Guns went free if they was carried in cases. Most everybody took their own food along because meals at them railroad eating places cost from four to six bits, and they didn't care what they served, because they wouldn't be seeing you again.

Julia and Jim had traveled light coming out from Grand Island. They sold most everything they had left, right there in Carbon. All I took West with me was my bed roll, extra clothes, double-barrel shotgun, rifle, and food to eat on the trip. We all had our own tin plates, cups, and spoons. Julia packed the cooking pot in with her stuff.

The train come through in the morning. Mama and Myra was the only ones down to see us off because the men was working in the pits. While we was setting on a bench, waiting for the train, Myra begun to put up a fuss about wanting to go too, but Mama put her arm around her shoulders and straightened her right out. She says, "Myra, some day you'll be leaving. Mothers and fathers always know it's coming. They think about days like this one, from the time their babies are born. But they don't really mind saying good-bye, so long as they know that their children are going on ahead. I'm happy, right now, because I know that Mont and Jim will be having good jobs and the baby will be drinking fresh milk, and Julia won't have to work so hard. It's a long way across, from east to west, but now we're almost there."

After we got on the train, Jim and Julia got a seat together, and took turns holding the baby while I set alongside a fellow I never seen before or since. I must of been thinking about Mama, with her arm across Myra's shoulders, talking to her, just like she'd talk to me. I seen why she figgered then that whatever come she wasn't going to quit, and she wasn't sending no bad news home to her folks, neither. Yep, I must of been thinking about something else, because I can't even remember crossing over from Wyoming into Utah, or nothing, excepting that there was a lot of country between Carbon and Ogden.

When we come to the valley that drained into the Great Salt Lake, we was all looking around to see what kind of a place them Mormons had walked to. They sure didn't have much to start with, but they was making something fine out of a desert. Mama always said, "The Lord helps those who help themselves." That sure goes for the Mormons; they ain't ever asked no favors of nobody.

When we was still living in Carbon, we'd seen many an emigrant train, heading west. We knowed they set on seats covered with rice-sacking, while passenger cars was upholstered and stylish inside. But we hadn't been on a train with folks going clean on through to the coast. We used to set on some rocks, close to our dugout and look at them folks on the emigrant train. They was sort of bottled up in there without no fresh air; that's why they'd pile off and walk back and forth while the train was taking on coal. Most of them was Americans, just like us, and they'd walk all around the platform, and then make a run for it when the whistle blowed. But them foreigners stayed in close to the steps, because they wasn't taking no chances on being left. Them women held on tight to big, shawl wrapped bundles, even when they just stepped outside long enough to get a breath of air.

But setting on a hill looking down at people traveling like that is a lot different from being one of them yourself. When we got off the coach at Ogden, we was emigrants too. A big, potbellied fellow stood there shouting at us, and pointing to a far siding where we was to carry our stuff and get on a train that was made up of freight cars back of the engine, two flat cars back of that, and then a whole bunch of wore-out, beat-up old coaches that had been brung out from the East coast, after the railroads back there couldn't use them no more.

I never seen so many different kinds of folks as I did on that loading platform at Ogden. But when they seen us get off the through train and knowed we was emigrants too, they was extra friendly, and took us right in with them. That whole trainload of folks had been cooped up together all the way from Omaha. Them days, the through trains on the transcontinental lines was averaging twenty-two mile an hour, but emigrant trains didn't run on a regular schedule; they set on sidings and let them fast trains go through. By the time that bunch got to Ogden they was real well acquainted, and laughing and joshing while they was carrying their stuff from the Union Pacific train, over to the emigrant train. Most of the folks that had little children big enough to walk, tied their pans, and tin cups, and things like that on ropes, hanging down their backs. That sort of stuff is light, but takes up room and is hard to pack. It come in as handy, keeping track of them children, as a bell does on a cow when she's browsing on brush and likely to get out of sight.

Soon as we got aboard, we begun piling our stuff in under the seats. The men put their guns and what else they could in the racks up overhead, but no matter how we worked it, we was still crowded. Thirty-six people in a car, along with their children, hand luggage, blankets, victuals, and pots and pans, sleeping curled up on them slippery matting seats and waiting in line to do their cooking on two little stoves in the corner, can't be strangers long. I set up all the way because there was four of us single fellows setting two by two and knee to knee, down at the end of the car. One family that had two part-growed children and a baby slept the best. They let the seats clean down so they had a solid bed. Then they pulled their bundles out and tucked their two children in under the seat. The woman and man and the baby slept on the bed part. But the rest of the folks done quite a bit of jawing about the way they had their stuff piled out in the aisle. Jim and Julia just had the one seat, so they leaned it back all they could without getting called down by the folks back of them, and took turns sleeping and holding the baby.

Golly we had fun on that trip. By the time that bunch had got to Ogden, the ones figgering on being in San Francisco at any certain time had give up and settled back to enjoy theirselves. Us young fellows got in a lot of rabbit shooting when we was parked at sidings along the way. We'd stay in close and keep a fellow posted to signal when the express come through so we could go on again. Most times it was several hours late. One day we was going back toward the train when one of the boys says, "What do you suppose they're hauling the empty coal cars the wrong way for?"

"Beats me," says I. "Carbon's back of us."

We knowed they was coal cars on account of having three-foot walls all around the outside of them. Us fellows was standing there, looking at them casual-like, when one of the boys says, "They brung them along to dance in."

So that's what we used them for. We got the fellow in the car ahead to play his fiddle, then we went up and down the aisles in all the cars, gathering up the young folks. From then on we spent more time out on them cars dancing and yelling and taking on, than we did inside where we belonged. When we got out on the flat cars we had to stay there until the train come to the next stop. But with the fiddler getting up on the back of the box car ahead of us, swinging his feet and calling the numbers, nobody wanted to go inside anyhow.

Nights, the men would gather around and tell yarns, and the women would set together and talk, like they will do. One fellow got awful tiresome. He told the biggest whoppers I ever listened to, and he kept stopping to say, "Don't you believe me?" Then he'd tell some more and say, "Don't you believe me?" We didn't, but we tried to act like we did.

Jim got tired of listening to him. So he took over and told a terrible whopper. He told it straight-faced, and it was real long. Once in awhile he'd throw in "Don't you believe me?" and the fellow that had been doing all the talking would nod his head.

When Jim got all done he looked right at that fellow, and says, "Don't you believe me?" When the fellow nodded his head, Jim says, "Well, you're a damned fool if you do."

Of course, we was close to being broke and crowded and wondering about what was on beyond, but we had so much fun on that emigrant train that it makes me feel sorry every time I go downtown and see the streamliner go by. I sort of hate to think about all them folks inside, setting there in little rooms, traveling from coast to coast. No sir, there's a lot worse things than going by emigrant train, and getting to know other folks along the way.

We was all looking real close when we come to the California state line. I sure was surprised when the country on the other side looked just like Utah. Folks in our car had quieted down. They was all reading them printed folders that had brung them west. Jim always skipped over the part that said they needed tourists and investors the most. He liked the place where his book said they was short of settlers and that many a man—getting there with his pockets empty after paying his railroad fare—was making it just fine.

Them pamphlets wasn't all alike. There was an old lady, setting across from Julia, that put in all her time reading one from the Fountain of Youth. I ain't sure just what she looked like, because she was so drawed over with the crippling rheumatism that I never seen nothing but the back of her neck. I got to know her two sons well. They was farm folk from Iowa. A lot of different doctors back there had give up her case before this fellow from the Fountain of Youth had heard about it. He come clean out to their farm, and

give them a written guarantee that she'd be cured. They'd had to pay
in advance for the treatments to hold a place for her because so many
other folks was waiting, too. Both the boys had come because they
couldn't move her unless they made a chair by crossing hands and
holding tight to their wrists. Anyhow, they'd had to sell their place
to get money for the trip and the treatments. When the three of them
was together they'd set and talk about how she'd soon be cured, and
they'd make a new start on a homestead out West. But Julia used to
go along to stay with her when the boys carried her to the little room
at the end of the car. Julia said when the old lady was by herself she'd
cry with the pain in her joints. I've often wondered what become of
them and that guarantee.

The farms along the way kept getting smaller, but the houses and
barns was getting bigger. It didn't take a section of land to make a
living in the valleys out West. Jim begun smiling and pointing places
out to Julia. She held the baby up close to the window so he could
see the cows. After a while we come to the Sacramento River where
Hapgood and Hume canned the first salmon on the Pacific Coast. I
was real glad that the first big river I come to, on my way to the
Columbia, where I was going to learn the cannery business too, was
the one where them pioneers built that little floating cannery, way
back in 1864.

Our train was run onto a ferry that took us back across the Sacramento River to where the tracks begun again on the other side. When
we finally reached the Oakland pier, we got off the train, gathered up
our stuff, went through a housed-in place, and across a gangplank
onto a big ferry. We was so busy getting our stuff moved and keeping
track of our tickets and the baby that we never seen nothing until
we clumb a flight of stairs to the upper deck of that ferry boat, taking
us across San Francisco Bay to the depot at the foot of Market Street.

Golly, that San Francisco harbor is a sight for sore eyes when you're
looking across it from the Oakland pier. I didn't have no idea what
to expect, but that wasn't it. At first, all I seen was the water, and the
big ships, and the little sailboats scuttling back and forth. You ain't
got no idea how I felt seeing all that water going to waste in San
Francisco Bay, when the folks back in Carbon was paying twenty-
five cents for a whiskey barrelful.

Then I looked up to where Julia was pointing, and I seen San

Francisco with all them buildings down close to the water, and the houses spreading back across the hills. The sun was shining on them white buildings over there. It ain't no wonder they've got to calling California the golden state. No, sir, you can't get away from it, there's something about the place that gets under a man's hide. After he's once been there he gets to itching to go back and see it all over again. I knowed we couldn't write and tell Mama what it was really like, so I told Julia I was going to send her one of them picture cards, and say, *We got here safe, August 30, 1883, and we're all doing fine.*

It was noon when we walked off the ferry and into the depot at the end of Market Street. I never heard so much hollering and racket any place else in my whole life. One of them hotel fellows would run up, grab onto a fellow's bags, and yell, "Stay at our hotel for a dollar."

Then another fellow would get ahold on the other side, and screech, "I've got better rooms than his for six-bits."

With all them fellows grabbing at us, and tugging every which way, and shouting in our ears, and yelling mean things back and forth at each other, and the horses' feet clip-clopping on the cobble-stones, and all the folks from the train yelling about where they was going to stay or saying good-bye, I couldn't even hear myself think.

Finally, Jim and me got on each side of Julia, who was holding the baby, and we stood guard over our stuff while we watched for a few minutes. We was trying to figger out what to do next. We seen a big, tall greenhorn from Nevada, who'd come in with us, get mad when them city slickers grabbed hold of his bed roll and bundle. He run after the hotel man who was putting it in his carriage, figgering on taking it and him off to stay at his place. He reached in and took his blankets out of there. Then he doubled up his fist and knocked that fellow cold. Some of the rest of us boys waded into a few others that was buzzing around, bothering us. We had them laying all over and was teaching them smart alecks a real good lesson, when the police come.

Them policemen was fine fellows, and just as honest as anybody you'd ever hope to meet. They said all we was doing was protecting our own property, and that them hotel fellows didn't have no busi-ness grabbing our bags and loading them like that, unless we told them to. When the police seen how them fellows was doing, they run a copper wire up the dock and tacked it down. They told them hotel fellows if they crossed that line and grabbed any more bags, they'd be throwed in jail. After they made that rule, things was lots better, but, of course, them fellows was still on the other side of the wire there, waiting to pounce as soon as a man made up his mind and stepped over the line.

One of the boys from our train said his brother knowed of a real nice hotel that wasn't too expensive. We went up there with him. It was more like a boarding house, and was called Lodgings, or something like that. After I washed up and changed my shirt, Jim and Julia and me went down to eat at a "three for two." They used to have them all over, but I ain't seen one for quite a spell. A "three for two" is a restaurant where you get three things—soup, meat, and dessert—for two-bits. Lots of places charged four-bits or better after you got inside. That's why working folks watched for them places. If you see a sign that says "three for two," that's the place to do your eating.

A bunch of us young fellows had agreed to meet that night and see the town. We knowed we was greenhorns, but we was smart enough to stay together. We didn't have no money to waste, and we wasn't hankering to get into trouble, so we kept out of things and seen everything we could free. Just like when we went down to the Tar Flat on the Barbary Coast. All we done was look at the outside of the old Bella Union House, that was said to be the toughest place in the country. I've listened to enough stories about that place to figger it must of been.

We seen Chinatown, and we seen signs other places, saying to boycott the Chinese. A lot of folks favored starving out the ones that was here already so they'd leave because they was through using them building the Central Pacific Railroad. A bunch of the signs told about thousands of white men walking the streets looking for work. Men was stopping us, asking us for handouts. I begun to wonder about what kind of luck Jim would have getting a job. He'd gone to bed right after supper because he planned on making an early start, come morning.

But I figgered I could do my sleeping on the boat. We walked for hours, shouldering our way through the crowds, just looking. But of all the places I seen, the one I liked best was the Studebaker Headquarters, down on Lower Market Street. I knowed they manufactured wagons, but them shiny carriages with the fringed top was really elegant. Any young fellow would of give his eyeteeth to be setting in one of them in a derby hat and a linen duster, driving a matched span of high steppers.

Next morning, we was setting close to the window in a restaurant, eating breakfast, when I noticed Jim stop with a spoonful of oatmeal mush about halfway to his mouth, and put it back down again. He says, looking straight out the window, "Julia, don't that girl walking along on the other side the street, make you think of Sadie?"

Julia was awful understanding with Jim. All she said when she reached out and patted his hand was, "Yes, Jim, so many things do." But there was something in her face that made me wonder if it ever bothered her, knowing she hadn't been chose first. She went back to spend the day in the rooming house because the baby was too heavy for her to carry.

Jim and me walked on down the street together to where I was turning off to check on my sailing date at the Pacific Coast Steamship Company's office. He told me he'd bought a paper the night before, and the only "help wanted" ads he could find was for woodcutters to go way out to a camp where they was paying a dollar and a half a cord, and for an experienced fireman to go to work right away to take the place of a fellow who'd been drowned. It paid fifty dollars a month, but meant shipping out in a collier that run up the coast as far as Tacoma. It just wasn't no job for a man with a family. He went down to check on it anyhow, and found he wouldn't do because he didn't belong to the union.

Everything around the port was organized. He knowed something about tanning hides, but he didn't belong to the Tanners' Mutual Protective Association. He was a husky fellow with a strong back, but he didn't belong to the Longshore Lumbermen's Protective Association. He'd learned the blacksmith's trade, he'd worked building the shops in Grand Island, but everywhere he went to ask for work, he'd find hundreds of men waiting in line. They figgered close to fifty thousand men had come into California looking for work that year. And that didn't count the surplus that had been building up from clean back at the time of the gold rush in '49. The real Californians that wasn't promoters knowed it wasn't right, and said so.

But they didn't have nothing to do with sending out them free booklets.

Next day Jim went over to the land office to find out about homesteads. It sure beats all, that them fellows doing the writing hadn't checked up on free land first. California had been settled by the Spanish ahead of any other place out West. They'd had private ranchos, and sheep barons, and railroad grants. Why clean back in 1872, Henry Miller and Charles Lux had got title to forty mile of land on the west side of the San Joaquin Valley. Miller had nearly a hundred thousand cattle, and owned half a million acres of land. Other estates, almost that big, was being held together and passed on from father to son. Jim didn't have money to pay down on a farm. Land that could be used for raising oranges and mulberry trees had been snapped up and planted. If he wanted to homestead, his best chance would be to locate somewhere farther north.

Because Jim was married and had a wife and baby, it slowed him down considerable. He couldn't follow the fruit, or take off for the canneries, or work on the big ranches where the men slept in the bunkhouse, and got their meals dished up at a long table in the ranch house. He had a family, it was up to him to get a roof over their heads, quick.

That night we set and talked late. Next day, Jim looked for work again. On the way back he stopped in at the land office, and they give him a copy of the homestead laws and a map of Oregon. I knowed their money was going fast, but it wasn't my place to help them decide. After I booked my passage, I'd left what money I could spare with Mama. I was running so short myself there wasn't no way I could help them. I'd be leaving Saturday morning on the *State of California*. That left me two more nights in San Francisco. So I got Tom, who was lodging there, and we took off for the evening, to give them a chance to talk things through alone.

Next morning, at breakfast, they told me they was heading north, to homestead. Jim and me hurried right down to Goodall, Perkins, and Company, at Number 10, Market Street, to see if they could sail Saturday, too. That outfit was the agents for both the Pacific Steamship Company, and the Oregon Railway and Navigation Company. Anybody wanting to go north on one of the four "New A.I. Iron Steamships" had to book passage with them. The sailing dates was

Wednesday and Saturday, on *Queen of the Pacific, Columbia, State of California,* or *Oregon.* Somebody had turned in some space, so we could leave together the next morning. Jim and me took a little while walking along the harbor. We was looking at the Spreckles yacht, and the revenue cutter, the *Corwin,* and all of the rest of the ships that was in. Neither one of us had no idea how late it was until twilight come. We hurried right back to the lodging house where Julia and the baby was setting in the room waiting for us to take them out to dinner at the "three for two." Julia never said a word about us being late.

Later on that night, a knock come on my door, and there stood Julia. She had her coat on and her scarf tied over her head. I could see she'd been crying. She says, "Mont, I can't go in the morning without seeing something of San Francisco. The baby's so heavy, I haven't been able to carry him far. Nights, when Jim's come back from looking for work, he's needed to have me stay right with him. They're both asleep now. Will you walk with me tonight?"

That's how it come that Julia and me stood in the shadow, watching the carriages coming down from Nob Hill, and seen the women that lived in the big houses with the pointed roofs and round towers, getting out of the carriages and going into the Grand Opera House to see Ada Deavers playing in *Romeo and Juliet.* We seen the man standing at the door of the Palace Hotel, to open it for the kind of folks that belonged inside. When we stood looking at the signs on Woodward's Gardens, where they had the museum and the educational exhibits, she says, "I've always sort of wished that Mama had got to see the Magic Pictures and the Statuary and all the rest when we was in Washington."

"Me, too," says I. But I never thought till after we was on the boat that Julia might of took that way to say she'd like to see what was inside at Woodward's Gardens. Julia was sort of hard to understand because she wasn't no hand to ask for things.

She done most of her looking in the windows on Market Street. I thought I'd never get her away from them yellow-haired figures, dressed in pink, blue, and green dresses, with sashes, and lace, and roses pinned on here and there. Them Sullivans and Dolmans didn't have no real warmth in them to wear out of doors, and them cashmere suits and India muslin dresses was just plain flimsy. I showed

Julia men's suits, selling from ten to twenty dollars, that was made good and didn't have no wear-out to them. But I never seen a woman yet that showed much sense about liking clothes for the way they'd wear.

Julia and me walked so far, we was both wore out before we got back to the lodging house. When I left her at their door, she says, "Thank you, Mont. I won't ever forget the folks, and the lights, and all the pretty things on Market Street. Now, I'm all ready to finish packing."

We got up real early next morning because we was sailing for Astoria and the Columbia River. Hardly nobody was out on the streets. When the driver stopped the horses to let us out, down on the pier, the fog was so thick you could of cut it with a knife. After they checked our tickets and bed rolls and bundles, we went through onto the lower deck. A fellow showed us Jim and Julia's stateroom. Then he took us to where I'd be sleeping in an upper berth because another fellow had got there first and took the lower.

After I left my stuff, I went back to see if Jim and Julia wasn't coming up on deck to watch them cast off. Julia had got things straightened around. The baby was sleeping in the berth. Jim was setting alongside reading the homestead laws and studying the map of Oregon.

The fellow at the land office, who had give him the map, said he could still find good land out in the little valleys, where there wasn't no roads going over the mountains. The folks coming west by covered wagon had filed on everything in the Willamette Valley. No homesteads was left, except on beyond.

Jim was watching his money close, trying to stretch it enough to buy a horse, so Julia and the baby could ride. He figgered that with what he could carry in his pack and tie on the horse in back of her, they'd have enough along to get started. He could make it all right on foot, and lead the horse over Neahkanie Mountain, where they'd have to climb, because there wasn't no way to go around. The men telling Jim where to go had said to follow on down the beach from Astoria. The worst part of the whole trip would be crossing Neahkanie Mountain, where the whole side was sheered off straight, and dropped down hundreds of feet to the ocean below. It was the hardest stretch to get over along the whole Oregon Coast, but other folks, picking their footing careful on that narrow trail, was making it. Jim figgered they could too. From there on the going would be easier and the trail clear marked.

It wouldn't be much more than a hundred mile over the mountains until they come to the Tillamook Valley, where they'd find good spring water, timber for a cabin, and plenty of game. A man couldn't ask for better land nowhere, and they'd be living close to the Pacific Ocean, where the rainfall was heavy and the pasture stayed green, year around. Soon as they got a little money ahead, they could buy a cow and have milk for the baby. The grass growed tall, and didn't freeze or get covered with snow in the Tillamook Valley in Oregon.

When I come in, Julia asked Jim if he'd like to bring the baby up on deck, so he could get a last look at San Francisco. He said he'd already took his, that nobody there had wanted to see him, so he'd looked around real careful when he packed to see he hadn't left nothing, because he wasn't aiming to come back. But if she wanted to come up on deck with me, he'd be glad to take care of the baby while he went on with his reading. He didn't see no point in looking back when he should be spending his time finding out about a valley where a man could still get hold of some free land and make a living for his family.

When we got up on deck, Julia walked over to the rail, looking back toward San Francisco. But there wasn't nothing she could see —nothing but fog. So she straightened her shoulders and turned away. Then she walked clean on down to the bow of the boat, where she stood, trying to see ahead.

Me and Julia had growed up together, but I never noticed her looking like Mama before. I seen it first when I was following her along the deck, but I sort of passed it off because they wasn't no blood kin. But when I got up close to her, I knowed it was more than just the way she walked or the set of her shoulders. It was something in her eyes, and around her mouth, and in the way she held her chin when she says, "San Francisco must be an awful nice place to live, for folks that's got money, and jobs, and belong there. I know what the covered wagon pioneers went through, crossing the plains first. They've more than earned all they've got up there in the Willamette Valley. We wasn't among the first, so it's up to us to make the best of what's been left. I don't want my folks worrying about Jim, and the baby, and me. We'll be all right, and we'll make it, because we're young and strong. I talked it over with Jim last night, and we're not sorry we're going on. There's rivers, and trees, and mountains ahead."